LIBERALISM AND IDENTITY POLITICS
Puerto Rican Community Organizations
and Collective Action in New York City

LIBERALISM AND IDENTITY POLITICS
Puerto Rican Community Organizations
and Collective Action in New York City

José E. Cruz

Copyright © 2019 by Centro Press, Center for Puerto Rican Studies. All rights reserved. No part of this publication may be reproduced, distributed, or transmitted in any form or by any means, including photocopying, recording, or other electronic or mechanical methods, without the prior written permission of the publisher, except in the case of brief quotations embodied in critical reviews and certain other noncommercial uses permitted by copyright law.

Library of Congress Cataloging—in-Publication Data
Names: Cruz, José E., 1953- author.
Title: Liberalism and Identity Politics : Puerto Rican Community
   Organizations and Collective Action in New York City / José E. Cruz.
Description: New York, NY : Centro Press, Center for Puerto Rican Studies,
   2019. | Includes bibliographical references and index.
Identifiers: LCCN 2017006438 | ISBN 9781945662089 (pbk. : alk. paper)
Subjects: LCSH: Puerto Ricans--New York (State)--New York--Ethnic identity. |
   Puerto Ricans--New York (State)--New York--Politics and government. |
   Puerto Ricans--New York (State)--New York--Social conditions. | Community
   organization--New York (State)--New York. | Social action--New York
   (State)--New York. | New York (N.Y.)--Ethnic relations.
Classification: LCC F128.9.P85 C78 2018 | DDC 305.868/72950747--dc23
LC record available at https://lccn.loc.gov/2017006438

Printed in the United States of America

Centro Press
Center for Puerto Rican Studies
Hunter College, CUNY
695 Park Avenue, E-1429
New York, NY 10065
centrops@hunter.cuny.edu
http://centropr.hunter.cuny.edu

Cover photos (clockwise from top): Richie Pérez protesting police brutality (Richie Pérez Papers); Alice Cardona at a protest (Alice Cardona Papers); Protest to save Hostos Community College (Elsa Cabrera Papers). The photographs are from the Center for Puerto Rican Studies Library and Archives, Hunter College, CUNY. Cover design by Kenneth J. Kaiser.

For my children Elena, Gabriel, and Víctor, and in memory of my brother-in-law Mark W. Allen (1963-2018), a courageous and wise man.

TABLE OF CONTENTS

viii .... List of Figures and Tables

viii .... List of Acronyms

xi .... Preface and Acknowledgments

17 .... Introduction

34 .... **CHAPTER 1**
　　　　　　　　The Context of Strategic Action and Demand-Protest

50 .... **CHAPTER 2**
　　　　　　　　To be Accepted as an American

64 .... **CHAPTER 3**
　　　　　　　　We Have our Own Problems Here

84 .... **CHAPTER 4**
　　　　　　　　Racism Cannot be Fought with Silk Gloves

102 .... **CHAPTER 5**
　　　　　　　　Liberals for Justice and Progress

119 .... **CHAPTER 6**
　　　　　　　　The Most Serious Problem

137 .... **CHAPTER 7**
　　　　　　　　The Eyes and Ears of the Community

153 .... **CHAPTER 8**
　　　　　　　　We are All Liberals Now

172 .... Notes

204 .... Bibliography

209 .... Index

218 .... About the Author

LIST OF FIGURES AND TABLES

Figure 1.1   Federal Transfer Payments as a Fraction of Personal Income in Puerto Rico, 1940-1990

Table 1.1   Puerto Ricans in New York City, 1940-1990

Table 1.2   Age Structure of the Population of New York City, 1970-1990 (in percent of total population)

Table 1.3   Poverty Rates in New York City, 1970-1990 (in percent)

Table 1.4   Percentage of Non-movers, Movers from Puerto Rico, and All Other Movers in Metropolitan Areas with Largest Puerto Rican Populations, 1990

Table 1.5   Mean Household Income in New York City, 1970-1990

LIST OF ACRONYMS

AFL-CIO   American Federation of Labor-Congress of Industrial Organizations
APRED   Association of Puerto Rican Executive Directors
CAFA   Committee Against Fort Apache
CAP   Council Against Poverty (Also NYCCAP)
CCFIS   Citywide Committee for Integrated Schools
CDA   Community Development Agency
CHE   Comunidad Hispana Para Educación [Hispanic Community for Education]
CNPP   Comité Nacional Pro Plebiscito [National Pro-Plebiscite Committee]
CPCR   Committee on Police Community Relations
CPVBNY   Comité Pro Voto de Boricuas en New York [Committee for the Puerto Rican Absentee Voter]
EHTC   East Harlem Tenants Council
HHC   Health and Hospitals Corporation
HPC   Harlem Parents Committee

IPRP	Institute for Puerto Rican Policy
LULAC	League of United Latin American Citizens
LUPA	Latinos United for Political Action
MFY	Mobilization for Youth
NAACP	National Association for the Advancement of Colored People
NAPRA	National Association of Puerto Rican Affairs
NAPRCR	National Association for Puerto Rican Civil Rights
NACOPRW	National Conference of Puerto Rican Women
NCPRR	National Congress for Puerto Rican Rights
NIE	National Institute of Education
NPRC	National Puerto Rican Coalition
NYCCAP	New York City Council Against Poverty
PRIDE	Puerto Rican Inter-American Dynamic Educational Foundation
PREA	Puerto Rican Educators Association
PRISA	Puerto Rican Students for Action
PRCDP	Puerto Rican Community Development Project
PRLDEF	Puerto Rican Legal Defense and Education Fund
SEEK	Search for Education, Elevation, and Knowledge Program
UBP	United Bronx Parents
UFT	United Federation of Teachers
UPAW	United Parents Against the Wall
UPR	University of Puerto Rico
VRA	Voting Rights Act

x

Every people has a past, but the dignity of a history comes when a community of scholars devotes itself to chronicling and studying that past.

—Sonia Sotomayor, *My Beloved World*

PREFACE AND ACKNOWLEDGEMENTS

When I first read the above quote in Justice Sonia Sotomayor's 2014 memoir, it struck me instantly as the best justification for my work on Puerto Rican politics and an excellent rationale for ethnic studies as well. I think her statement is profound. It suggests that whatever meaning or significance HIStory—already biased from within by designation—may have, it is extrinsic, the product of an act of recognition. It also indicates that there is value added to the task of chronicling and studying the past. Hers is a humanistic assessment that goes beyond the professional or commercial value of intellectual inquiry and scholarly activity. Implicitly, this assessment suggests that the past has not only meaning but also implications that go beyond the content of historical treatments and evaluations. Somebody writes our history, therefore we exist, and long after we are gone, we can still make our mark.

Instead of focusing on an abstract working-class, the marginalized subject par excellence in a substantial number of historical works, I have focused here on Puerto Ricans in part because that is an element of my identity. I think of and about myself in terms of the very identity that this book singles out as its vantage point. I have made a serious effort to make sure that I did not go native. And I believe I have avoided this trap not so much out of professional fear or methodological awareness but simply because while Puerto Ricans may be my people, they are not, alas, my community. This has insulated me from the risk of partiality, as I feel I have no personal stake in presenting the community in a rosy light. More important, I believe I was successful precisely because of, rather than in spite of, identity; I could not possibly stop being Puerto Rican in order to become Puerto Rican.

Clearly, the underlying premise of this book and one of its key justifications is the belief that there are positive lessons to be abstracted from its account, chiefly that there is a legitimate place in liberal politics for politicized identity. One of the most hostile disagreements with this proposition in the literature can be found in Arthur Schlesinger's book *The Disuniting of America*, where politicized ethnicity is either a ploy to advocate for economic interests or a dangerous cult that atomizes the civil society, contaminates the political society, and generally threatens the integrity of the political culture and the pursuit of the common good. But even recognitions in the literature of the idea that politicized ethnicity has a legitimate place in politics are more lamentations about the absence of general support for the idea and tend to be short in the specifics of its value. One prominent example is the otherwise excellent book by Arlene Dávila, *Barrio Dreams, Puerto Ricans, Latinos, and the Neoliberal City*, where the main thesis is that the commercialization of culture is more acceptable than the politicization of ethnicity.

For some time now, I have respectfully disagreed with prominent historians over the notion that there are no lessons in history and with the idea that politicized ethnicity is a pathological feature of political systems. In this book, I take the position, based on the empirical account offered, that there is much to learn from looking backward at politicized ethnicity—indeed, much that could be useful in the future. I also believe that there is much positive consequence for liberal politics in the politicization of ethnicity, and that the benefits can be specified. After reading Sotomayor's *My Beloved World*, I realized something else, namely, that in writing about Puerto Ricans, whatever other conscious or nonconscious goals I was pursuing, whether to further vindicate the notion of lessons in history or to continue to explore the possibility whether politicized ethnicity was dangerous and undesirable as opposed to positive and affirmative, I was also fulfilling a human value.

This goal may sound grandiose, and it may be rejected by readers if the investiture of dignity is understood to occur only in accounts that highlight moments or trajectories of triumph and glory as opposed to those that simply recognize human struggle. Puerto Ricans (and others) may disagree with my claim but whether they do or not, this book brings attention to Boricuas, recognizes their actions and contributions, acknowledges the flaws in their participation, and generally suggests that, contrary to what the late mayor of New York, Edward Koch indicated at one point during his incumbency, they are somebody and do count.

Anyone who visits the section "Many Voices, One Nation" at the National Museum of American History, which is dedicated to specifying the role of ethnic and racial diversity in the making of the United States, will learn that Puerto Rico is a territorial possession where slavery was a Spanish institution and where Snow White sugar was manufactured once the U.S. took over the island in 1898. They will not know that Boricuas were an integral part of the civil rights movement unless they watch carefully the short video featured as part of the display about the Poor People's Campaign in Washington, D.C.—the project the Southern Christian Leadership Conference carried out in 1968 after the assassination of Martin Luther King, Jr.—and they are able to identify the director of the Office of the Puerto Rican Commonwealth in New York, Joseph Monserrat, as he addressed a crowd expressing solidarity with "our brothers and sisters." They will realize that Puerto Ricans were there if they recognize the founder of the Congress of Puerto Rican Hometowns in New York, Gilberto Gerena Valentín, standing behind Ralph Abernathy—who took over the leadership of the Campaign in the absence of King, Jr.—as Abernathy delivered a speech that highlighted the contributions of blacks to American history. There is one poster in the exhibition that alludes to the participation of Puerto Ricans in the Campaign, but this will be clear only to visitors who know Spanish.

Thus, this book is an addition to the growing literature that stands as a corrective to a case of monumental ignorance about Puerto Ricans in the United States generally and in New York in particular. This ignorance must be corrected not just because Puerto Ricans deserve the recognition but also because the use by Puerto Ricans of ethnic identity was generally beneficial to their social and political aims and to the city. In addition, their experience is important because, by practicing identity politics, they provided evidence that while theoretically liberal tenets may seem antithetical to that kind of political practice, the two are reconcilable.

My academic career has been shaped by a Marxist ethos. Before readers recoil from that admission, I must explain: I do not mean a materialist ethos that reduces consciousness to social being but one that acknowledges that while "all that is solid melts into air," transformation is not always a process of destruction or of leaving everything behind. In fact, the opposite can be true: by delving into the past we can shape the present and influence the future. My ethos is Marxist in the sense articulated by Marx in a letter to his friend Arnold Ruge from 1849. I have cited that letter many times before, in conversation and in writing, to the point where those who know me may start to think of me as a one-note samba. Yet, the passage in the letter where Marx suggests that true revolutionaries are uncompromising in two ways—in being critical without fearing conflict either with the powers that be or with the results of their critique—reflects an aspect of my approach to research and scholarship that defines me decisively.

I have tried my best to live up to that Marxist prescription in the execution of this project. It would be presumptuous of me to think that anything I have done, this book included, has been in any way threatening to the powers that be. But I do know that at least my work has been unconventional, in terms of how I deploy my understanding of interdisciplinarity, and in how my presentation style does not always conform to the stylistic standards of routine scholarship, but also in the sense that it combines scholarship and advocacy and tries to develop insights and standards that may have political value.

I have never worried about the question of "fit" too much and the consequences of that attitude have not been negative in any way I can discern. I do worry about being misunderstood and I have tried not to be afraid to follow the path dictated by the facts of the case. This may seem antithetical to the notion of imbuing the past with dignity. Yet the dignity of history emerges not from its embellishment but from the recognition that no matter how dreadful the past may have been, there is always something of value in its consideration. Of course, it is more pleasant to bask in the glow of achievement than to dwell in the agony of failure. And while it is true that failure can be instructive, here the emphasis is on the positive, simply because the case study helps craft an interpretation about politicized ethnicity and its relationship to liberalism that challenges the idea that they represent an aporetic mix.

This book has been too long in the making not so much because the work was challenging but because all too often life got in its way. I mention this not as an alibi but simply to highlight the fact that during the time that I worked on this project I became indebted to many, many people—too many to remember and list name by name at this moment. Some will read the book, most will simply know that it has finally been published, and all who read this much will recognize themselves in the previous sentence. A big thank you to them all.

I must mention a few people by name because they helped me in substantial ways: at the Center For Puerto Rican studies, Nélida Pérez and Pedro Juan Hernández were indefatigable allies and collaborators. Mining archival sources can be a mind-numbing exercise, but their assistance ameliorated the inevitable distress that comes from doing archival research. Over the years, I have benefitted from many conversations about all things Puerto Rican and beyond with Edgardo Meléndez, Felipe Pimentel, Carlos Vargas-Ramos, and Xavier Totti. I thank Xavier Totti in particular for providing a home for my work.

At the University at Albany I have enjoyed unconditional freedom to pursue my academic interests. My colleagues and students in the political science department and the department of Latin American, Caribbean and U.S. Latino studies have been a source of major support. I am especially grateful to Edna Acosta-Belén and Carlos E. Santiago, two distinguished scholars of Puerto Rican politics who are also aware that ethnic identity and objectivity can go hand in hand. A million thanks go to Elizabeth Allen for her editorial assistance and for everything else that matters.

Lastly, I am grateful to three anonymous reviewers for Centro Press. Their assistance is the most recent and therefore the easiest to remember. I heeded many of their recommendations with great benefit, and others I ignored at my own peril. Ultimately, all credit for the merits of the book I share with those who lent me a hand, and all its flaws I accept exclusively as mine.

INTRODUCTION

This book is based on research that was meant to recall and analyze elite- and community-level politics in New York City between 1960–1990. For reasons of space and for the sake of offering separate but complementary theoretical interpretations of two aspects of the same story, that single narrative is now split in two, each part somewhat overlapping in content with the other.

The elite-level recollection can be found in *Puerto Rican Identity, Political Development, and Democracy in New York, 1960–1990.*[1] In *Puerto Rican Identity* the emphasis is on the fundamentally liberal democratic character of Puerto Rican politics at the elite level and generally. Here the connection between identity politics—understood as a politics seeking integration, progress, and redress of grievances using a collective identity as the basis for social and political mobilization—liberalism—understood as a theoretical approach that emphasizes individuality, autonomy, and choice and gives pride of place to society over the state—and community politics is emphasized.

Thus, this is a chronicle of the role of ethnic identity—understood here as a sense of self shaped by national origin, culture, and history that changes in context—in Puerto Rican community-based activities and collective action, as one way of understanding the relationship between liberalism and identity politics.[2] The argument that flows from the empirical account is that the aporetic relationship between liberalism and identity politics can be transcended in practice.

LIBERALISM AND IDENTITY POLITICS
This is not a book of political theory and therefore, I will treat the so-called incompatibilities between liberalism and identity politics concisely. My objective is to substantiate a basic proposition about the relationship between liberalism and identity politics through a pragmatic assembly of ideas and events. The latter can assist in logically establishing what I would call a hypothesis for practice—that is, a general proposition about liberalism and identity politics that may be useful in the world of politics. My exegetical effort is minimal. I do not develop a grand critique of liberalism or identity politics but rather suggest that the aporetic relationship between the two can be challenged.

My objective is not to argue for a tolerance of conceptual inconsistency but to suggest that, to paraphrase Nicholas Rescher, the resolution of a theoretical incompatibility must be minimally based on abstract rationality but it cannot be accomplished through abstract rationality alone.[3] This approach distinguishes this book from other treatments about liberalism and identity politics, which either focus on their relationship from a strictly theoretical point of view and/or eschew the possibility of compatibility between the two in practice.

CLAIMS IN THE LITERATURE

The alleged aporetic relationship between identity politics and liberalism is not fully or explicitly argued in the literature. But the argument can be deducted from corollary claims that are related to exclusion as a condition of political viability in liberal societies. Some claims are also based on these propositions: that a system of group rights is undesirable; that group rights and liberalism are incompatible; or that liberalism itself is deficient. In the case of Puerto Ricans, as well as in the case of African Americans, treatments of their politics often focus on identity but either ignore the ethnic component of identity or simply fail to consider the possibility that it may have a role to play in liberal politics. Let me specify these aspects of the literature in turn.

In *Philosophies of Exclusion: Liberal Political Theory and Immigration,* Phillip Cole argues that "the existence of a liberal polity made up of free and equal citizens rests upon the existence of outsiders who are refused a share of the goods of the liberal community."[4] Although Cole does not refer to identity politics, his idea of exclusion as a feature of liberalism is predicated on the distinction between citizens and non-citizens and more generally on a category of "outsiders" that could be citizens or could simply be any group who is ascriptively considered unworthy. This is the most extreme version of aporia between liberalism and anything that may come close to a politics of identity.

Cole's view is shared by Melissa Williams, although in her case, the problem is represented as a *failing* of liberalism that may be amenable to correction. Nevertheless, because she suggests that marginality is simply a correlate of disadvantage, the agency of marginal citizens is a mere response to unequal status that excludes the possibility of responses that may be animated by the liberal ethos itself. In fact, her argument is that group-based representation is the only fair *alternative* to liberal representation.[5] In other words, identity politics can only find its place in a communitarian or socialist rather than a liberal system.

A different view of exclusion is articulated by Thomas W. Pogge, who rejects group rights based on ethnic identity only if the groups excluded from enjoying the benefits extended to others are different "in a way that renders them ineligible for the rights in question."[6] In this case, exclusion is not aporetic in character but one wonders what would happen if the criteria for ineligibility was suspect. For example, it is well-known that some within the African American community object to the extension of affirmative action benefits to Latinos and other groups. A typical complaint by minorities about affirmative action is that it has benefitted largely white women, and the tone of this complaint is often one of indignation and suggestive of illegitimacy.

Chandran Kukathas strongly and unequivocally states that in a liberal society there is absolutely no room for group rights. To him the only legitimate freedom is the freedom of association. He concedes that within the archipelago of associations that naturally will follow from the exercise of that freedom, competing and overlapping jurisdictions will be the norm. Thus, he unwittingly suggests that the adjudication of rights and benefits must follow some kind of group identity compass. But no, Kukathas insists that in his concept of the liberal archipelago there is no room for unity and hierarchy but rather for "a society of societies which is neither the creation nor the object of control of any single authority, though it is a form of order in which authorities function under laws which are themselves beyond the reach of any singular power."[7]

To him, human diversity is so strong and intractable that the best thing liberalism can do is create an institutional context that allows for diverse individuals and groups to coexist. Political obligation under these terms eludes the question of group rights and reduces it to a commitment to whatever institutional context "preserve[s] an order in which people who differ can coexist."[8] But even this is not acceptable if it means that identity politics produces a liberalism of compromises that "reflect[s] not any principled resolution of philosophical differences but varying patterns of mutual accommodation among people and groups whose principled aspirations [...] pull in different directions."[9]

Then there is Steven Kautz, who describes liberalism as a public philosophy in crisis, no longer capable of providing a political compass that can allow citizens to find the right path in their pursuit of the common good. Kautz describes "classical liberalism" disparagingly, suggesting that the idea of community it espouses is the purview of "romantic utopians or dangerous authoritarians." But his key question regarding contemporary liberalism is not so much whether it requires exclusionary norms or is incompatible with identity politics, but whether it serves any legitimate purpose as a public philosophy.[10]

A keen reader could argue that *contra* Kautz, Carol Horton not only substantiates a case for liberalism but bridges the gap between individuality and group rights with her concept of social liberalism. Her concept, however, is predicated on a possibility rather than a fact. In other words, for social liberalism to be possible, equality of opportunity must translate into equality of results, and for that to happen, government must intervene in society and the market. This is a fair, although problematic and highly contested, conceptualization of expanded liberalism, but it says nothing specific about identity politics, which is the vantage point from which the present recollection follows.[11]

On the other hand, Will Kymlicka has shown that there is a history of a relationship between liberalism and minority rights that is consonant with my view that the relation is aporetic in theory but not in practice. According to Kymlicka, it is possible to secure equality through the promotion of group rights. However, when he makes his case for liberalism and group rights, his focus is *culturally* plural societies; he is more concerned with cultural maintenance and its place in minority rights than with the problematic that distinguishes identity politics as I have defined it here. Similarly, while Iris Marion Young acknowledges the importance of recognizing and accepting *difference*, her prescription has less to do with reconciling identity politics and liberalism and more with suggesting that fruitful social interaction between diverse participants begins with the recognition of their diverse identities. Her concern is not with liberalism but more generally with social justice. In 2000, David Ingram also made a case for a positive relationship between equal citizenship and group rights. But his main concern regarding identity was cautionary: ways must be found to avoid assuming that identities are uniform.[12]

In the work of Kenneth Hoover, dating from 1975, there is not even a hint of this concern. Unlike Horton, he does not qualify liberalism but suggests that liberal values can be realized by individuals contracting with others in ways that are consonant with communitarian approaches to political action. To him, the problem is not liberal values but liberal solutions that fail to appreciate the communal dimension of liberal values, thereby emphasizing approaches to social problems that glorify private property and the market.[13] His prescription, alas, is vague and lacks insight into how identity politics and liberalism can come together to bring about methods that can effectively help realize liberal values, beyond pure individualism and reliance on the market. To wit: "Organized groups must go beyond concretizing short-run or lowest-common-denominator formulations of their 'interests' in search of an evolutionary development of member's interests and potentialities."[14]

According to Santosh C. Saha, when ethnicity mediates the process of identity formation and state-building, it can be destructive. At the same time, there is sufficient research that suggests the opposite: ethnic attachments can help assist in the reconstruction of state structures.[15] How does this address the question of identity politics and liberalism? It does not, because, politically, state structures can be of any kind.

The case of the Black Panthers in the U.S. could suggest a place for identity politics in a liberal society. In his analysis of their ideological trajectory, Paul J. Magnarela argues that their brand of identity politics was not exclusionary; the party did not endorse reverse racism. Instead, the Black Panthers were convinced, at least rhetorically, that their black revolutionary nationalism had the potential to overcome capitalism and help build a new national American identity free of racism. To the leadership of the party, ethnic identity was a tool for the pursuit of respect and dignity. Huey Newton, in particular, believed that this had to be done in cooperation with others rather than in isolation.[16] This meant, however, that identity politics required reaching out to members of out-groups but only to pursue systemic transformation rather than to realize liberal values.

By the early 1990s, the question of identity and its relationship to the politics of Puerto Ricans in New York was addressed by Angelo Falcón. However, unlike Antonia Pantoja's analysis, noted below, Falcón's was not a synthesis of a position held in the past. He was not recapitulating the Puerto Rican experience but making a projection for the future. Further, his focus was not ethnic identity. He specifically explored how non-African American groups saw themselves racially. His main concern was not with how Puerto Ricans could use their ethnic identity to advance a political agenda—liberal or otherwise—and under what terms. Instead, his main question was whether race would play itself out as the engine of a new civil rights movement—encompassing groups other than African Americans—or as a wedge leading to increased competition for limited resources.

Falcón predicated the answer to the previous question as partly dependent on how Puerto Ricans saw themselves racially and how this affected their relationship with African Americans rather than on how they translated a racial identity into political action on their own and for their own benefit.[17] In his analysis, he cited a 1972 unpublished paper that suggested that "[A]n awareness of what the process of becoming conscious of one's Puerto Ricanness may allow the Puerto Rican to program Puerto Rican identity, resulting in that self-positive image which is the prerequisite for Puerto Rican pride and self-determination."[18] In this view, to act on the basis of identity required an awareness of how one became aware of one's identity. It suggested nothing regarding the relationship between liberalism and identity politics.

Going back to the question of exclusion, there is an important view that opens up the possibility that its grounds may be related to human nature more than to political values or a theoretical approach as Cole, Williams, and Pogge suggest. In this view, exclusion is not predicated on the viability of a particular ideological order but as a condition of political viability in general. While this may seem similar to the views on this issue considered above, there is a crucial difference regarding the basis for exclusion that is relevant to my argument.

The idea of exclusion as a condition for the existence of a viable polity goes quite far back, all the way to *The Politics* by Aristotle, where the exclusion of free women and workers from citizenship is a pre-condition of political well-being. But a close look at Aristotle's rationale for exclusion reveals a critical difference with the view that exclusion is required by a particular kind of order.

According to Aristotle, the defining characteristic of a citizen is the faculty of giving judgment and holding office.[19] At the same time, he claims that anyone who is a member of an association can be considered a citizen. "The task of all citizens," Aristotle wrote, "however different they may be, is the stability of the association, that is, the constitution."[20] For citizens to be able to perform this function, they all had to possess the intrinsic virtue of being able to preserve political stability. But in his view, in the context of human diversity, it was impossible for all human beings to be endowed with that faculty.

What does that mean? It means that, if there was to be exclusion within the political society, the reason for it was the variety of human endowments rather than the normative principles of any given doctrine, philosophy, or ideology. Human beings do segregate themselves according to ideas and principles but these are malleable. What is unchangeable is human nature and, therefore, if a citizen must be capable of governing and being governed, not everyone can be a citizen because not everyone is endowed with that capacity. In Aristotle's vision, women and workers did not have that capacity as humans, and therefore exclusion from citizenship was necessary. The important point for my account is that exclusion was not dictated by a particular kind of normative order but as a result of different types of individual endowments.

In sum, pre-required exclusion, incompatibility between group-based representation and group rights and liberalism, and the rejection of liberalism itself as a public philosophy are key aspects of the literature on identity politics and liberalism that are at odds with the key proposition of this book, namely, that the theoretical aporia between identity politics and liberalism can be transcended in practice. The analysis in the literature of two important cases in New York City that were expressions of identity politics—the cases of Puerto Ricans and African Americans—does not consider that particular angle.

Here, the Puerto Rican case provides evidence that supports the idea that identity politics can be a sustaining force of liberalism because Puerto Ricans were endowed with the capacity to pursue a liberal agenda from the vantage point of a group identity. Ultimately, this is a case for agency that avoids what I call the theory trap, that is, the idea that theory is a blueprint rather than a roadmap for practice. Of course, agency is always exerted in context, as Tamar Carroll shows in her study of identity-based organizing in New York. That study, however, is different from mine in two ways: it gives pride of place to the role of the state in fostering or curtailing identity-based mobilization; and it focuses on the relationship between identity politics and coalition-building.[21]

THE PUERTO RICAN CASE

A word must be said at the outset about the meaning of being Puerto Rican. Although I am fully aware that categories tend to essentialize their object, I am not concerned here with the Russian-doll problem of categories that obscure categories, as if the existence of layers of meaning and consequences embedded in the coexistence and interaction of subordinate, subsidiary, and superordinate categories somehow make it impossible to focus on, and ascribe epistemic value to, singular dimensions of identity or ascription, such as "Puerto Rican." Yes, there are different ways of being Puerto Rican, but here I have chosen to focus on Puerto Rican as a collective identity based on documentary-defined ascriptions. In other words, I accept what the documentary record tells me about how Puerto Ricans understood their collective identity and how others adjudicated that identity, even if it is true that there is ample room there for unpacking based on class, race, gender, and nativity, among other descriptors.

In the end, everything cannot be assessed in light of everything else, but if I wanted to be post-modern in my approach, and unpack the label "Puerto Rican" to show how it obscures more than illuminates, I could. Other treatments of ethnic identity have been concerned with how it is generated, transmitted, and transformed. Here I take documentary-defined ascriptions of identity for granted. My interest is in how documentary-defined ethnic identity was used by Puerto Ricans as the basis for community-based activities and collective action in order to assess the relationship between liberalism and identity politics.

Ultimately, my view about Puerto Rican identity corresponds with the notion that, however fixed and essential it may seem, it is dynamic. As A. L. Epstein put it in *Ethos and Identity,* identity is "essentially a concept of synthesis. It represents the process by which the person seeks to integrate his various statuses and roles, as well as his diverse experiences into a coherent image of self."[22] When identity is under attack and transforms into identity politics, identity conforms to the definition so eloquently expressed by James Baldwin in his essay "Princes and Powers," which I here paraphrase: it is a process whereby individuals cling to habits of thinking, feeling, and acting developed in a given context in the face of forces that demand their substitution for habits developed by others in a different context.[23] This view suggests resistance and preservation but in the end the kernel of identity changes even if its shell remains the same.

What this case study adds to the literature is a grounded theoretical argument for a positive relationship between liberalism and identity politics from the perspective of questions that are specific to identity politics, understood not only as a politics seeking integration, progress, and redress of grievances using a collective identity as the basis for social and political mobilization, but also as a set of political actions in which a particular group participates on the basis of self-definition as well as external ascriptions of self. Puerto Ricans didn't need to know how they became Puerto Ricans to know that they were treated poorly. Their knowledge of self was enough to make them organize and mobilize, using their identity to demand first-class citizenship within the framework of liberal values.

Puerto Ricans in New York established grassroots organizations to advocate for Puerto Rican interests, to fight mistreatment, to promote upward mobility, and/or to provide community services. Some of these institutions began locally in neighborhoods and branched out to the city and/or national level. Collective action included activities and mobilization around issues as well as specific instances of demand-protest ranging from occupation of governmental offices to rallies and marches to urban riots. Identity politics was the glue that held these aspects of Puerto Rican community politics in New York City together. All in all, the community was dynamic and well-organized, contrary to the conventional wisdom that has characterized it as riddled with "collective pathologies, marginalization, generalized apathy and individual disorganization."[24]

Self-sufficiency vs. Identity
An important documentary point of departure of this recollection and analysis is Antonia Pantoja's "Puerto Ricans in New York: A Historical and Community Development Perspective," published in 1989. Using this article to frame the recollection

of a process that culminated after the article was published may seem odd. Yet, this is appropriate because, when she wrote it Pantoja was recalling what she had done as well as the conditions of her actions. In this article she laid out not only an account of Puerto Rican community development in New York City, but also a vision of the principles she honored and the strategic path she followed, in hopes that Puerto Rican community institutions would do the same in the future.

"Long before a War on Poverty ever existed," she wrote, "we started to develop our own institutions."[25] These institutions were designed to acculturate Puerto Ricans through service provision, cooperative economic development, and electoral participation. But they were also a means used to maintain their native language and cultural heritage. Puerto Ricans had an island background but they were not insular; for example, advocacy organizations and political clubs defended movements for liberation in Latin America. This was also a sign of the importance of ethnic identity for them.

In offering a recollection of Puerto Rican community-based activities and collective action, I wish to bring into view their fundamentally liberal character. I argue that while Pantoja's vision provided an important framework for action, ethnic identity was the engine that propelled and sustained community efforts consistently over time. Pantoja talked about ethnic pride, but in her vision, self-sufficiency was the key strategic goal. More than a politics of self-help, however, Puerto Rican community politics was a politics of identity, that is, a politics of mobilization based on a collective sense of self to seek integration, progress, and redress of grievances. More important than ethnic pride was ethnic status, although these two aspects interacted symbiotically. In other words, hostility, abuse, and racism correlated with ethnicity and ethnicity anchored the responses to these forms of oppression.

Before 1960, Puerto Ricans had organized within other Hispanic groups. "We called ourselves Puerto Ricans and effectively challenged and replaced the non-Puerto Rican leadership who had elected themselves spokespeople for Puerto Ricans in the larger society," Pantoja commented in her article.[26] After 1960, the "Puerto Rican" category expanded to become "Puerto Rican New Yorkers," and that identity structured professional, service-provision, academic, and political initiatives.

For Pantoja, community development had to be the work of Puerto Rican institutions. But ultimately, self-sufficiency and identity worked hand in hand. She concluded:

> The community, through its working units, selects the problems and the strategies of action to be undertaken. In this approach, the people who are members of the community are participants in the resolution of their own problems and they grow in acquiring knowledge, skills and value positions. But they also become owners and controlling elements of as many of their own institutions as possible.[27]

Community Politics

Carlos Vargas-Ramos notes that Puerto Rican political participation is mixed: exceedingly high when it comes to protest activity, higher than the participation of the Mexican-origin population in electoral politics, but lower than the participation of other groups. According to Vargas-Ramos, Puerto Ricans are most active in the kind of political participation that is the least effective.[28] But what is the measure of effectiveness?

What the following chapters suggest is that through community-based activities and collective action, Puerto Ricans articulated a liberal form of identity politics in which ethnic identity and the idea of group rights provided a platform for the assertion of individuality, for claims to autonomy and choice, and for the production of both individual and collective goods. There is a far distance between this and what Ernest Gellner called a "liberalism [that] absolutizes a relative position [...] a philosophy of sour grapes of rootless men who have lost all full identification with a community or commitment to a set of values [...]."[29] And because of that, the Puerto Rican contribution to bridging the gap between liberalism and identity politics in practice is important and a good measure of effective politics.

In 1938, in his profile of Oscar García Rivera, the first Puerto Rican elected to public office in the United States, journalist Art Shields wrote: "The Puerto Rican people of Harlem are a living force for democracy." García Rivera went to the State Assembly in Albany, New York, in 1937, fighting Tammany Hall as a progressive Republican with backing from the communist-sponsored American Labor Party.[30] Shields wrote for the *The Daily Worker*, so it is likely that, to him, the democracy he thought Puerto Ricans wanted was socialist rather than liberal. Nevertheless, nowhere in his profile did Shields suggest that the trajectory of the Puerto Rican struggle in New York was headed in that direction, and García Rivera himself went to Albany not to smash the system but to make it deliver on its promises. In that sense, García Rivera's agenda mirrored Puerto Rican community politics.

Pantoja's vision was appealing to Puerto Ricans who engaged in community-level activism, advocacy, and politics in New York City. But while that vision may have animated aspects of community institutional discourse and practice, it was never fully realized. Despite generating, overall, a positive balance sheet, action was not always informed or productive. Self-sufficiency was predicated and exalted, but it remained largely elusive, in no small measure because, I would argue, it is a myth. And this is relevant to a review of what went on before her article was published because Pantoja's ideas then were part and parcel of the standard that she tried to follow from the onset of her participation in community development activities in the 1960s.

In other words, what she articulated in 1989 was the template that she purported to follow with the establishment of two key Puerto Rican institutions, the Puerto Rican Forum in 1957 and ASPIRA in 1961, even though institutionally these groups were ever anything but self-sufficient.[31] Nevertheless, these organizations became the model for future community organizations and the principles and strategy that Pantoja articulated in print in 1989 constituted a roadmap, even if in the 1960s the map was imaginary—not in the sense of being a fantasy but in the sense of being a scheme propelling and driving action.

If action was possible, it was not so much because participants desired to *co-exist* with the mainstream of politics and society but because they wanted to be *integrated*. Integration was pursued by Puerto Ricans on their own terms, that is, as *Puerto Ricans* with obligations as well as benefits; in other words, through a politics of identity. As for collective action, the idea of self-sufficiency receded into the background, overtaken by the idea of ethnic pride as the anchor of participation seeking respect, inclusion, and equal treatment within the civil and political society. It is reasonable to suggest that this type of identity politics has been part and parcel of Puerto Rican politics in New York for quite some time.

FRAMEWORK FOR ASSESSMENT

The literatures on identity politics and liberalism are vast, and so far I have only referred to a subset of critical works that help establish the general contribution of this project. In this section I focus on the work of Michael Kenny because it offers a comprehensive theoretical review and analysis of identity politics. For the purpose of establishing a framework for my assessment of Puerto Rican community-based activities and collective action as a form of identity politics against claims that the relationship between identity politics and liberalism is aporetic, Kenny's work suffices.

In *The Politics of Identity*, Kenny notes that identity politics has been regarded as troublesome not just because it substitutes the group for the individual but also because individual interests and ideology are replaced by group allegiance and culture. In other words, the lens of identity politics is illiberal since it focuses on belonging as opposed to being.

Another alleged problem is that it brings back the parochialisms and vestiges of tradition that prevent the emergence of the modern, universal citizen. Culture becomes heritage and, consequently, ways of being in time lose their dynamism; life becomes a museum's permanent collection. Further, identity politics "is inherently subversive of established ideas about the appropriate boundary between questions that are political and those that are not."[32]

For example, are the questions, *Who should I support as a presidential candidate* and *Should a man marry a man*, both political? In the identity politics metric they both are. To some, this is something close to a new barbarism, which is another way of saying that it is foreign and out of place. Kenny does not agree. He does not see identity politics as the terminal illness of liberal democracy. In fact, he argues that Romanticism, moral pluralism, and philosophical monism are Western philosophical traditions that have provided a basis for identity politics.

But identity politics is an international phenomenon that varies according to local, regional, and national contexts. Within Anglophone political theory, it is the recognition of social mobilization on the basis of suppressed or neglected collective identities, for example, the women's and gay liberation movements. It is a phenomenon of the 1960s, which sets groups as opposed to individuals apart in society and politics in virtue of shared characteristics that define their collective interests. Social, economic, and political demands are made on the basis of these collective interests whether putative members of these groups like it, need it, or not. The Puerto Rican case fits smoothly within this framework.

What unites all identity politics? One answer to this question is that all identity politics share the imposed character of identity: you do not choose to be female, gay, black, or Latino. But this can go only so far, since some identities can be chosen. Religious identity is an example. In this case, the costs associated with satisfying the religious imperatives of a minority can be seen as inherently unfair by the majority. For example, why should I as a taxpayer bear the costs of private Catholic education if Catholicism is not natural but a historical choice made by some Americans? A possible answer is that choice loses its relevance if once a choice is made it is irreversible. And this is the case, if the act of choosing is foundational. Once a foundational choice is made, the boundary between belonging and being is obliterated, and membership becomes transcendental, inevitable, natural, not in essence... but as a matter of choice!

In the context of the United States, the question of choice has come up in the case of race, despite the fact that race is clearly an ascriptive trait—in other words, you cannot choose between being black or white. Similarly, if you are born and raised in Puerto Rico and then move to New York, you cannot will Anglo-conformity into your outlook, as even New York-born Puerto Ricans eventually find out, if Anglos reject your overtures and if assimilation means cultural and/or linguistic suicide.

The liberal solution to this problem has been to separate the public from the private and to confine identity politics to the private sphere, in effect removing the political from the question of identity. In other words, at home you can be Puerto Rican, practice *Espiritismo*, and speak Spanish, but in society you relinquish these parts of yourself to be a model American citizen. In 1994, Renato Rosaldo suggested cultural citizenship—that is, membership from the vantage point of difference as opposed to commonality—as an alternative.[33] With this concept, he tried to validate identity politics as a legitimate form of liberal democratic participation.

If cultural citizenship is a way of organizing values, beliefs about rights, and practices affirming cultural as opposed to political belonging within a nation,[34] then, until an earlier reference is found, the concept was first proposed by Maria Teresa Babín in 1956, in a short article in *La Voz de Puerto Rico en U.S.A.*, a newspaper founded in that year by the National Association of Puerto Rican Merchants, based in Brooklyn, New York.

Babín argued that cultural citizenship existed at the level of "costumbres, la actitud hacia la vida, la tradición y la herencia ideológica," [customs, attitudes toward life, tradition, and ideological heritage], and that it was in the vernacular language—in this case Spanish—where the essence of culture resided, separate from the laws that ruled the political destiny of people and of the "ciudadanía que se adquiere jurídicamente por las circumstancias y los vaivenes de la historia" [citizenship acquired legally as a result of the vagaries of history], which was a clear reference to the acquisition of U.S. citizenship by Puerto Ricans in 1917.[35] In this view, the practice of cultural citizenship was embodied in the practice of speaking Spanish, which was conceived as a group right.

Another common thread among varieties of identity politics is that identity politics always and everywhere "challenges the boundaries and conventional content of politics."[36] But this is also problematic, according to Kenny. Socialism, communism, fascism, and other political phenomena throughout history have threatened socio-political norms before identity politics emerged in the 1960s. Is identity politics therefore intrinsically illiberal? How can this be when, as the chapters that follow show, practitioners of identity politics often do so from the vantage point of a commitment to liberal democracy and modernity?

Post-modern invectives against identity politics are arguably less compatible with the discourse of liberalism and modernity than identity politics itself because these invectives see the tacit acceptance of the fluidity of primary and secondary identities by the subscribers and practitioners of identity politics—for example, I am Puerto Rican first, but if my fellow Puerto Ricans choose a fascist for President, I will not be with them—as inherently unstable and impossible to pin down. In the post-modern approach, if someone asks the question, What makes me a Puerto Rican?, all the possible answers, if refracted by gender, race, and class, are not just a sign of fluidity but indeterminacy.

Thus, the inevitable conclusion is that if all Puerto Ricans are not like me but I consider myself Puerto Rican, others must not be part of my group, and if they are, I cannot be one of them. Put differently, since it is impossible to establish an essential criterion for Puertoricanness, Puerto Ricans do not exist. Thus, following the post-modernist logic, liberal democracy is neither liberal nor democratic and identity politics is nothing but a swirling chaos of incoherence and deception, except intersectionally, although the problem with this is that no one really lives intersectionally, except in their own mind. With Marx, post-modernists could just call politics and culture a sleight of hand leading to the universal representation of particular class interests. This, of course, does happen, but it is a mistake to reduce politics to false consciousness.

During the 1960s, for every anti-liberal supporter of the Black Panthers you could find at least three liberal supporters of the Southern Christian Leadership Conference; for every supporter of Malcolm X, you could find three supporters of Martin Luther King, Jr. In the case of Puerto Ricans, for every supporter of the militant Young Lords during the 1960s, you could find ten supporters of Herman Badillo. And, in the end, the Young Lords themselves ended up trading the practice of politics for the study of politics, the challenge of the legal system for entry into its corridors, the streets for the library, the mass demonstration for institutional media, El Barrio for the gentrified city block or suburbia. For Puerto Ricans, identity politics was the point of entry to the liberal democratic stage. Their attacks on sexism and patriarchy, on racism and poverty, on political exclusion and police brutality, on monolingual education, were attacks staged from the trenches of modernity against the forces of backwardness and tradition.

Kenny emphasizes that trying to define identity politics in terms of a common theme or grand narrative is less important and more difficult, than *specifying the impact of identity politics and its capacity to raise new and important questions.* The key question, for him, is not whether identity politics is really a barbarian at the gate of liberal democracy. Instead he suggests that the importance of identity politics is related to the following questions:

1. Who are its protagonists, and what are their interests, histories, and ideologies?
2. Is the pluralism of identity politics a pluralism of diversity or a pluralism of difference—is conflict in identity politics about interests or about principles?
3. Is the idea of citizenship, comprised of individuals equal under the law, replaced by the idea of singular group personality, groups unequal under the law and therefore each requiring their own law?
4. Is it true that under identity politics each group has an "irreducible individuality and that each must struggle to achieve its self-realization, whatever the social and political costs"?[37]
5. Or is it true that under identity politics, groups simply "make demands that imply the extension and realization of some of the central norms of liberal politics—democratic inclusion, non-discrimination, and equality of respect above all"?[38]
6. What kinds of issues do identity politics bring to the forefront? Do these issues bring new interest and commitment to the political process, or do they create deeper and/or irreconcilable conflicts?
7. Does identity politics produce "rival visions of public life and social authority" that are incompatible?[39]
8. Do we lose a sense of "shared moral and political purpose" when we support or engage in identity politics?[40]
9. Does identity politics substitute the ideal of a democratic community for a "democracy of communities," and if so, is this undesirable?[41]

A simple set of summary answers could be BOTH to questions 2 and 6; NO to questions 3, 4, 7 and 8; YES to question 5; and YES and NO to question 9. At the conclusion of this empirical recollection, I will elaborate on these short answers.

In the historical *collage* that follows, the protagonists—in other words, the answer to question number one—are Puerto Ricans from working-class, professional, and academic worlds, some originally from the island and some native-born New Yorkers. To a post-modern analyst, these would be different kinds of Puerto Ricans, acting politically with different sets of interests and achieving outcomes that were in line with the variety of their backgrounds and motivations.

This is logical and generally true in the sense that within one family, say, the family of Martin Luther King, Jr., Martin and Coretta were irreducible to each other. The flip side of that coin is that, ultimately, just as in the outside world the individual differences between Martin and Coretta were reduced to the category of black and each was treated on the basis of that collective identity, documentary and practical life ascriptions reduced the singularities of Puerto Rican types to a collective identity that provided the basis for their racialization which in turn catalyzed mobilization as a collectively identifiable group.

The empirical account shows that in carrying out community-based activities and collective action, the protagonists in this narrative behaved based on a sense of a group identity—as Puerto Ricans—despite the existence of shades of Puertoricanness that make the group situationally and existentially a differentiated whole. Their interests were social, economic, cultural, and political and most sought recognition as first-class citizens, feeling entitled to the benefits of liberal democracy, with a sense of commitment and obligation to the liberal democratic notions of individual rights and equal justice for all.

To be sure, some were interested in systemic transformation and their activism was inspired by revolutionary aspirations. In the end, however, they pushed left to get to the center and as a result, unwittingly reinforced the central norms of liberal politics.[42] As will be clear below, the organizing principle for this enterprise was Puertoricanness. And this enterprise broke the theoretical aporia between liberalism and identity politics, between the value of individualism and the validity of group rights that identity politics is purportedly incapable of surmounting.

The past is ultimately definitive and shaped by clear boundaries, but it is not immune to interpretation. Therefore, the reader must remember this: other accounts of Puerto Rican politics may offer alternative interpretations to the one offered here. Mine is circumscribed to the period recalled for analysis and to the particular cast of characters that populated the process of community-based activities and collective action during that period. It is entirely possible that others looking at the same period may offer a different interpretation based on a different focus, different sources, and a different theoretical outlook.

METHODOLOGY AND SOURCES

The argument of this book—that the aporetic relationship between liberalism and identity politics can be transcended in practice—is illustrated empirically in seven chapters that describe Puerto Rican community-based activities and collective action between 1960 and 1990 in the manner of what I call a historical *collage*. A historical *collage* is an ensemble of events that produces a coherent narrative, using juxtaposition as its primary tool.[43]

This technique is a useful counterpoint to the tendency to present analytical reconstructions of historical events as faithful renderings of history. While this is sometimes possible, there are also cases in which the fragmentary and incomplete historical record only allows for interpretive recollections such as the one I offer here.

The *collage* of events assembled here is based on the review of archival sources, newspapers, videos, photographs, secondary sources, and also by listening to informants, conducting interviews, watching interviews, and reading interview transcripts about Puerto Rican political participation at the community level in New York City. The final product is a *recollection* rather than a *recreation* of community-based activities and collective action. As such, the book is a survey of behavior by groups and individuals acting strategically or through demand-protest actions over time. The recollection does not produce a narrative in the conventional sense since there are gaps in the record that were impossible to fill; it is in that sense that the book recalls rather than recreates. Its flow is fundamentally chronological and detailed. Not everything is serially connected, but all groups and events have been selected for their salient, emblematic, illustrative, or little known previously but interesting character.

Historical writing is often called "narrative" and this book narrates the process of Puerto Rican community-based activities and collective action only to the extent that it follows a chronological sequence. As noted earlier, there is much juxtaposition in the chronicle. I have re-structured the order of events to make for a more digestible rendering, but overall the order of presentation corresponds to their actual sequence.

The recollection provides the material for the construction of a singular explanation: community-based activities and collective action were forms of identity politics that were facilitated by a liberal democratic milieu. They sustained the consensus that shaped and informed that milieu, and expanded its vocabulary.

Puerto Rican politics in New York City is an example of a politics of community seeking inclusion, participation, recognition, and redress of grievances along liberal democratic lines. In other words, it is a politics that blends liberalism and identity politics not *naturally* but *empirically*, emphasizing inclusive difference. Thus, the Puerto Rican record of community-based activities and collective action is an example of a kernel of identity politics cum cultural citizenship within the shell of liberal democratic politics.

In this recollection, I highlight movement from beginning to end through a series of alternative openings, all connected and, ultimately, seen as a whole, presenting a story that has significance, coherence, and structure. The book recalls the community-based activities and collective action *trajectory* Puerto Ricans followed in New York City within that framework. The resulting "story" provides an opportunity to say something about politics, specifically about identity politics and its kinship to liberalism as *grounded theory*.

In order to provide some measure of control over bias and distortion in newspaper accounts, I reviewed relevant coverage by the *New York Times* and *El Diario-La Prensa*, the two newspapers of record in New York in English and Spanish, respectively. As far as providing a good sense of the overall story, these newspapers complemented each other. In my archival forays, however, I came across clippings from other newspapers, such as *El Diario de Nueva York, El Imparcial, El Mundo, El Tiempo, La Voz de Puerto Rico en U.S.A., New York Newsday, Noticias del Mundo, The Guardian, The New York Telegram and Sun, The Worker,* and *Vida Hispana,* which provided useful details and perspectives.

SCOPE AND CONTENT

I focus on the years 1960-1990 because during the 1960s the Puerto Rican community in New York reaches a critical demographic mass that makes it into a group of significance. During the 1960s and 1970s, some of the most interesting and meaningful developments in its social, cultural, and political trajectory in New York take place. The year 1990 seemed an appropriate cut-off point because, after charter revision, the city became a completely different place politically. To be sure, there were changes between 1960 and 1989 that altered the context of participation, but charter revision in 1989 set an entirely different stage, worthy of designation as a threshold for a new set of developments. While charter revision had more of an impact on the political process than in terms of community-based collective action, it seemed reasonable to use that signal moment in the political life of New York to bring the narrative to an end.

The underlying premise of this decision was simply that a new political context might require a new vantage point and framework for an account of subsequent developments. For example, as a result of charter revision, political representation in the city council was expanded, making electoral politics a more meaningful arena of competition and action than before. This created a threshold of significance for community-based collective action, marking the period after 1990 as different from the years preceding charter reform.

The common theme of the forthcoming chapters is community-based activities and collective action. The chapters chronicle the *trajectory* of the community to produce a hypothesis for practice, namely that liberalism and identity politics can be reconciled empirically, from the ground up. I do not offer this as a definitive explanation but as an interpretation of Puerto Rican politics that doubles as a roadmap for political action. I first came across the idea of theory as a roadmap for politics in Alasdair MacIntyre's "The Indispensability of Political Theory." In that article, MacIntyre uses the metaphor of a roadmap to suggest that theory is ultimately a template that offers guidance without providing a faithful rendering of reality.[44] Nothing in this account is fabricated or fanciful, but my interpretation is open-ended, and the directions of the roadmap that flow from the account can be recalculated.

Chapter 1 sets the context for the historical recollection. Chapters 2 through 7 are a selective chronicle of events and activities that follows my *collage* strategy of narrative development. Community-based activities and collective action provide the empirical thread that runs through the account. The narrative is assembled according to that framework.

I distinguish between institutional and grassroots actions as separate markers in the thematic organization of the chapters to differentiate strategic from demand-protest action. Strategic action was mostly proactive and deliberate, whereas demand-protest was mostly reactive and contingent. Actions driven by specific issues are placed within either one of those two categories. The content within each category is different in each chapter, and each chapter is different in terms of the issues highlighted, depending on what was happening during the period recalled and based on my judgment for inclusion, which was guided—as already noted—by whether the events were salient, emblematic, illustrative, or little known previously but interesting. Throughout the chapters I offer commentary *passim*.

Chapter 8 concludes the book with a brief account of the general trajectory of Puerto Rican politics in New York City, arguing that community-based activities and collective action blended liberalism and identity politics. As noted previously, the questions regarding identity politics formulated above are directly addressed in Chapter 8 in light of the preceding empirical account.

The narrative shows that in some instances the tension between self-sufficiency and identity politics was typically resolved in favor of the latter. It is also clear that Puerto Rican community-based activities and collective action were variegated not only in terms of issues and orientation, but also in terms of the mix of characters. In some cases, city government sought to co-opt community mobilization and in others, seemingly non-political events were used to promote an identity politics agenda. Ethnic identity was both a resource and a hindrance, and competition was never in short supply regardless of ethnic identification among protagonists. Puerto Rican electoral politics has been historically characterized as deficient but this aspect of political participation is better conceived as the tip of an iceberg that included community-based activities and collective action around issues such as education, housing, police brutality, racial relations, and the adequacy of governmental responses to Puerto Rican needs. Community institutions and groups that chose strategic action and demand-protest as methods of participation addressed these issues from the vantage point of a Puerto Rican collective identity. In doing so, they blended liberalism and identity politics in practice. Let us now turn to the recollection of this three-decade process.[45]

CHAPTER 1

THE CONTEXT OF STRATEGIC ACTION AND DEMAND-PROTEST

Historically, the growth of the Puerto Rican population in the United States has been fundamentally driven by migration. In the aftermath of the social and economic devastation caused in 2017 by Hurricane María, migration is once again the main force behind population movements between the island and the mainland. The larger context of migration—historical and contemporary—is colonialism, capitalist development, and economic crisis. This context explains why the majority of Puerto Ricans migrate to the U.S. but does not fully account for their settlement, adaptation, and political incorporation. Capitalism and economic crisis shape the context of action differently on the mainland, while colonialism recedes into the background.

This time around, the leading recipient of migrants fleeing after María is Florida, followed by Pennsylvania and Massachusetts, with New York coming in fourth place.[1] A story in the *Washington Post*, detailing the efforts of Miguel Joey Aviles, a self-described diversity coach in the town of Branson, Missouri, to bring Puerto Ricans to the Ozarks to fill labor shortages in the town's tourist economy, suggests that beyond Florida and the Northeast, this new migration will bring Puerto Ricans to the least expected destinations straight from the island.[2] This is not unprecedented, but it has not been a distinctive feature of Puerto Rican migration to the U.S. for some time.

In his study of Puerto Rican migration, Edgardo Meléndez demonstrates beyond reasonable doubt what intuitively and based on bits of information—both scholarly and anecdotal—has been known for a long time: that the Great Migration of Puerto Ricans to the U.S. during the 1940s and 1950s was sponsored by the government of Puerto Rico.[3] In the aftermath of María, the Puerto Rican Commonwealth is once again sponsoring migration, even if this time it is largely doing so by the default mechanisms of powerlessness and incompetence. Overpopulation is once again a factor but in the Marxist sense of surplus labor rather than the Malthusian sense of fertility run amok.

Just as in the past, when businesses recruited Puerto Ricans to work in the sugarcane fields of Hawaii, the tobacco fields of Connecticut, and the vegetable farms of New Jersey, the government is being assisted by a variety of agents.[4] Some, like universities on the mainland that are opening their doors to students in need, are driven by good intentions. Others, like Miguel Joey Avilés, are hustlers who tell businessmen that to lure Puerto Ricans as cheap laborers, they must offer Goya products and learn how to dance *merengue*.

To think that people are going to settle from Puerto Rico to the middle of nowhere for culinary reasons is ludicrous. Further, this so-called diversity coach should know that *merengue* is a Dominican musical genre. Regardless, it is also ridiculous to think that Puerto Ricans would move to Branson if they could dance to *their own* rhythms of *bomba* and *plena*. Fortunately, there are also respectable firms involved, in places like Maine, Wisconsin, and Indiana, whose incentives of housing and cars are more substantial than dancing, Goya plantains, or coconut water. Unfortunately, the U.S. government has also "sponsored" migration through its callous treatment of islanders.

While this book looks backward to the period between 1960-1990 in New York City, the theme of Puerto Rican migration and its circumstances—colonialism, capitalism, economic crisis, natural disasters—is an element of continuity between past and present and an important element of the context in which Puerto Ricans carried out community-based activities and collective action. Once Puerto Ricans set foot in the U.S., everything changes. Elements of continuity become abstract forces, but the one factor that emerges prominently and structures the socio-economic and political life of the migrants is their Puerto Rican identity. How exactly Puertoricanness will play itself out politically in Puerto Rican communities post-María remains to be seen. My hope is that this examination of the past provides political lessons for what may be a new era of Puerto Rican identity politics and liberalism in the United States.

PUERTO RICAN NEW YORK

By 1970, the impetus for Puerto Rican population growth in New York City provided by migration from the island had waned and was replaced by the natural increase in population. Politically, the prequel, during the mid-1960s, was the emergence of the Nuyorican generation. This was a cohort of Boricuas who made their mark in the music (e.g., Willie Colón and Eddie Palmieri), literature (e.g., Pedro Pietri and Tato Laviera), and politics of the city (e.g., Herman Badillo, though he was born in Puerto Rico; the Puerto Rican Socialist Party; the Young Lords; and United Bronx Parents). While by 1990 Puerto Ricans remained a relatively young population compared to the rest of the city's residents, the gap in age structure had closed over the years. Table 1.1 shows the growth of the Puerto Rican community in New York over time, and Table 1.2 shows that by 1970 approximately 75 percent of Puerto Ricans residing in New York City were younger than 35 years of age compared to 53 percent for the city as a whole. Twenty years later that 22-percentage point gap fell by half to 11 percentage points.

In 1960, Puerto Ricans in the United States numbered over 856,000.[5] The New York City component represented 72 percent of the U.S. total. The median age of the group was close to 28 years old. According to the Democratic Party's State Committee, more than 200,000 Puerto Ricans voted in New York City in the 1960 election out of a total of 3.6 million voters. While one-half of one percent of the vote was not impressive in absolute terms, Puerto Rican leaders highlighted the impact of this small proportion of voters. According to the Mayor of San Juan, Felisa Rincón de Gautier, commonly known as Doña Fela, Puerto Ricans were a significant voting bloc, significant enough to claim they had helped the election of mayor Robert Wagner in 1961.[6]

Table 1.1. Puerto Ricans in New York City, 1940-1990
Total Population and Average Annual Growth Rate

YEAR	NEW YORK CITY	AVG. GROWTH	PUERTO RICANS	AVG. GROWTH
1940	7,454,995	—	61,463	—
1950	7,891,957	—	245,880	—
1960	7,781,984	—	612,574	—
1970	7,881,284	—	844,303	—
1980	8,215,920	0.42%	887,500	0.50%
1990	8,408,590	0.23%	887,573	0.0001%

Sources for total city population: 1940: https://www.census.gov/population/www/documentation/twps0027/tab17.txt
<Accessed July 22, 2014>. 1950: https://www.census.gov/population/www/documentation/twps0027/tab18.txt
<Accessed July 22, 2014>. 1960: https://www.census.gov/population/www/documentation/twps0027/tab19.txt
<Accessed July 22, 2014>.
Sources for Puerto Rican population 1940, 1950, 1960: Campbell Gibson, Population of the 100 Largest Cities and Other Urban Places in the United States: 1790 to 1990, United States Census Bureau, June 1998; Department of City Planning, City of New York Puerto Rican New Yorkers in 1990, Table 1-1, December 1993.
For Tables 1.2, 1.3, 1.5:
1. The data for 1980 and 1990 are extracted from the Public Use Microdata Sample, 5% New York State files, for the New York City MSA or PMSA.
2. The data for 1970 are extracted from the Integrated Public Use Microdata Sample 5% for SMSAs.
3. The 1970 PUMS does not include the household income variable.

Political Economy Context

In the United States, a period of unprecedented economic expansion during the early 1960s was followed by slowdown by the end of the decade and the early 1970s. The period from the mid-1970s to the early 1980s was marked by stagflation and crisis.[7] Despite the 1987 stock market crash, a period of recovery continued during the later years of the decade. This pattern of growth, stagnation, and recovery was also evident in New York City and was reflected in the changing socioeconomic status of Puerto Ricans in the city between 1960 and 1990.

The 1960s was a period of buoyant economic growth in the United States. The decade represented the longest economic expansion on record at the time, and the inflationary pressures brought on by military expenditures during the Vietnam conflict had not been fully realized. The economic high-water mark was 1965. From 1960 to 1966, real output grew at the average annual rate of 4.8 percent per year, despite interruptions in expansion in late 1962 and early 1963. There was a recession only in the first half of 1967.[8]

In 1964, fiscal policy was driving the economy forward. President Johnson's dual wars—one on poverty and the other in Vietnam—in conjunction with a major tax

Table 1.2. Age Structure of the Population of New York City, 1970-1990 (in percent of total population)

AGE GROUP	NEW YORK CITY			PUERTO RICANS		
	1970	1980	1990	1970	1980	1990
0-34	53.24	53.57	51.54	75.57	69.95	62.60
0-15	25.93	22.34	20.40	43.38	35.20	29.20
16-24	13.89	14.70	12.65	15.93	17.97	15.55
25-34	13.45	16.53	18.49	16.26	16.78	17.45
Over 34	34.42	33.21	35.38	21.85	26.24	31.93
35-44	11.46	11.93	15.25	11.24	12.07	14.08
45-54	11.81	10.78	11.12	6.61	8.75	10.62
55-64	11.15	10.50	9.01	4.00	5.42	7.23
Over 65	12.34	13.22	13.08	2.58	3.81	5.87

Source: See Table 1.1.

decrease in 1964 led to full employment by 1965. The fiscal engine was at full throttle, and monetary policy was supporting it rather than serving as a restraint. By the second half of 1965, money supply was growing at a very expansive 10.6 percent annual rate. From a projected government surplus of $8.6 billion in the first half of 1965, policymakers found themselves with a deficit of $9 billion by the end of the year.

The Puerto Rican economy was also undergoing a dramatic restructuring as the agricultural sector continued to decline while attempts were made to attract more capital-intensive industries that could better withstand the vicissitudes of the U.S. business cycle.

In New York City, similar patterns of economic expansion were coupled with evidence of problems to come. There was clear advance warning of the difficulties down the road. But beginning with Mayor Robert F. Wagner, the city managed to muffle the sounds of trouble for years, by overstating income and underestimating expenses. This produced budgets that were balanced only on paper.[9]

Both John V. Lindsay, who succeeded Wagner as mayor and served in that capacity from 1966 to 1973, and Abraham D. Beame, who succeeded Lindsay as mayor in 1974 and soundly criticized both Wagner and Lindsay for these practices while City Comptroller, fell into similar patterns of "fiscal gimmickry." Ten years after Wagner's last year in office (1965), New York City was on the brink of financial default. This was to have serious repercussions on the socioeconomic status of Puerto Ricans, both those living in New York and those on the island.

Once the 1975 fiscal crisis hit, operating expenses rose rapidly with the growth of social programs and city services.[10] The recession drove more and more people to the welfare rolls while inflation increased costs and operating expenses across the board. Short-term borrowing increased dramatically to close the gap between expenses and revenues and inflationary pressures pushed the costs of borrowing ever higher. When the banks and the investor community lost confidence in the city's ability to manage its affairs and reduce expenses, they refused to buy the city's bonds.

Robert Abrams, a Bronx borough president from 1970 to 1979, whose constituency was largely Puerto Rican, decried the interference of the banks in managing city affairs. But few alternatives were available if default was to be averted.[11] Cutbacks in city services, layoffs, the closing of community programs and schools, reduced funding for the City University of New York, the elimination of capital construction projects, and increases in taxes in combination with a national downturn in economic activity and rising inflation squeezed the more vulnerable groups in society. Puerto Ricans were hit particularly hard.

By the end of 1975, Governor Hugh Carey created the Municipal Assistance Corporation—known as Big MAC—and the Emergency Financial Control Board. It did not take long for the public to realize that the city was being managed by both Big MAC and the Control Board and that fundamental decisions were being made by the governor in Albany and not the mayor. At this point the city was on the brink of default, and the only option available was for the federal government to step in to underwrite the existing mountain of debt.

Earlier, President Gerald Ford resisted attempts to get involved and used the city's situation as an example of profligate Democratic Party spending. The *Daily News* provided the most acerbic summary of the urban policy of the federal government under Ford in its famous October 30, 1975, front page headline: FORD TO CITY: DROP DEAD, Vows He'll Veto Any Bail-Out.[12] Fred Ferretti, a reporter with the *New York Times*, portrayed Washington's stance on New York City as an attack on Puerto Ricans and other minorities, arguing that Washington thought of them as "arrogant smart asses who didn't give a damn about the rest of the country [...]."[13]

President Ford eventually relented and agreed to federal involvement that averted the default at the very last minute. There was more than enough blame to go around for this state of affairs—it would be heaped on the city's leadership, the financial community, the labor unions, the feds, and the state—but the bottom line was that the residents of New York City found themselves paying more for fewer services, facing precarious prospects for continued employment, seeing needed capital infrastructure projects postponed or cancelled, and, overall, experiencing a decline in the quality of life.[14]

The Puerto Rican community found itself disproportionately affected by these developments. In 1960, its socioeconomic status was already dismal. Puerto Ricans were at the lower end of the income scale and at the higher end of the unemployment rate. Families with incomes under $3,000 were 34 percent of the total compared to 27 percent for blacks and 12 percent for whites. The unemployment rate for Puerto Rican males was 10 percent compared to 7 percent for blacks and 4 percent for whites. At 11 percent, the unemployment rate for Puerto Rican females was higher, while black females were on a par with Puerto Ricans males with a rate of 7 percent, compared to 5 percent for white females.

Older Puerto Rican males were twice as likely to be unemployed than all older New Yorkers (9 and 4 percent among those 45-64 years old, respectively) and 20 percent of Puerto Ricans 14-19 years of age were unemployed compared to 11 percent of all New Yorkers in the same cohort. The story was similar for older Puerto Rican females: 10 percent of those between 45-64 years of age were unemployed compared to 5 percent for females citywide; 9 percent among the 35-44 year-old cohort were unemployed compared to 5 percent for their city counterparts. The median school years completed by adults over 25 years of age in 1960 were: 8 years, Puerto Ricans; 10 years, blacks and all New Yorkers.[15]

With the fiscal crisis, the poverty rate—already high by any standard—skyrocketed among Puerto Ricans. In 1970, almost one-third of Puerto Rican residents had income levels that fell below the poverty line (see Table 1.3). By the end of the decade, that figure increased to over 42 percent, while for New York City residents as a whole, the poverty rate rose from 14 percent to 18 percent over the 1970-1980 period.

While the federal government was reluctant to provide resources to an increasingly insolvent New York City, it did take measures to contain island migration. Federal monies began flowing to Puerto Rico in earnest in the early 1970s (see Figure 1.1). The expansion of the safety net on the island reduced incentives to migrate, thus lowering the pressure disadvantaged new arrivals might add to an already beleaguered city.

There is also evidence that Puerto Rico's full participation in the Fair Labor Standards Act in 1976 that led to the elimination of differences between island minimum wages and the federal statutory minimum had the effect of forestalling migration to the U.S.[16] Here again was a situation where the federal government imposed conditions on the island that fundamentally impacted the labor market, and hence,

Table 1.3 Poverty Rates in New York City, 1970-1990 (in percent)

	% OF PERSONS IN GROUP UNDER POVERTY LEVEL	
YEAR	NEW YORK CITY	PUERTO RICANS
1970	14.48	32.92
1980	18.34	42.04
1990	17.25	37.26

Source: See Table 1.1.

Figure 1.1 Federal Transfer Payments as a Fraction of Personal Income in Puerto Rico, 1940-1990

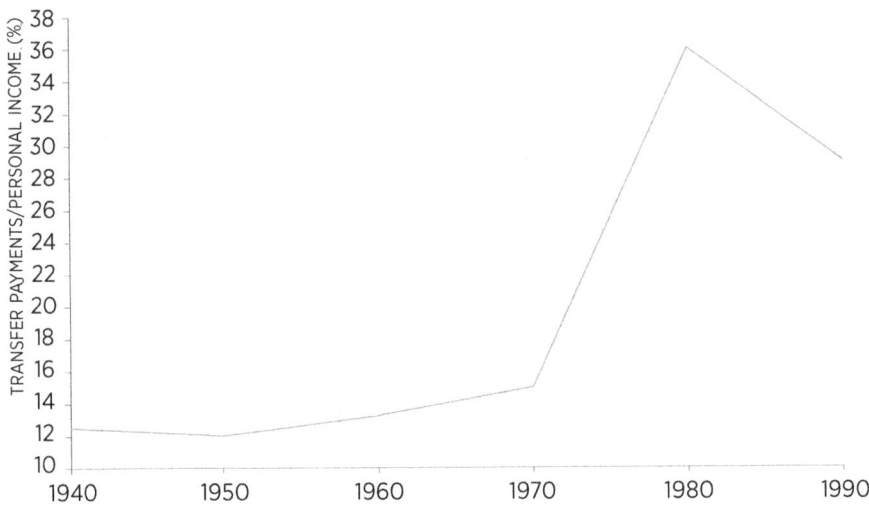

Source: U.S. Census of Population, Puerto Rico: Detailed Characteristics, various years.

migration. The data show this effect as a result of the closing of the nominal wage gap between Puerto Rico and New York City and of the extension of federal benefits to island residents.[17] The other crucial factor in this equation was that conditions in New York City were deteriorating rapidly for Puerto Ricans in the mid-1970s.

By 1980, in the national context, Puerto Ricans had the lowest incomes, highest poverty rates, low labor force participation, high welfare dependency, high numbers of single female-headed households, and low levels of educational attainment. Yet, given their high concentration in New York City and the calamity that befell that city from 1974 on, could things really have been any different? By 1990, positive change was taking place.

While migration from Puerto Rico picked up in the 1990s compared to the previous decade, New York City was not the main destination for Puerto Rican migrants. As Table 1.4 shows, of the metropolitan statistical areas with largest concentration of Puerto Ricans in the U.S., New York City ranks last in terms of the fraction of its population that came from Puerto Rico in the five years prior to the survey date of 1990. In 1990, 63 percent of the Puerto Rican population of New York City had not moved in five years, while 33 percent had moved within the city or across state and municipal lines. Only 3.5 percent of the city's Puerto Rican population moved directly from Puerto Rico in the previous five years.

The stability of the Puerto Rican population during the 1980 decade was also reflected in the population's income growth over that period. Table 1.5 compares

Table 1.4 Percentage of Non-movers, Movers from Puerto Rico, and All Other Movers in Metropolitan Areas with Largest Puerto Rican Populations, 1990

METROPOLITAN STATISTICAL AREA	NON-MOVERS	MOVERS FROM PUERTO RICO	ALL OTHER MOVERS
Lawrence-Haverhill, MA	24.2	26.5	49.3
Worcester, MA	37.3	20.3	52.4
Waterbury, CT	29.3	16.1	54.6
Rochester, NY	29.3	11.1	59.6
Lancaster, PA	29.6	12.9	57.6
Tampa-St. Petersburg, Clearwater, FL	31.0	15.4	53.6
Reading, PA	31.6	14.9	53.5
Springfield, MA	32.0	17.7	50.3
Miami, FL	33.7	12.4	53.9
Buffalo, NY	33.7	15.3	51.0
Boston, MA	35.8	11.5	52.6
Hartford, CT	35.9	14.5	49.6
Bridgeport, CT	38.0	9.6	52.4
Cleveland-Lorain- Elyria, OH	38.5	12.1	49.4
Allentown-Bethlehem-Easton, PA	39.9	11.7	48.4
Trenton, NJ	41.0	10.9	48.1
Chicago, IL	42.4	5.1	52.5
Los Angeles-Long Beach, CA	43.6	4.8	51.6
Newark, NJ	44.7	9.1	46.2
Philadelphia, PA	44.9	7.5	47.6
Lorain-Elyria, OH	47.4	5.3	47.2
Jersey City, NJ	50.6	5.7	43.7
New York City, NY	63.0	3.5	33.5

Source: U.S. Department of Commerce, 1990 U.S. Census of Population and Housing, 5% Public Use Microdata Sample (PUMS); tabulations by Carlos E. Santiago.

Table 1.5 Mean Household Income in New York City, 1970-1990

	NEW YORK CITY		
YEAR	MEAN HOUSEHOLD INCOME	PERSONS IN HOUSEHOLD	MEAN HOUSEHOLD INCOME PER CAPITA
1970	—	2.73	—
1980	$18,645	2.54	$7,352
1990	$42,043	2.56	$16,412

	PUERTO RICANS		
YEAR	MEAN HOUSEHOLD INCOME	PERSONS IN HOUSEHOLD	MEAN HOUSEHOLD INCOME PER CAPITA
1970	—	3.72	—
1980	$10,802	3.10	$3,490
1990	$24,028	3.03	$7,926

Source: See Table 1.1.

mean income per capita in New York City and among its Puerto Rican residents, in 1980 and 1990. Puerto Rican mean income growth (per capita) kept pace with that of the city in general and the gap in mean income per capita closed somewhat by 1990. While the picture was not great, it was certainly different from what one might have expected if trends dating back to 1970 had continued.

The modest economic improvement experienced by Puerto Rican New Yorkers during the 1980s was offset by the fact that in 1990 they had lower socioeconomic status compared to the Puerto Rican population in the U.S. overall. The mean household income per capita of Puerto Rican New Yorkers was below the average for the overall Puerto Rican population by 5 percent. For Puerto Ricans in New York, the poverty rate in 1989 was 36.5 percent compared to 30.3 percent for Puerto Ricans in the country.

Nevertheless, the economic progress experienced by Puerto Ricans in New York City was similar to that of Puerto Ricans elsewhere in the nation. The increase in mean household income per capita of Puerto Ricans in New York during the 1980s was 28.8 percent, just about the same as the 29 percent for Puerto Ricans overall. While remarkable by national standards—although only in a relative sense—the gains of Puerto Rican New Yorkers were not unusual in New York City. The second half of the 1980s were years of solid economic growth for the city and this was reflected—however pale a reflection—in the income gains of many racial and ethnic groups in the population. Unfortunately, while the 28.8 percent growth in household income per capita among Puerto Ricans was close to the average gain of 27.1 percent for the city as a whole, the 40 percent increase for non-Hispanic whites meant a huge gap between the two groups that expanded during the 1980s.[18]

POLITICAL CONTEXT

Generally, Puerto Rican engagement in political activity is lower than that of non-Hispanics and non-Hispanic whites. In many states and localities, Puerto Ricans have achieved parity in descriptive representation and have made inroads into bureaucratic positions in municipal and county governments. Representation has not fully translated into policy responsiveness. Why not? This is the case in part because the most significant form of Puerto Rican political activity is protest, which is considered to be the least effective of all; they also have limited access to resources that contribute to increased participation; and elected officials, especially in New York, are insulated from political challenges and thus are generally less responsive. Since their numbers are small, they also have less leverage over their peers.[19]

There are exceptions to the pattern of responsiveness. After Hurricane María hit and devastated Puerto Rico, the first responders on the ground came from New York in a plane provided by Jet Blue filled with bottles of water and other supplies. This effort was orchestrated by the Governor of the State, Andrew Cuomo. Almost a year later, to the day, at a roundtable in the Somos el Futuro Legislative Conference titled "NY Stands with Puerto Rico," the dozen or so participants effusively thanked the governor for his concern with Puerto Rico and for his intensive and sustained support. The panelists included academics, elected and bureaucratic officials, representatives from the government of Puerto Rico and international organizations, and non-profit and business executives with a special interest in Puerto Rico, whether commercial or humanitarian in kind.

Sadly, however, as important, necessary, and welcome as the focus of attention on the impact of María was, the hurricane hit the island, not New York. The directly affected were Puerto Ricans in Puerto Rico, not in Brooklyn, and therefore this break in the pattern of selective inattention that is typical of the relationship between Puerto Ricans and elected officials meant very little, except symbolically, to Puerto Ricans in New York. During the roundtable at Somos el Futuro, the Bronx Borough President had nothing to say, and the chair of the Puerto Rican/Hispanic Task Force in the state legislature, who quickly became Governor Cuomo's point man for the state's relief effort, mentioned the Bronx only because that was his place of residence.

When the state's Lieutenant Governor mentioned that in April 2018 the state had sent a tactical assessment team that deployed students and teachers on the island to assess damages, bring supplies, and work in rebuilding homes, I wondered what kind of disaster would be necessary to deploy those kinds of resources in Puerto Rican neighborhoods in the Bronx. When Assemblyman Marcos Crespo gushed over the fact that New York State was the first responder in Puerto Rico, setting up a New York State Office in San Juan to coordinate relief efforts and to provide resources to address economic and public health issues, I wondered why the state, or the Puerto Rican/Hispanic Task Force for that matter, did not have a special office to coordinate the provision of technical assistance, job training, access to resources for economic development and education for Puerto Ricans throughout the city.

The answers to the questions above are related to the nature of political representation in city and state government and to the political trajectory of Puerto Ricans in New York. First, if there is no office in the city or the state comparable to the New York State Office in San Juan, it is because Puerto Ricans in the Bronx, Manhattan, Queens, and Brooklyn who happen to have Puerto Rican or Latino representatives in the city council, the state legislature, or Congress, have some of their needs attended through constituency services. Second, Puerto Ricans have resorted to a diverse set of means for action, including electoral politics, social movement politics, lobbying, and litigation to pursue the satisfaction of individual and collective interests. Third, their incorporation—that is, their access to political representation and representation in the policy process—has been facilitated to some extent by the labor movement and largely by community-based activities and collective action instead of political parties. This is a variant of the main argument of this book: Puerto Ricans pursued the benefits of a liberal order through collective action and their claims were driven by identity.

The War on Poverty
When the Johnson administration declared a War on Poverty in the United States, the last thing that was expected to happen was that this particular policy turn would provide a context for a political practice that reconciled identity politics—understood as a politics seeking integration, progress, and redress of grievances using a collective identity as the basis for social and political mobilization—and liberalism—understood as a theoretical approach that emphasizes individuality, autonomy, and choice and gives pride of place to society over the state.

By the time the War on Poverty was officially declared in 1964, Puerto Ricans already had a history of community activities and collective action in the city. The Hispanics Young Adults Association, which despite its name was mostly Puerto Rican, had been established a decade earlier, the Puerto Rican Forum had been around for seven years, and ASPIRA was in its third year of operation. A school boycott had called attention to the needs of Puerto Rican students in the public education system and a riot had unfolded in response to police brutality. What Johnson wanted to accomplish, Puerto Ricans had already started with private resources on their own.

The public at large was mostly indifferent about poverty, and Johnson had to take steps to change this attitude. The first was taken during his 1964 State of the Union Address, when he categorically declared that "this administration, here and now, declares unconditional war on poverty."[20] He then repeated his goals without being specific to various types of audiences, ranging from university students to the

Business Council to the AFL-CIO. He visited poor communities, he cajoled businessmen into becoming part of the administration's rhetorical campaign in favor of the policy, articles and books were written advocating for this unusual "war," lobbyists were enlisted in the effort, and all was done in terms that emphasized the common interest while downplaying any association between poverty and race. Of course, most poor people in the United States were white, but the Democratic Party was concerned that the initiative might be construed as largely a program to benefit blacks.

In a short period of time, the War on Poverty won its first battle. Johnson managed to sway public opinion in support of his program, enlisting as advocates and supporters liberal intellectuals, government bureaucrats, southern Congressmen, key labor leaders, and local elected officials. When the Economic Opportunity Act of 1964, the centerpiece legislation of the War on Poverty, was proposed, one of its first advocates was the U.S. Conference of Mayors. Opponents were not shy: Senator John Tower of Texas declared that the War on Poverty was a war on local control and representative government. Senator Millard Simpson of Wyoming, claimed that it was a scam, a policy designed to make "the deceitful seem honest, and the fraudulent seem trustworthy." And Senator A. Willis Robertson from Virginia objected to being pressured to vote for a bill on purely symbolic grounds. To him, the Economic Opportunity Act was long on purposes and short on justification.[21]

What is interesting about the War on Poverty is that it was a liberal program that provided a rationale for identity politics. Zarefsky notes that "from the colonial period onward, the dominant belief was that poverty was an individual, not a social problem. [...] The mid-nineteenth century humanitarian reform movements reinforced this approach, since their emphasis was on *individual* actions to improve one's life." He adds, "The Progressive movement contributed the argument that poverty was a social phenomenon, not an imperfection of the individual, and that powerful social groups had an economic stake in its perpetuation."[22] In his view, this led to a perspective that was more tolerant of individual shortcomings and derelictions, but still insisted that even if poverty was social in scale, private, voluntary measures to address it were better than public interventions. During the 1930s, this belief was modified by the subsidiarity principle, which meant that the level of intervention should be determined by the limits of action. The structure of the argument for the subsidiarity principle was that individual, private level efforts were best as first resort measures; and collective, governmental level action was best as a last resort intervention, once it was clear that all lower level efforts were insufficient or ineffective.[23]

The War on Poverty changed all that, not thoroughly and definitively, but in a substantial way. To put it in terms of one interpretation of the role of race in American political development, the policy was one element of the transformation of the American racial order from white supremacist to transformative egalitarian.[24] In other words, a coalition of actors enabled a policy that shifted the grounds of intervention on a social policy issue, favoring principle over expediency, emphasizing equality of opportunity, but providing resources to ensure equality of results. The legitimacy of the use of the power of the state for social purposes was "increased," but it was not "new" because this was not the first time that governmental action had provided a context for mobilization on the basis of a collective identity to seek institutional support for individual and group uplift and redress of grievances. But it was in this particular context that Puerto Rican community activities and collective action took place between 1960-1990, even if by the mid-1970s they were back on their own, using the same strategy for action in their pursuit of first-class citizenship from the vantage point of difference.

Community-Based Activities and Collective Action
Puerto Rican organizations during the early 1960s in New York City emerged in a context in which participatory, grassroots democracy was normatively juxtaposed to representative government. This was a period of intense normative dissent when disaffection from political elites and the rejection of political hierarchies by large swaths of the public was very strong. Emerging community organizations were not only shaped by this *zeitgeist* but, in addition, saw themselves as distinct and even alienated from the more traditional community leadership. This leadership was seen as island-centered and divorced from the people. In this context, what began as resentment of "an arm of the Puerto Rican government attempting to represent Puerto Ricans in New York,"[25] transformed into a general anti-establishment attitude. But it was an attitude that meant different things to different political actors.

Puerto Rican community leaders and their organizations were disaffected from the Puerto Rican and Anglo political elites they saw as unresponsive to Puerto Rican needs. They wanted to focus on their status in New York, not in Puerto Rico. And their anti-establishment sentiments stopped at the War on Poverty resources shore. Disaffection from the political system, including criticism of the War on Poverty as a conspiracy against the unity between Puerto Ricans and blacks, was the hallmark of left-wing individuals and organizations. But the *zeitgeist* of the 1960s counterculture had its limits, and it did not fully or consistently permeate the thinking and actions of most Puerto Rican community organizations.

In the War on Poverty context, at the community level, the quest for empowerment quickly transformed into the saga of service provision. Previously, during the Kennedy administration, loads of money began to flow to New York City to fight juvenile delinquency and poverty. Among Puerto Rican organizations, the Puerto Rican Forum became the main recipient of funds. These were used to set up day care services and the Puerto Rican Family Institute, among other initiatives. The Puerto Rican Community Development Project was another example. The War on Poverty further institutionalized these initial efforts.

Yet are these examples enough to characterize the organizational politics of the community during the 1960s? An inventory of Puerto Rican organizations during the

1960s carried out by the Migration Division tallied 263 groups.[26] Were all of these caught in the service provision web, unable or unwilling to promote political empowerment? The majority may have been, simply because organizational development at the time was so dependent on government funds. But it is hard to say with certainty that such was the case because, despite prohibitions to engage in partisan activism and political activities, so many organizations found ways around the rules to endorse, provide resources to, or engage in electoral and/or demand-protest actions.

The chronicle that follows suggests that community groups were not divorced from political action. Some even participated in cases where demand-protest was the principal form of collective action. In practice, both strategic action and demand-protest illustrated a reconciliation between identity politics and liberalism; these actions were focused on the provision of individual services from the vantage point of a collective identity and a platform of group rights.

For community activities, take the example of the Puerto Rican Forum. The Forum was created before 1960, but it provided the basic template for the community institutional development efforts that followed from 1960 thereon. Its emphasis was on self-help, focusing on the Puerto Rican family, Puerto Rican youth, and the educational needs of the community. In 1964, the Forum sought anti-poverty funds to promote bilingual education and Puerto Rican studies.[27] Political organization to achieve representation was not part of the agenda, and the agency believed that ethnic identity and solidarity were essential to the task of educating Puerto Rican youth.[28]

Politics, however, was not outside the organization's radar; it was there, but bleeping in its own fashion. The political strategy of leaders like Antonia Pantoja, Josephine Nieves, Frank Bonilla, and others was one of brokered representation in positions within city government. From these positions they hoped to shape and influence public policy to benefit Puerto Ricans.[29] Puerto Ricans were the focus of action, and the perspective of action was liberal democratic; its values and objectives were choice, autonomy, individual advancement, and civic and political engagement; its means were community-based activities and collective action based on a group identity. In this politics of identity, Puertoricanness provided a platform for the reconciliation of difference and equality.

Organizations like the Forum had a triple function: to provide services, to set a context for leadership development, and to facilitate the process of brokered representation of Puerto Rican interests. None of the original leaders of the Forum was ever elected to office. But Pantoja was recruited to work for the Commission of Intergroup Relations, Bonilla went to head the Center for Puerto Rican Studies at Hunter College, where he championed a model of political participation that included research advocacy and community activism, and Nieves used her position in state government to promote political incorporation from within the bureaucracy.

As for collective action, demand-protest was its main expression and the National Congress for Puerto Rican Rights (NCPRR) was one of its main exponents.

On October 6, 1986, the leaders of NCPRR held the National Puerto Rican March for Justice in Washington, D.C., originally scheduled for October 4.[30] The Congress expected 2,000 participants.[31] It is uncertain how many actually marched, but judging from the fate of other initiatives it is likely that numbers were small. For example, the Women's Task Force of the New York chapter of NCPRR attempted in 1986 to focus on the issue of day care but could not get its initiative off the ground.[32] Nevertheless, the march was a clear example of identity politics and was preceded by other events. Members commemorated the birthday of Martin Luther King, Jr., held a successful dance to raise money, and attended several conferences and activities in support of striking workers.[33]

In 1989, NCPRR decided that a voter registration campaign was the vehicle to make an impact on the lives of Puerto Ricans in the city. "We are looking forward to incorporating in that campaign forums [...] and finally developing a Latino agenda," wrote Isabel Malavet, chair of the New York City chapter, in the group's newsletter. According to Malavet, the goal was to make City Hall address the needs of Latinos in general and of Puerto Ricans in particular.[34]

A similar concern was expressed by Eddie Baca in February on behalf of the newly formed NY Puerto Rican/Hispanic Voter Analysis Project, which intended to serve as a clearinghouse of information for anyone interested in the development of the Puerto Rican/Hispanic vote in the city. The Project focused on analyzing the Hispanic vote and on mobilizing Puerto Rican and Latino voters.[35] Voting was certainly not demand-protest, but its pursuit by NCPRR and others illustrate the permeability of the boundaries between different types of community-based action and shows how a politics of liberalism infused group behavior even for groups that worked hard to distinguish themselves from the liberal establishment.

The focus of this book is community-based activities and collective action in part because these have been prominent venues for Puerto Rican political participation but also because the trajectory of these activities show the compatibility in practice of liberalism and identity politics. The examples of the Puerto Rican Forum and the National Congress for Puerto Rican Rights illustrate the overall context and orientation of Puerto Rican community politics as a mix of these two allegedly aporetic companions.

The chronicle of the Puerto Rican experience in the city laid out in Chapter 2 through Chapter 7 suggests that community activities and collective action were predicated—explicitly and tacitly—on the belief that the society was "open," as Glazer and Moynihan claimed in *Beyond the Melting Pot*. This was true as far as it went but it certainly did not exclude the existence of artificial and unfair hurdles for minorities.[36] In light of those hurdles, political action was varied, and despite the fact that between 1960 and 1990 there were over two hundred Puerto Rican candidacies for political office in the city, strategic action and demand-protest were no less important, and based on what they represented for the relationship between liberalism and identity politics, no less productive.

Puerto Rican community organizations sought to promote community uplift both through self-help and government support and Puerto Ricans rallied for better education, better housing, protection against police brutality, and to promote electoral participation as steps on the ladder towards integration without sacrificing their cultural background. In doing so, they added an identity component to their social liberalism. The pages that follow highlight a series of activities and actions that, whether strategic or demand-protest, were practical expressions of a liberalism with a New York attitude, that is, a politics that reconciled identity politics with liberal values.

CHAPTER 2

TO BE ACCEPTED AS AN AMERICAN

In 1964, a series of articles published in the *Daily News* provided an assessment of Puerto Rican status and identity in New York. One article described the Puerto Rican as "a stepchild torn by two loyalties" at the same time that it displayed a photo of Commissioner of Relocation Herman Badillo, a native of Caguas, Puerto Rico, who was socialized as a New Yorker and whose politics best exemplify the simultaneously (discursively) aporetic and (empirically) integrated character of the relationship between liberalism and identity politics.

His political career was an exercise in cultural citizenship under the liberal banner of "one nation, one standard." Shortly before his death, he published a memoir with that banner as the title. Badillo called himself an "ex-liberal" at the time, but he used the label only to mean that he was no longer a Democrat, that he did not believe anymore in the power of government to make Puerto Ricans first-class citizens, and that to move up socio-economically and politically Puerto Ricans could only count on themselves.[1] A statement by a Puerto Rican teacher in the *Daily News* article could have been proffered by the earlier Badillo: "We do not object to becoming part of another country's culture. [...] To be an American is a great honor and it is the ultimate goal of many of our people to be accepted as an American. However, the majority of Puerto Ricans who have some knowledge of their heritage do not want to adopt such a culture at the expense of discarding their own."[2]

Culture was one important concern in the politics of the community but not the only one. As this chronicle shows, to be accepted as an American also meant fair treatment in matters related to policing, housing, education, and equal opportunities for political participation. Instances of collective action were also part of the mix, always related to an issue that flared at a particular moment as a violation of liberal democratic norms.

STRATEGIC ACTION

Literacy requirements to vote, lack of educational opportunities, poverty: these were some of the issues that concerned Puerto Ricans in New York. The scope of their impact was collective, and the approach to address them was group-based. Yet the expansion of political opportunities, increases in access to quality education, and socio-economic uplift was dependent on the concerted action by individuals inspired by liberal promises of autonomy, choice, and economic well-being. Liberalism was the question; and identity politics, the answer.

Electoral Politics

In October 1963, a number of Puerto Rican groups led by the Office of the Commonwealth of Puerto Rico, also known as the Migration Division of the Department of

Labor of Puerto Rico, or Migration Division for short, and the League of Women Voters were busy registering voters. Rather than wait for a court decision on *Camacho v. Rogers*, the case that initiated litigation against literacy requirements to vote in New York, or for the approval of an amendment to the state constitution that would allow literacy tests in the vernacular of the voters, Puerto Rican leaders and organizations staged a massive campaign to bring the estimated 70,000 Puerto Ricans who were English-proficient onto the rolls.

The estimate of the State Democratic Committee was that 230,000 of the 254,000 voters with Spanish surnames were Puerto Rican, a veritable electoral force that was stymied by New York's requirement of English literacy to register and vote.[3] A different estimate put the number of Hispanics in New York at 700,000, of which 300,000 were estimated to vote regularly.[4] The 300,000 figure was in keeping with a Census Bureau estimate for 1960. According to the Office of Puerto Rico in Washington, given that the migratory flow from the island was at a low point, it was likely that the 1960 figure was still accurate in 1963.[5]

In July 1964, the Commonwealth Office continued its registration and voting campaign, holding meetings with Puerto Rican organizations and other groups as well as interested individuals. In New York City, according to its report on monthly activities for July, the Office distributed close to 118,000 pieces of literature to over one hundred organizations and individuals. Flyers were distributed also among non-Puerto Rican organizations. This was the tenth consecutive campaign of its kind conducted by the Office.[6]

During the summer, the Legion of Voters in New York City tried to register as many voters as it could. The group had just begun its activities and the organizers decided to make the Legion a permanent organization "concerned with all problems relating to the right to vote of every Spanish-speaking citizen."[7] Commenting on another effort, journalist Luisa Quintero wrote: "The voter registration campaign that the Democratic Party will be conducting in the city is of transcendental importance. Nothing will ever be accomplished until all qualified voters are registered."

According to Quintero, Puerto Ricans Eugene Rodríguez, a candidate for the 4th District assembly seat, and Gil Sánchez, President of The Voters Club in the Bronx, were actively registering voters in their county. In Brooklyn, Luis Hernández, had been elected president of the Young Democrats for Johnson and was committed to conducting a vigorous registration campaign. Also working on voter registration were the Ponce De León Democratic Club, headed by Iván J. Vice, and the Seneca Democratic Club, headed by George Swetnick.[8] According to community leader John Carro, by the end of the summer, an estimated 50,000 Puerto Ricans and Hispanics had been newly registered. Another 25,000 were expected to sign up during the last stretch of the campaign, from October 7th to 10th.[9]

Organizational Activities

In 1964, an analysis by the Puerto Rican Forum of the state of the Puerto Rican community in New York suggested two key developments: 1. The evolution of Puerto Rican leadership was substantial; and 2. The basic obstacle to Puerto Rican progress in the city was lack of educational opportunities. Observers noted that the Forum was proof that Puerto Ricans had moved from small-scale, mutual aid efforts, to a more diversified and complex set of institutional initiatives.[10]

This analysis noted that Puerto Ricans were at a disadvantage due to language and a lack of skills. Contrary to public perceptions, the study argued, Puerto Ricans were not successfully adjusting to their new reality, and they needed help. To help Puerto Ricans help themselves, the Forum created the Puerto Rican Community Development Project (PRCDP), with Antonia Pantoja as executive director. At a press conference held on November 6, 1964, Blanca Cedeño, executive director of ASPIRA; Francisco Trilla, president of the board of directors of the Forum; Pantoja, and Josephine Nieves, president of the Forum, announced their intention to seek funding for $12 million for the Project from government and private sources. To document conditions that kept Puerto Ricans at the bottom of the socio-economic ladder, the PRCDP cited municipal employment statistics. Puerto Ricans were only 3 percent of the municipal workforce compared to 23 percent for blacks and 74 percent for other groups including whites.[11]

Manuel "Manny" Díaz, Jr., offered two different versions of the origins of the PRCDP. The first version is told in writing in an undated document titled "Outline of the Puerto Rican Community Development Project," signed by Díaz as executive director and chief consultant. In this document, Díaz dates the founding of the organization to December 1964 and claims that it began as a Board of Directors including "a group of citizens representing the major sectors of the Puerto Rican community in New York City."

In April 1965, this Board made a grant request to the Anti-Poverty Operations Board amounting to $13,350 and with that grant staff was hired to begin work on June 1 of that year. In his interview with Lillian Jiménez, Joseph Erazo claims that these initial funds were facilitated by the president of the City Council, Paul Screvane, a former sanitation commissioner.[12] Additional funding was requested from the Anti-Poverty Operations Board in August. Díaz indicates that he acted as executive director of the Project until August 1966, when he became regional director of the Equal Employment Opportunity Commission, and was succeeded by José Morales in September of that year.[13]

In the second and more colorful account, Díaz begins by talking about the triumvirate that controlled federal juvenile delinquency dollars—Harlem Youth, Inc., Bedford Stuyvesant Youth and Action, and Mobilization for Youth (MFY). These groups dispensed their resources mostly to black and Jewish community organizations. "The Puerto Rican community was getting zilch," he said in 2004. The convergence of Díaz at MFY, Josephine Nieves as an intern for City Administrator Henry Cohen, and Antonia Pantoja from the Puerto Rican Forum and ASPIRA, produced the PRDCP initiative. This group wondered why Puerto Ricans were getting nothing.

Díaz consulted with his friend Richard Cloward, who advised him to "form a holding company that can negotiate for the total community of Puerto Ricans in New York City." That holding company became the PRDCP.

On a trip to Washington, D.C., Díaz, along with community leaders Gilberto Gerena Valentín, Darío Colón, Joseph Erazo, and Louis Núñez met with Sargent Shriver, from the Johnson administration, who told them to submit a proposal. The next day, the group met again with Shriver, who, after glancing at their hastily produced document "for 20 seconds," approved it on the spot. Díaz's explanation for this is that Shriver needed to spend all his money before the end of the fiscal year and was desperate to do so.[14] These two stories are not contradictory and probably mark key moments in the development of PRCDP rather than conflicting accounts of its origin. The second version is supported on the record by Joseph Erazo who added that Shriver told the group that he would consider a proposal if it was on his desk the following day by 9:00 am. "Get thee to a hotel room, get thee a secretary, and get thee a typewriter," Shriver said to them. "Yeah, it was just crazy," recalled Erazo.[15]

The funds received were distributed in small grants to 300 Puerto Rican organizations throughout the city. Evelina Antonetty, Nydia Velázquez, Dámaso Eric, Víctor Alicea, and Frank Espada were some of the community leaders who got their start employed in some capacity with PRCDP money.

PRCDP was beset by internal conflict from day one. According to Díaz, in the first round of conflict, a faction led by Ramón Vélez prevailed over another led by Gilberto Gerena Valentín.[16] Vélez has been characterized as a Democratic Party regular who took advantage of War on Poverty resources to build a political machine in the Bronx, and Gerena has been characterized as a radical politician and activist, but, in effect, despite their differences in style, strategic approach, and relationship to the political parties, they were two sides of the same coin: two Puerto Rican cultural nationalists seeking equal treatment under the law for Puerto Ricans as citizens of a liberal democracy. For them, identity politics was not a strategy but an affair of the heart, full of nationalist sentiment and righteous indignation.

For its part, the Office of the Commonwealth of Puerto Rico in New York continued to promote self-help efforts and inter-ethnic alliances within the community. These were the main objectives of its community organization program in 1964. The program intended to make Puerto Ricans active in the civic and social life of their neighborhoods, to create an environment of mutual understanding and acceptance between ethnic groups, to assist them in creating their own organizations, to advocate for services, and to promote new leaders. Unfortunately, these goals were not in sync with the resource level of the program. This financial obstacle was ten times more significant than the theoretical incompatibility between liberalism and identity politics. The Office of the Commonwealth had the theory figured out; what it lacked was the money to move forward in practice. During fiscal year 1964-65, its capacity was at a 50 percent level, due to staff resignations and a hiring freeze.[17]

DEMAND-PROTEST

Does identity politics produce visions of public life and social authority that are only applicable to individual groups and are therefore incompatible with general interests and concerns? The issues that prompted group action among Puerto Ricans could not be said to be exclusionary in nature. Education, housing, police brutality were issues of general concern. There was specificity to Puerto Rican demands but none entailed an illiberal or undemocratic way of life and all were pursued within the bounds established by generally accepted social, legal, and political standards. Civil disturbances were beyond the pale but even these did not constitute a serious threat to the liberal polity. They were actions that forced measures necessary to bring into alignment liberal-democratic promise and performance.

Education

In November 1962, the effort to establish a Department of Hispanic Studies at City College-CUNY became heated as a so-called Committee of Six threatened to picket the college charging discrimination favoring the study of French in the Department of Romance Languages. At the time, City College was one of the few institutions of higher education in the city where immigrants and minorities had the opportunity to achieve a post-secondary education. Tuition was free. The Committee of Six consisted of Francisco Trilla, Antonia Pantoja, Josephine Nieves, Alberto De León, Yolanda Sánchez, and Ruperto Ruiz. Also involved was Gilberto Gerena Valentín, presiding over a separate committee called Puerto Rican Cultural and Social Action.[18]

In response to these charges the newspapers *El Diario de Nueva York* and *La Prensa* donated $500 towards the purchase of books in Spanish for the college's library.[19] Groups such as United Bronx Organizations, headed by Monserrate Flores, supported the creation of the Department of Hispanic Studies, rallied behind the Committee of Six, and were even willing to participate in demonstrations.[20]

In contrast, the Council of Students taking evening classes at City College decided not to support the proposed demonstration. The council was presided by Puerto Rican Eunice Irizarry.[21] During the fight between Hispanic faculty and the college's administration, mistrust between the parties was evident. When the invitation to come to City College extended by a Hispanic professor to University of Puerto Rico's chancellor, Jaime Benítez, was annulled by the college's administration because the professor had not followed proper administrative procedure and protocol, Hispanics cried discrimination. In turn, the college's president, Dr. Buell Gallagher accused them of conspiring to embarrass him and his administration.[22]

Other charges against the college were that Hispanic faculty were denied promotion and tenure and that French language instructors were allowed to teach Spanish. The administration explained that Hispanic representation along the ranks of tenured faculty was a matter of time and that it had been the policy of a previous president to hire faculty that could teach more than one language.[23] Charges and countercharges emerged daily as Puerto Ricans presented evidence of dismissals of Hispanic faculty, and the college defended the firings.[24] Ironically, President Gallagher was a 25-year member of the NAACP and a supporter of Spanish-language literacy tests for voters.[25]

The controversy even took an international dimension when representatives of Spain's Ministry of Education protested the lack of a Hispanic Studies Department at the college.[26] Meanwhile, ASPIRA announced the creation of a Center for Puerto Rican Studies within the organization. The Center was part of the college-bound program at ASPIRA and included courses in literary history, Ibero-American civilization, and Latin American culture and development.[27]

On February 4, 1964, the front-page headline of the *New York Times* read: BOYCOTT CRIPPLES CITY SCHOOLS; ABSENCES 360,000 ABOVE NORMAL; NEGROES AND PUERTO RICANS UNITE. According to the authorities, 45 percent of enrolled students did not attend classes on February 3. The one-day boycott was a protest against racial segregation in the public school system. The boycott ended with a march and rally in front of the headquarters of the Board of Education in Brooklyn by 3,500 demonstrators chanting "Jim Crow Must Go" and "We Shall Overcome." The organizer of the boycott, civil rights leader Bayard Rustin, called it the largest civil rights protest in the nation's history. But more significant than the number of participants, some of who admittedly stayed out of school out of fear of violence, was the fact that blacks and Puerto Ricans had worked together to make the boycott a success, Rustin said to the press.[28] The United Federation of Teachers (UFT) did not endorse the boycott, and only 8 percent of the city's teachers participated.[29]

•••

On January 12, 1965, *The Worker* reported on a picket line held in front of the homes of nine Board of Education members. The demonstrators alleged foot-dragging on the part of the Board on integrating schools. This action was used to announce a citywide boycott of segregated schools throughout the city. The group behind the action, the Citywide Committee for Integrated Schools (CCFIS), demanded a timetable for desegregation, improvements in the so-called "600" schools, which enrolled students considered "maladjusted," the promotion of 200 black and Puerto Rican teachers to supervisory level, and the revision of the school construction program.[30]

On January 22nd, another boycott was launched from Junior High School 139 by the Harlem Parents Committee (HPC). The schools involved in the action were majority black and Puerto Rican. CCFIS joined HPC as a sponsor organization. Inadequate facilities, poor quality education, and segregation were the basic grievances motivating the boycott, dubbed "Operation Shutdown." In Brooklyn, for example, Junior High School 64 was built for a maximum of 1,200 students, yet it housed over 1,900. By early February, organizers expected the 31 segregated junior high schools targeted by their action to join the boycott.[31]

By February 9, 1965, eighteen schools were reportedly engaged in Operation Shutdown.[32] Two additional schools joined a week later, bringing HPC and CCFIS closer to their goal.[33] In a letter supporting the boycott, the Rev. Graydon E. McClellan, General Presbyter of the New York Presbytery, wrote: "The Negroes and Puerto Ricans had it. They have waited for the rest of us to respond to the shocking studies, to exhibit concern for the full education of all children. They have complained, they have pleaded. And basically we have done nothing."[34]

Housing

Housing issues were also prominent during the 1960s. In 1961, Manuel and Maria Ruiz, a Puerto Rican couple from Massapequa, Long Island, took two residents of Massapequa to court alleging they had prevented them from buying a home in the Lake View section of Massapequa out of prejudice. "Far from wasting their time complaining about prejudice, the Ruizes defended their citizen rights by going to court. Their example is worthy of emulation," wrote columnist John Ortiz.[35]

Between 1960 and 1962 the state of New York released funds for the construction of only 427 low-rent housing units. In 1963, it held more than $50 million that could be allocated for housing. In that year New York City had over 200,000 low-income families in need of subsidized housing. To meet this need, the city could count on resources from the Federal Government, but the state seemed to "look the other way when it is a matter of low-income housing for New York City."[36] Ironically, Puerto Rican leaders played a role during the 1960s in the process of displacing their compatriots from New York's West Side. But through relocation, they also helped many families to move out of welfare hotels to permanent housing.[37]

In November 1963, *El Diario-La Prensa* called attention to the practice of block-busting, used by real estate speculators to promote white flight from neighborhoods using racial tactics and in turn sell the properties to blacks and Puerto Ricans at prices above their market value. Minorities were less likely to obtain first mortgage financing, and this left them vulnerable to the lure of second and third mortgages at exorbitant costs.[38] Also, during visits by the newspaper's mobile unit to various neighborhoods around the city, hundreds of Hispanics commonly and frequently complained about their housing problems, often accusing landlords of failing to provide contractual services.[39]

During the first week of the month, 150 tenants from Harlem picketed City Hall demanding better housing. A week later, the residents of three buildings in the neighborhood initiated a rent strike to denounce the "slum conditions" in which they lived. The strike was organized by the Community Housing Council. The Council expected residents of another fifteen buildings to join the strike and by December 1st, the group hoped to have tenants of 100 buildings participating.[40]

During that same week, about 110 families, mostly Hispanic, who had been on strike with support from the Congress on Racial Equality since November 1st, met to discuss their strategy against their landlord Hyman Kaplowitz. Their building was on Eldrige Street in Lower Manhattan. Kaplowitz had been cited three times for 410 code violations, and he faced jail if these were not corrected by November 8, 1963.[41]

•••

Sometimes, crimes committed by low-income or poor people, are assumed to be politics by other means. More often than not, the assumption is not supported by evidence. But in the case of an East Harlem fire that destroyed three apartment buildings on November 6, 1963, leaving 18 families homeless, one of the arsonists admitted that he started the fire because "I hate my landlord. My apartment is full of rats and roaches and my complaints have been futile. The landlord has ignored my complaints."[42] This was not a political act strictly speaking, but it certainly was not a purely criminal action either. In Brooklyn, a number of civic and political organizations took a more constructive approach to the problem. The Civic Community Center, the Brownsville Spanish Community Club, and the Ponce de León Democratic Club met to develop an advocacy campaign to make government agencies enforce housing codes and punish delinquent landlords.[43]

•••

On January 26, 1965, *The Worker* reported on another demonstration at City Hall, this one for better housing. This action was organized by residents of West and East Harlem. From the East Harlem Tenants Council (EHTC), Santa Landrau said: "We planned that if the mayor would not see us we would sit down in front of his office. About 400 of our families are in a desperate situation." On the street, one little girl was seen carrying a sign that said: MAYOR WAGNER, I'M COLD.[44]

After John V. Lindsay took over the mayoralty in 1966, the protests continued. Immediately after the transit strike that welcomed Lindsay to office was settled, City Hall was stormed by members of EHTC demanding to see the mayor. They wanted Lindsay to fix their buildings and to make sure there was heat during the winter. Lindsay's Press Officer, Woody Klein, told them the mayor was not available and was able to mollify them by bringing the spokesperson of the protesters into his office. Klein then called Ted Vélez, the head of EHTC, and, while the spokesperson listened, he asked him to give the mayor time to address their demands. "I'm asking you to go easy on us until we have a chance to get started," Klein told Vélez. Vélez agreed to call off the sit-in, persuaded that Klein would do something for EHTC later on.[45]

Later on, in March, 1965, a sit-in took place in the offices of the city's Housing Administrator, Milton Mollen. Mollen was already at home when he learned about the demonstration and rushed back to the scene. He failed to appease the demonstrators who remained locked in for several hours until the water was shut down and the toilets and telephone booths were closed off. For one year, all the protesters had received from the city was a large volume of correspondence. Now, their action exacted a promise of heat and hot water from Mollen but no more.[46]

Police Brutality
During the 1960s, police brutality was a prominent concern among Puerto Ricans in New York. There was the case of Antonio Pagán, a 23-year-old shot to death in May 1963 while shielding himself with a garbage can cover from the blows of a policeman. In November 1963, Víctor Rodríguez and Máximo Solero were shot in the backseat of a patrol car. In February 1964, Frank Rodríguez (in some press accounts he is referred to as Francisco), designated Student of the Year by the Boys Club of America, was shot in the back by a rookie policeman. In September 1964, Gregorio Cruz was shot three times and was crippled for life.[47]

Another example was the case of Ernesto Rodríguez, a 22-year-old Puerto Rican from the town of Mayagüez, who was beaten by two policemen in October 1965. As often was the case, the victim became the accused. In November, a Grand Jury deliberated to determine who should be charged, Rodríguez or the policemen.[48] In September 1966, Luis Rodríguez, who was mentally disabled, was killed, shot in the chest. A few days later, Trífilo Rubero, a 44-year old war veteran, was shot three times in the Bronx.[49]

And then there was the case of Puerto Rican merchant Luis Hernández, who was shot and killed by a police detective on October 31, 1966, in the social club that he managed on the Upper West Side. As a result of the shooting, a group of Puerto Ricans organized the Comité Boricua Contra la Brutalidad Policíaca [Puerto Rican Committee Against Police Brutality]. The group was successful in taking the Hernández case to a Grand Jury. The detective who shot Hernández claimed self-defense, but the members of the Comité were skeptical. The policeman's story was not confirmed by witnesses, and a Comité spokesperson declared that even if Hernández had been armed, the policeman had no right to shoot to kill.[50]

The case of Frank Rodriguez generated an intense response. After the killing, over 250 people picketed the 23rd police precinct on 104th Street in East Harlem to chants of "Assassins!," demanding an end to police brutality. The following day, a silent march took place involving over 300 persons, mostly Puerto Ricans. The marchers went from the funeral home where Rodríguez lay on 103rd Street, past the 23rd Precinct, to the Church of the Holy Agony on 101 Street and Third Avenue, where a high mass was held for the deceased.[51]

Later on, another march and rally was held, during which an integrated crowd of more than 6,000 picketed the city's Board of Education headquarters in Brooklyn. According to *The Worker*, one third of the marchers were Puerto Rican. This event was education related but at the rally, Gilberto Gerena Valentín announced an upcoming demonstration in Albany on March 10 to protest the "stop and frisk" and "no knock" laws, and a second school boycott, planned for March 16th. Gerena Valentín warned that those laws would be applied mostly to blacks and Puerto Ricans and urged the crowd to remain unified in the fight for first-class citizenship.

Other Puerto Rican leaders present were Joseph Monserrat, director of the Office of the Commonwealth of Puerto Rico; Irma Vidal Santaella, deputy commissioner of the Department of Corrections; Assemblyman Carlos Rios, and the Rev. Pablo Cotto. In his address to the marchers, Monserrat declared: "Today we Puerto Ricans are really proud of being Puerto Ricans. Demonstrations are a new concept to Puerto Ricans. This is a beginning."[52]

A few days later, Ralph Martinez handcuffed himself to the grill outside the office of Police Commissioner Michael J. Murphy, demanding an end to police brutality against blacks and Puerto Ricans. Next to him were Flora Santiago and José Sánchez, from the group Progressive Youth of Puerto Rico and later notable as the pro-independence folk music duo Pepe y Flora. The three were arrested along with three leaders from the group that organized the demonstration, the Congress for Racial Equality.[53]

In March 1964, reporter Mike Davidow declared Puerto Ricans "in revolt against police brutality and all forms of second class citizenship." The occasion was a march to City Hall to protest the killing of Frank Rodríguez.[54] The killing spurred the organization of the Committee on Police Community Relations (CPCR), chaired by Héctor Vélez, a worker with the Narcotics Commission of the East Harlem Protestant Parish.[55]

According to Gerena Valentín, when it came to Puerto Ricans, the police behaved as if they were "running a plantation." Valentín had just beaten red-baiting charges by a group called the Puerto Rican Committee for Democratic Justice with a 204 to 4 vote in his favor among the delegates to an assembly of the groups organizing the march. The assembly met at Club La Ronda on 103rd Street and Broadway.

"A great alliance is taking shape in 1964," Davidow wrote, referring to the collaboration between Puerto Ricans, major civil rights groups, and key labor unions such as Local 1199, the Drug and Hospital Workers Union and District 65, and the Retail, Wholesale and Department Store Employees Union.[56] "There are unmistakable signs," he concluded, "that the Civil Rights Revolution has finally swept the Puerto Rican Community into its orbit."[57]

Only days after the march on City Hall, Puerto Ricans mobilized once again, this time against the "stop and frisk" and "no knock" laws passed by the state legislature in Albany. These laws gave the police unprecedented and sweeping search powers. Even though court approval was still needed to search the homes of citizens, now the police could do so without warning. Also, anyone suspected of having committed a crime could be stopped and searched in public. "What no demagogue or dictator could do, the Republican controlled N.Y. State Legislature has done," declared Representative William Fitts Ryan, commenting on the legislation. Puerto Ricans condemned the Assembly's action and joined the NAACP in protest against the new laws. Héctor Vélez, from the CPCR, described the laws as "running counter to local morality and national jurisprudence. We have enough police brutality without those laws."[58]

Added to all this were the many suspicious suicides of Puerto Ricans while in custody or in jail: of Oswaldo Rivera, Juan Santiago, and César Ruiz Zapata in 1965; of Jaime González and Alfonso Betancourt in 1966; all of them found dead by hanging.[59] Public remarks in 1969 about the suicide rate among Puerto Rican convicts came and went without causing much reaction. A year later, when Victor Maldonado died in a Bronx county jail, the president of the city's corrections board, William Vanden Heuvel, reacted with dismay. "This kind of tragedy could be avoided," he said. "We need more Spanish-speaking personnel and more Puerto Rican judges." Vanden Heuvel announced a program also sponsored by Herman Badillo to offer humane treatment to Puerto Rican convicts in local, state, and federal prisons. "We are trying to reform our penal system," said Vanden Heuvel, "but we have a ways to go."[60]

Sometime in the spring of 1965, the National Association for Puerto Rican Civil Rights (NAPRCR) announced that it would picket the four police stations in Manhattan, Brooklyn, and the Bronx where four Puerto Ricans had allegedly committed suicide by hanging between February 3 and March 22. "We will picket every Saturday until the mayor launches an investigation of the hangings," said Gilberto Gerena Valentín. Puerto Rican demands for an in-depth investigation of the deaths had been rejected by Deputy Police Commissioner Walter Arm. As a result, NAPRCR decided to suspend all talks with the police until Mayor Wagner ordered Police Commissioner Murphy to take the concerns of the Puerto Rican community seriously.[61] The first of these demonstrations took place March 27 in front of Police Headquarters on 240 Centre Street at 12:00 noon.[62]

Following the first demonstration, the police department announced the creation of a program to improve relations with Puerto Ricans. The program was run by committees of Spanish-speaking leaders in selected police precincts, and it was modeled after a committee system established after the July 1964 Harlem riots (see below). The designated leaders would meet once a month with the police inspector in charge of uniformed policemen and the captains of the selected precincts. The initiative was sponsored by the Police Department, the Commission on Human Rights, and various Puerto Rican leaders. "This is definitely a good step," said Ramón Vélez, on behalf of the National Association for Puerto Rican Affairs (NAPRA), "but we have a long way to go before we have amicable relations between the police department and the Puerto Ricans in this city." Vélez and about 200 members of his group had picketed City Hall, police headquarters, and the 5th Precinct of Manhattan for three hours only days before the program was announced.[63]

On April 3rd, over 300 Puerto Ricans picketed 18 police stations in the Bronx, Manhattan, and Brooklyn demanding an investigation into the hangings as well as an investigation into the deaths and injuries while in police custody of another eleven Puerto Ricans. When people learned that in 1964, John Carro, now an assistant to Mayor Wagner, had been taken into custody after protesting police brutality and held at a Bronx police station for two and a half hours, even after identifying himself as a mayoral aide, their confidence in the explanations provided by the police diminished further.[64] On April 6th, more than thirty Puerto Rican leaders met with Mayor Wagner to reiterate their concern about the deaths of Puerto Rican inmates by hanging, and to express their conviction that all the cases investigated by the police had been "whitewashed." Wagner offered to study the situation further.[65] On April 10th, a smaller group of about thirty-five picketed police headquarters. They demanded the resignation of Commissioner Murphy. This demonstration was organized by NAPRCR, and it also demanded the creation of a civilian review board to look into complaints about police behavior.[66]

In May, the City Council finally seemed to be moving in the direction sought by the protesters. A council sub-committee recommended the establishment of an independent board to examine questionable police actions. The only problem with this proposal, according to its critics, was that the board would consist of city council members. Its director would be Deputy Mayor Edward F. Cavanagh, Jr. How independent could such a body be? Puerto Ricans wanted minority representation on the board. Mayor Wagner and Commissioner Murphy did not. In fact, Murphy's position was that he'd rather resign than be subject to a civilian board. But a board controlled by the mayor and the city council was acceptable to him.[67]

The council proposal drew fire from all sides. It was unacceptable to Republican and Conservative councilmen, who felt it went too far, and unacceptable to Puerto Ricans and blacks, who felt it did not go far enough. "[I'm being] blasted from pillar to post," said the sponsor of the proposal, councilman Dominick Corso. There did not seem to be much reason for Commissioner Murphy to worry about the proposal, but he resigned nevertheless, ostensibly lured by a more attractive position in the private sector. In all likelihood, he was driven out by the pressures to establish the review board.[68] When mayoral hopeful John Lindsay jumped into the fray, suggesting the addition of four civilians to the existing police-controlled review board, he was thanked for expressing an interest, but his proposal was rejected by all.[69] At the end of June, after five thousand policemen picketed City Hall in protest, the council tried to force a vote on the proposed board. The motion was defeated 27 to 8. Action on the bill was then deferred, and public hearings were set for July 13th and 14th.[70]

The day after the hearings concluded, it was clear that no independent review board would be forthcoming. Instead, a new proposal emerged: to establish the position of deputy police commissioner in charge of relations with minority groups.[71] Earlier, speaking on behalf of Puerto Ricans in the city, Gerena Valentín suggested the citywide adoption of Operation Friend, a program operating out of the 24th Police Precinct that consisted of classes of Spanish and of Puerto Rican culture to policemen, a police training program to recruit Puerto Rican youth, and regular meetings between the police and community residents.

Gerena Valentín had been severely beaten by the police while picketing in the Bronx. From his hospital bed he once again used the "plantation" simile, but this time to refer to the way the police treated everyone in the city, not just blacks and Puerto Ricans. He added: "If all precincts with heavy Puerto Rican populations adopted the program of the 24th, there would be a big improvement of the situation."[72]

Was this alternative considered? While the council waited to act, the police shot and killed another black man in Brooklyn, prompting the Congress on Racial Equality to demand an investigation, organize protests, proffer warnings about racial riots, and call again for the establishment of the civilian review board.[73] In the end, the proposed board was not established. Instead, the operating procedures of the existing board were modified to allow for the cross-examination of witnesses in cases of alleged police brutality, to make the activities of the board public, and for officers receiving complaints to wear civilian clothes.[74]

The concerns of Puerto Ricans regarding the suicides of inmates during the first half of the 1960s were not validated until August 1971, by the findings of an investigation conducted by District Attorney Eugene Gold into the death of Bernardo Cintrón at the Brooklyn House of Detention. The findings led to the suspension of a police captain and three corrections officers. In an editorial, *El Diario-La Prensa* acclaimed Gold's investigation and suggested that similar inquiries could go a long way to clarify why the percentage of Puerto Ricans who were killed in jail, gunned down on the streets, or met death by "suicide" in police precincts was so large.[75]

1964 Riot

On July 18, 1964, Harlem exploded in anger, seemingly out of the blue. But the convulsion was not arbitrary. On the morning of July 16th, policeman Thomas Gilligan shot James Powell, triggering six nights of bedlam during which thousands of New Yorkers looted stores, attacked the police, and committed acts of indiscriminate vandalism. One rioter was killed, 118 were injured, and 465 were arrested.[76]

The riot extended from Harlem to Bedford-Stuyvesant, in Brooklyn. This was mostly a black event but at one point, on July 20th, a drunken man yelled to the police: "You want war? We'll give you war. Wait'll the Puerto Ricans come over to help us."[77] Puerto Ricans, however, were busy fighting blacks in Brownsville. The result there was five men and a boy shot, six arrested, and several injured.[78]

The police alleged that Gilligan had shot Powell in self-defense. But no one saw Powell attack Gilligan, who approached Powell pointing his gun at him. Gilligan shot Powell three times and the shot that killed him went through his forearm, close to his wrist and into his chest. The police claimed that this wound indicated that Powell was at the ready to stab officer Gilligan but no one saw Powell holding a knife. His raised arm may have been a defensive gesture.[79] In any event, if Powell had a knife, Gilligan could have shot in the air to scare him off or could have simply told Powell to stop. Why would anyone be so crazy to try to stab someone aiming a gun at him?

On September 1st, a Grand Jury refused to indict Gilligan, based on his account and because of conflicting testimony on the part of witnesses.[80] Most residents of Harlem, rioters or not, were convinced that this was wrong, that Gilligan should have been able to disarm a kid, belligerent or not, without killing him. Reporters Fred Shapiro and James Sullivan, did not agree, using the example of an incident where a policeman had almost lost his life trying to disarm a knife-wielding aggressor; the key word in their argument was "almost;" the aggressor was not shot and the policeman did not lose his life. Also, in their example, the knife-holder was not a 15-year-old but a grown man.[81]

During the disturbances, Mayor Robert Wagner was away in Spain. He professed no intention of interrupting his trip to attend to the riot. City Council President Paul R. Screvane and Police Commissioner Michael J. Murphy were left to handle the situation.[82] Wagner's blasé attitude did not last long. On July 20, he canceled the remainder of his European trip and returned to New York.[83]

The riot started with a shooting and ended with a rain shower. Shortly after midnight, during the early moments of July 23, as rain started and then came down harder, the crowds dispersed and the rioting fizzled out. One cop noted: "Some of these people aren't afraid of horses, of nightsticks, even of guns. A couple of drops of rain and they run."[84] Commissioner Murphy summed up the riot as "a crime problem and not a social problem."[85]

Nevertheless, the riot was used as an opportunity to call for a civilian review board. The demand was supported by U.S. Senators Jacob Javits and William Fitts Ryan, the Manhattan Democratic Organization, the Police Community Relations Board, and the Social Action Committee of Grace Congregational Church. The basic argument against it, expressed by Commissioner Murphy, was that it would hamstring the police force.[86] Mayor Wagner decided that the review board would not be established.[87]

It is hard to say whether it was worth it, given the $4 million cost of the damages, but the riot accomplished this: the police promised to assess the procedures of its own civilian complaint review board, to recruit more minorities, and to increase the number of black patrolmen in Harlem; through a community affairs committee, the police would increase its interaction with the neighborhoods and City Hall would work towards better communication with citizens, meaning blacks and Puerto Ricans.[88] Whether this was worth it or not, it was too little even if it was not too late.

CHAPTER 3

WE HAVE OUR OWN PROBLEMS HERE

On May 22, 1966, a group of community leaders and activists met at Las Vegas Restaurant, on the corner of Broadway and Myrtle Avenue in Brooklyn, to discuss the future of a new organization. They could not agree on a name, but all agreed that it should be a federation of groups focused on Puerto Rican issues in Brooklyn. Participants were enthusiastic about the future of the organization and determined to jolt political leaders out of their indifference to Puerto Ricans. Some wanted the federation to focus on civic issues. Others argued for political involvement. All were clear that the group should not be "a continuation of island politics because we have our own problems here." Someone affiliated with the Johnson Administration and with the NAACP suggested that Puerto Ricans should join blacks to seek joint solutions to their common problems. Interestingly, the suggested logo of the organization was an image of El Morro, the fort built by the Spanish in Puerto Rico to fend off their colonial rivals in the Sixteenth Century.[1]

What did it mean for Puerto Ricans to focus on their problems in New York, while doing it through an organization that defined itself with a cultural reference to Puerto Rico? In a meeting at City Hall with 75 Puerto Ricans on February 2nd, Mayor John Lindsay had told them that his administration would not give special treatment to any ethnic group and exhorted them to consider themselves Americans first, New Yorkers second, and Puerto Ricans last.[2] The attendees did not take this remark well but afterwards, in a Western Union telegram stamped March 11th, the President of the American Committee for Puerto Rican Civic Integration, Ramón Colón, thanked the mayor for his statement.

Colón claimed that Puerto Ricans needed such exhortation because they were "civically confused, they are uncertain of what they are," as a result of Puerto Rico's ambivalent relationship with the United States. "A million Puerto Ricans living in New York," Colón wrote, "must fight for and honor their children born here."[3] It is unlikely that the proponents of El Morro logo were confused about who they were. And just as the chronicle that follows suggests, it is more likely that their reference to El Morro in the process of creating a new organization focused on issues in New York was indicative of a symbiotic relationship between their Puertoricanness and their status in the city.

STRATEGIC ACTION

One important concern about identity politics is that it can substitute the ideal of a democratic community for a so-called democracy of communities. That this should be a matter of concern is interesting given the long-standing and generally accepted notion that if the existence of particular group interests in any given society is inevitable, the greater their number the better the prospects for equality and justice. As Rousseau put it in *The Social Contract*, "If there are partial societies [in the state], it is best to have as a many as possible and to prevent them from being unequal [...].[4] When Puerto Ricans pursued their communal interests they were part of a sea of "partial societies," and they were in fact unequal. Since there was no great philosopher-king that could promote equality, they had to do it themselves, as a politicized ethnic group, but one whose objective was not to subvert the system but to make it more inclusive and therefore truly democratic.

Electoral Politics
During the month of August 1966, the Office of the Commonwealth of Puerto Rico in New York conducted its usual voter registration campaign by distributing close to 10,000 flyers. In September, the campaign intensified with the distribution of 178,000 "facts for voters," 8,000 posters, 15,000 literacy tests kits, and 15,000 flyers with voter registration information. In this effort, the Office worked with close to 30 groups.[5] The following year, perhaps because of the July riots (see below), the campaign took place in September rather than earlier as usual. The effort was not much different in content than others—it included distribution of literature, posters, press releases, and placement of radio spots.[6]

During fiscal year 1968-69, the staff situation at the Office deteriorated. The community organization program began the year with three community organizers, two of whom resigned early on; the third resigned at the end of the year. This notwithstanding, the program held 22 meetings for registration and voting purposes. Two registration campaigns were carried out in August involving the distribution of 30,000 copies of a pamphlet with registration information, 200,000 copies of another titled "Datos Para Votantes" [Facts for Voters], and 200,000 copies of an illustrated booklet titled "Juan Votó" [Juan Voted].

Because of staff losses, this work was carried out mostly by the regional directors and field representatives.[7] The reader may wonder: How is it that activities carried out by the Office of the Commonwealth qualify as community action? Strictly speaking, they do not. Yet a measure of conceptual laxity is warranted here because the Office acted as a surrogate for the community, its activities meant to spur community action, and they were carried out, after all, by Puerto Ricans.

These activities and materials were supposed to encourage community participation in the electoral process in the United States. Yet a plebiscite on the status of the island was scheduled to be held in Puerto Rico in 1967; and therefore, at the end of 1966, the issue of Puerto Rican voters in the United States participating in island elections took on extra significance. Two groups advocating for full participation by Puerto Ricans in New York emerged: The Comité Nacional Pro Plebiscito (CNPP) [National Pro-Plebiscite Committee], headed by Ramiro Medina, and the Comité Pro Voto de Boricuas en NY (CPVBNY) [Committee For the Puerto Rican Absentee Voter].[8]

Medina's group wanted to create a movement throughout the mainland to fight discrimination against U.S. residents of Puerto Rican origin in their right to have a say on the future direction of their homeland. In the city, 93 percent of 4,890 Puerto Ricans surveyed by *El Diario-La Prensa* expressed their desire to vote in the plebiscite.[9] The argument of the CPVBNY for participation was simple: If the majority of Puerto Ricans on the island chose independence, Puerto Ricans in New York would be forced to choose between U.S. and Puerto Rican citizenship. Therefore, they should have a say in a decision that would surely have an impact on their lives.[10]

On January 30, 1967, reporting from New York for *El Imparcial,* journalist José Lumen Román wrote:

> The plebiscite that will take place in Puerto Rico has driven the Puerto Rican community to a state of anxiety and vigilance. Restlessness is due to the probability that Puerto Ricans in the United States may be denied the opportunity to be a part of the decision concerning the future of the island. Everywhere the same outcry prevails: Puerto Ricans in the United States should participate. Such is the politics of reason which ought to prevail over the politics of partisanship.[11]

This was no ordinary election, Medina's group claimed, but an exercise in self-determination from which no one should be excluded. "If we are," the group argued, "and the plebiscite results in the creation of a republic, we will become foreigners in the United States without having had any say in the matter."[12] Interestingly, this suggested that Puertoricanness was the driving concern behind the question of voting. In the context of colonialism, Puertoricanness was protected by U.S. citizenship; the end of colonialism, paradoxically, would put this identity in jeopardy within the U.S.

On March 27th, another group jumped into the plebiscite fray. The position of Puertorriqueños Unidos Pro Estadidad de Puerto Rico, a group active since October 1966 and headquartered on 500 Willis Avenue in the Bronx, was that mainland residents had the right to vote in the referendum. According to Eligio Ramos, president of the group, "We have patiently allowed the intrusion of island politicians into our affairs, so we fail to see why we cannot help decide the political future of our homeland."[13]

On April 24th, *El Diario-La Prensa* reported that the Comité Boricuas Ausentes Pro-Voto Plebiscitario (this may have been the same group as the CPVBNY, but it is not clear from newspaper accounts) had decided to organize a series of activities to keep the issue of participation on the island plebiscite alive, including a trip to Puerto Rico dubbed "invasión de almas" [invasion of souls] during which a march and rally would take place from Isla Verde International Airport to the Capitol building in San Juan.[14] In the states, the Comité decided to arrange visits with members of Congress and a demonstration in front of the Office of the Commonwealth on 322W 45th Street in New York City. A petition drive was also contemplated with the goal of gathering one million signatures. The Comité decided that if none of this worked, it would boycott the plebiscite, asking Puerto Ricans on the island to abstain.[15]

Puerto Ricans on the island, however, did not need encouragement from New York to boycott the plebiscite. This they did on their own. Both the pro-statehood party and the pro-independence movement feared that if their supporters voted and the Commonwealth formula won the election, their days would be numbered. Pro-independence groups also argued that the plebiscite was meaningless if the U.S. did not relinquish its sovereignty over Puerto Rico first so that voters could freely decide whether to continue or change the island's political status.

Some supporters of the Commonwealth agreed with *independentistas* on this point. Opposition to the plebiscite from the statehood party, however, caused a rift within the leadership that undermined the pro-boycott position of the party. The plebiscite was held—without any input from Puerto Ricans in New York—but its opponents managed to persuade 30 percent of voters to stay home. The Commonwealth position obtained more than 60 percent support. The participant statehooders rejoiced after receiving 26 percent of the vote; only 4,204 votes were cast for the pro-independence option.[16]

Organizational Activities

On June 1, 1966, Rubén Darío Colón, chairman of the PRCDP, finally received a response from the mayor to his complaint of May 11th on the issue of Puerto Rican representation on the New York City Council Against Poverty (NYCAP).[17] According to Colón, PRCDP had only one delegate in the Council, and he did not serve in any of the Council's sub-committees. This was considered inequitable given that smaller organizations had two or more representatives on the Council. "I appreciate your concern," said the mayor, but "I would deem it unfeasible at the present time to make new appointments to the NYCAP." The mayor promised a reorganization of the Council in June along with his agreement that an "effective liaison" between the Council and the PRCDP was highly desirable.[18]

In contrast, within the Commission on Human Rights there was a genuine desire to develop contact and communication with Puerto Ricans. On June 19th, for example, Commission representatives attended an all-day commemoration of *El Día de San Juan* on Randalls Island and later the Puerto Rican Parade on June 26th. At both events the Commission distributed informational materials in English and Spanish, which reflected its sensitivity to the language status of the community. Earlier, in April, the Commission's Chair spent four days touring Puerto Rico "to gain added insight into the nature [...] and cultural heritage" of Puerto Ricans in New York. Of course, trips to the Caribbean in April could easily be seen as junkets, and Booth had already been the target of such criticism after trips to Mississippi and California, which were decried as pleasure rather than business excursions.[19] But according to the Commission's records, the Caribbean trip was part of a larger initiative dubbed "Operation Understanding," which included the hiring of Spanish-speaking staff.[20]

On October 6th, Luisa Quintero reported in her column that NAPRCR, now under the helm of Amalia Betanzos, had decided to support a suit filed in court in April by civic leader Nathan Straus demanding the elimination of discrimination in the selection of juries in New York. Under the law, jury members were required to own property, which made it very difficult for Puerto Ricans to be selected. Other requirements discriminated against young people and members of racial minorities. According to Straus, year after year, over 90 percent of jurors selected in New York were white, middle-class, and professional.[21]

In December, NAPRCR took the lead in the campaign to revoke the certification of Manhattan Supreme Court Judge Charles Marks. The Association was joined in its campaign by the Congress of Puerto Rican Hometowns, the Puerto Rican Organization of Brownsville and East New York, the Puerto Rican Independent Organization of Chelsea, and the PRCDP.[22] His certification, claimed the Association, is "an affront to the honor and dignity of the Puerto Rican community. His prejudice and groundless statements make him incapable of producing fair judgments in cases involving Americans of Puerto Rican origin." While sentencing a Puerto Rican offender, Marks declared from the bench that "we need tougher restrictions on access to the United States by these people. They should at least know how to read and write before coming here."[23] With remarks such as these being proffered by political elites at the highest level of office, how could Puerto Ricans eschew identity politics?

• • •

During the 1960s, Puerto Ricans controlled seven—or 27 percent—of the community corporations operating in designated anti-poverty areas: the South Bronx, Hunts Point, Lower East Side, Middle West Side, East Side, Sunset Park, and Williamsburg Community Corporations.[24] Their overrepresentation in this area (in 1960, they were about 8 percent of the city's population) was more an indicator of their greater representation among the poor than of disproportionate political power. The agencies receiving the largest share of anti-poverty funds were ASPIRA, the PRCDP, the Puerto Rican Family Institute, and the Puerto Rican Forum.

When communities began organizing community corporations, the process was often conflictive. In El Barrio, for example, nineteen groups came together at the end of 1966 to form one such corporation. According to Olga Méndez, who was spearheading the initiative, the groups that did not support the creation of the corporation were simply divisive and did not have the best interests of the community at heart. "We need to avoid that," she declared.[25] She did not say it, but at this point in the process, self-sufficiency had given way to identity politics as the mainspring of community action.

• • •

On February 28, 1967, a so-called People's Board of Education issued a proposal for the decentralization of the New York City public school system.[26] The call from the People's Board was an important shot in what would become a major political war. According to the People's Board, decentralization meant that the responsibility for the education of children would lie in local communities. Specifically, the call was for increased parental involvement in all aspects of the educational process, including budgeting, administration, educational policy, and curriculum development.

All these aspects were to be worked out independently by each community organized as a school district managed by a community school board. The central administration would only be a resource center. The Board offered its proposal as "a major stride toward reversing the alienation of ghetto communities from the public school system and presenting the possibility of a significant reversal of the present mis-education of black and Puerto Rican children."[27] This was a version of decentralization understood as a tool for redress of grievances based on identity.

• • •

On April 15, 1967, Mayor Lindsay opened the proceedings of a conference about Puerto Ricans, dubbed "Puerto Ricans Confront the Problems of Urban Society: A Design for Change." He exalted the event and praised the participants for overcoming their political differences to work together as a community. He also called on "business, industry and labor" to take a hard look at their policies and practices to insure greater opportunities for the community.[28]

About 1,000 conference participants gathered at the High School of Art and Design on Second Avenue and 57th Street. Twelve panels recommended, among other things, the establishment of a training institute for community development leaders, more aid for Puerto Rican businesses, more emphasis on experience rather than on academic credentials for civil service jobs, and easier access to unemployment and welfare benefits.[29] Even the communists saw the conference as a good thing—"an opportunity to initiate a dialogue between the Puerto Rican community and the city administration"—although they were convinced that "the committee in charge of invitations has been careful enough to avoid inviting [...] anyone even remotely suspect of being a communist."[30]

Maybe so, but the participants were a Who's Who of the community leadership. Characters as dissimilar as activists Antonia Pantoja and Gilberto Gerena Valentín, social worker and povertician Ramón Vélez, academics Frank Bonilla and Elena Padilla, musician and composer Amaury Veray, and labor leader Mario Abreu rubbed elbows at the conference. Other prominent participants included Cándido de León, an assistant to the chancellor of the City University of New York; Manuel "Manny" Díaz, Jr., regional director of the U.S. Equal Employment Opportunity Commission; Josephine Nieves, deputy regional director of the Office of Economic Opportunity; Felipe N. Torres, a justice of the Family Court; Louis Cardona, deputy commissioner of the New York City Manpower and Career Development Agency; and Herman Badillo.[31]

Other than illustrating a salient feature of Puerto Rican identity politics in New York, what did the conference accomplish? Looking at the record, one could argue that much more was written than was done. The gap between recommendations made and actions taken is wide. The memo outlining Puerto Rican demands was twelve pages long. The most important items were bilingual personnel, appointment of Puerto Ricans to key positions, language programs, and floodlights in ballparks. Only in the area of housing, can one appreciate the difficulty in meeting their wishes: Was the city prepared to increase the supply of low-income housing, reserving 50 percent of all new housing for low-income families?[32] What cannot be disputed is the fact that the conference elicited a serious response from the Lindsay administration. In late September, the mayor reiterated the intention of his administration to maintain communication with representatives of the community in a letter addressed to Antonia Pantoja.[33]

One measure related to the conference is worth highlighting because it proved beneficial to Puerto Ricans and beyond: the support from the Department of Social Services for a rule change requiring *written* notifications to welfare recipients of their right to a fair hearing after any changes in their budget. An ancillary decision by the Department was to provide this information in English and Spanish.[34] A meagre accomplishment? Perhaps. But its symbolic importance was high and its benefit transcended Puerto Rican interests.

•••

In September, the president of the State Human Rights Commission, Robert J. Mangum, met with a group of Puerto Rican civil service leaders to discuss possible collaboration between the Commission and their organizations. Puerto Ricans were represented by Manuel Fernández, president of the Fire Department Hispanic Civil Service Society; Iran Marfisi, from the society at the Police Department; Joe Rodríguez, from the society at the Corrections Department; Paul Torres, from the Civil Service Employees Society; Gil Zayas, from the society at the Transit Department; and Republican leader Edward Mercado. From this evidence it is not possible to gauge the strength of these organizations or the level of Puerto Rican representation in each of these departments. Yet, their very attendance is suggestive of a degree of representation, organization, and active participation by Puerto Ricans within the city's bureaucracy rarely acknowledged, except to note absence of parity in representation.[35] And they organized as Puerto Ricans in civil service rather than as generic civil servants.

•••

In 1967, Puerto Ricans were active within the community corporations in charge of managing War on Poverty resources. Elections to their Board of Directors were heavily contested with ample participation from citizens. That fall, for example, 476 candidates ran for twenty positions to the board of the Community Corporation for Lower Manhattan. The jurisdiction of this body was from 14th Street down to Battery Tunnel and from Broadway to the East River Drive. The election was held on October 1, 1967. The enthusiasm and activity in all the zones of lower Manhattan, including those heavily populated by Puerto Ricans, suggested that the issue of participation was not so much about the participants but about the arenas of participation: meaningful spaces induced involvement.

In 1968, the goals of the Grand Council of Hispanic Societies were to promote patriotism, tolerance, equality, and mutual understanding through conferences, lectures, forums and social gatherings. The Council comprised Hispanic Societies in the civil service such as the Corrections Department, Fire Department, Housing Police Department, NYC Police Department, Sanitation Department, and the Transit Police Department. In its first newsletter, the council offered its members fuel oil discounts, life insurance, home appliances discounts, as well as help with civil service exams. The President of the Council was Joe Rodríguez. Distinto Díaz was the 1st vice president and editor of the newsletter.[36] The Council remained active throughout the 1970s and 1980s. In 1988, its leaders were Luis Salgado, president; Inocencia Cosme, 1st vice president; and Fred Malavé, 2nd vice president.[37] In all likelihood, most of the members of this federation were Puerto Rican. In the out-group imaginary, Puertoricanness meant marginality and indifference; among Puerto Ricans (and Hispanics) it meant organization; for the latter identity politics was a path towards integration.

•••

On April 19 and 20, 1969, two years after the conference at the High School for Art and Design, the Puerto Rican Community Conference "Puerto Ricans Re-examining Problems of the Complex Urban Society" took place in the central auditorium of Baruch College, on 17 Lexington Avenue. According to Gilberto Gerena Valentín, the goal of the conference was to bring attention to the crisis of the Puerto Rican family in New York. But this was not all that was expected of the meeting. In declarations to the press in February he said: "We hope that the conference will influence the one-quarter of a million Puerto Rican voters in the city and that it leads to the registration of 50,000 new voters."[38]

How the one hundred participants would do this was not clear. But they were expected to define the problems affecting Puerto Ricans in the city and propose solutions. Mayor Lindsay was scheduled to address the participants on Sunday, April 20th.[39] However, recalling the earlier conference sponsored by the Lindsay administration, Herman Badillo remarked: "Many people thought that the presence of the mayor at the 1967 conference was a guarantee that action would take place. This is not true. We have to develop concrete programs that the government and the community can implement."[40]

At the conference, some participants were not ready to accept any substitutes for Lindsay. When the mayoral representative, Simeon Golar, president of the city's Human Rights Commission, rose to speak he was able to offer only greetings on behalf of Lindsay before he was drowned out by hostile chants. As he left the podium Golar noted how "no ethnic group has a monopoly on bad manners." But this was not just a case of ill-mannered individuals. According to reporter Luisa Quintero, the hostile contingent was the same group that had remained seated when the conference opened with the U.S. national anthem.[41] The event provided participants a platform to think about about and discuss Puerto Rican issues and problems in the city, but, ultimately, Badillo was right.

DEMAND-PROTEST

When Puerto Ricans demanded equal treatment, they did it from the vantage point of difference. In their view, descriptive representation was a social as well as a political concept. The criticism of identity politics that it replaces the idea of citizenship, understood as individuals equal under the law, by the idea of singular group personality, of groups unequal under the law which require their own law, is not one that can be substantiated by the Puerto Rican experience.

Yes, they emphasized their ethnic identity as the source of their inequality but did so in order to obtain fair access to resources. Community control of local education was not demanded for the sake of segregation but for the sake of autonomy and choice and as the only alternative to a system of centralized control that to their minds was unresponsive because it was centralized. Once again they were at the center of riots that threatened public safety, but the cause of the disturbances was not identity politics but the failure of the liberal order to do its best to protect the rights of individuals.

Education

WE WANT TO STUDY! IT IS OUR CIVIL AND CONSTITUTIONAL RIGHT! DOWN WITH THE STRIKE! This is how a poster held by one of hundreds of students rallying on September 13, 1967, in front of Central Commercial High School read as they protested a teacher strike that began on September 11th, following the so-called "Vietnam Summer" and "the summer of major urban riots." "They are already educated; what do they care about us?" "They don't care about students: they are too greedy and concerned only with money." "For the work they do and how little they teach us, they make enough money already." These were some of the statements made by some of the students interviewed at the rally by *El Diario-La Prensa*. To some, the strike was an extension of their summer vacation. But most were unhappy and harsh in their sentiments against the striking teachers.[42]

Parents were equally unhappy. In a statement made at a parents meeting held in the offices of the Lower East Side Community Corporation on September 14th, the president of P.S. 15 Parents Association, Mauricia Pérez, accused the Federation of Teachers of negligence and called the teachers irresponsible for calling a strike without consulting with parents. The meeting followed a demonstration against the strike by parents in front of the school. At the meeting, parents rejected an offer by the teachers to teach students outside the classroom in so-called liberty schools, and they repeated the claim made by some students that teachers did not deserve better compensation. One of the parents claimed that in Puerto Rico students learned more even though the teachers were not as well paid, and schools had less resources. "So, what is the benefit of higher salaries, better facilities, and so many strikes?" asked an angry parent. No one was able to answer the question, and parents and teachers agreed to meet again to continue the discussion.[43]

Leaders of the group El Grito del Barrio used the strike to call attention to the disparities in access to War on Poverty funds experienced by Puerto Rican organizations. "East Harlem has the lowest level of educational attainment so we ask, Why not give us better schools and better teachers?" They noted that Puerto Rican groups had requested $3.6 million in anti-poverty funds but had received only $2 million. Further, they were dissatisfied with the distribution of the funds because they were disproportionately allocated to the larger community organizations.[44]

•••

On May 20, 1968, a group of students from the W.E.B. Dubois Club and the Brooklyn League of Afro-American Collegians, occupied the registrar's office at Brooklyn College, demanding the admission of 1,000 black and Puerto Rican students by fall, a required course on black history, and the hiring of more black and Puerto Rican faculty, counselors, and staff. The occupation was the culmination of a campaign initiated in the fall of 1967 by a student-faculty coalition that included the Dubois Club, Students for a Democratic Society, and approximately thirty faculty members. "We made it clear all along that we were willing to go through channels," said the chair of the Dubois Club, Ruth Portnoy. But the college failed to act on the proposal submitted by the student-faculty coalition, thus prompting the demonstration. As a result of the action, thirty-five students were expelled from the college.[45]

This was the higher education expression of a strand within the movement for educational reform initiated in 1967 that advocated for community control of the school system and for descriptive representation for minority students. Within the movement, some arguments for descriptive representation were incendiary and warranted close monitoring of its proponents by governmental agents. This is illustrated by the case of one Ralph Poynter, a school teacher and activist, whose writings in the newspapers *The Guardian* and *Workers World* were cited by government agents reporting to their superiors as examples of radical and inflammatory proposals such as excluding white teachers from the system and the burning of "whitey" textbooks.[46] This was identity politics at its worst.

∙ ∙ ∙

A key educational battle in the city took place in 1968 over community control of local schools. The main event of this battle was the 55-day strike led by the UFT over the job rights of its members. The strike kept public schools closed for two weeks since September 9th as a result of the firing of ten white teachers and 100 teachers who supported them from the Ocean Hill-Brownsville district in Brooklyn. The teachers were fired by the district board, presided by the Reverend Herbert Oliver, allegedly because they obstructed the school decentralization plan.

In Jerald Podair's account of the community control/decentralization battles of 1968, there are scant references to Puerto Ricans. One reference mentions that United Bronx Parents, the group led by Evelina Antonetty, wanted more study of African culture and of figures such as Marcus Garvey, Malcolm X, and Stokely Carmichael to balance discussions of classical antiquity and of Western history.[47]

The account offered by Anthony De Jesús and Madeline Pérez suggests that Puerto Rican participation was driven by the conviction of parents and community leaders that community control was the only way to secure a good education for their children. They also suggest that the idea of community control emerged as a result of the failure of desegregation policies.

De Jesús and Pérez credit Puerto Ricans with the idea that decentralization did not necessarily entail community control and that their leaders preferred the latter over the former. They document how, to some, decentralization was just a step toward community control; in other words, it was seen as a half-way measure that left considerable power and jurisdiction over neighborhood schools in the hands of the central Board of Education, whereas community control decentralized power and jurisdiction AND removed the central board completely from the equation.[48]

Overall, Podair casts the conflict as black and white; "whiteness" is represented as "middle-class values" and as an umbrella for Catholics and Jews. What did Puerto Ricans have to say? We learn nothing about it from his book. Years after the fact, Luis Fuentes, one of the Puerto Rican protagonists, suggested that the strikes were "the system's reaction to the rising tide of the black and brown liberation movements. [...] Inside the events of 1967 and 1968, inside the schools of Ocean Hill and Intermediate School 201 in Harlem the union made its war on the children of the poor."[49] Fuentes was the first Puerto Rican appointed as principal of a public school in New York City. He took his position at P.S. 155, in Brooklyn, in September 1967. A similar claim had been made earlier by Diana Caballero, who placed the responsibility directly at the feet of the state's Decentralization Law.[50]

During the confrontation, Héctor I. Vázquez, executive director of the Puerto Rican Forum and the first Puerto Rican appointed to the Board of Education, jointly with Ana Alvarez Conigliaro, another Puerto Rican at the Board of Education, told Luisa Quintero in an interview that:

> extreme militancy and violence scares the city. We need to keep up the struggle but with moderation. Puerto Ricans must not allow the imposition of racial distinctions that in Puerto Rico have no validity upon them. Puerto Rico is a unified country without racial distinctions. This is a feature that ought to serve as a model for this nation. We cannot allow difficulties in Ocean Hill-Brownsville, which have acquired racial overtones, to derail the movement towards decentralization and greater participation in school matters. The strike affects Puerto Ricans more than any other minority group because we are not concentrated in any one district. Only Puerto Ricans should speak for our children, we cannot allow others to speak for us or determine what is best for our children.[51]

Put differently, identity politics and autonomy went hand in hand; one could not work without the other. Vázquez and Conigliaro were not the only Puerto Rican leaders protesting the teachers' strike. Also joining the condemnation were a number of prominent figures in the community, including Luis Quero Chiesa and Louis Núñez, from the Board of Higher Education, and State Senator Robert García. Besides Chiesa, Núñez, and García, sixteen others declared publicly that the teachers were failing to fulfill their most important responsibility. "This is a strike against the community and it is the worst kind of blackmail. The union is acting like the incompetent teacher who punishes the whole class due to the bad behavior of a few students," reads their statement. "Decentralization is a must in this city; parents must have the opportunity to shape the educational future of their children."[52]

The Congress of Puerto Rican Hometowns joined its voice to the chorus of opposition. According to its president, Vicente Vélez, the Congress deplored the lack of good faith and delaying tactics by the Board of Education in the contract negotiations with the teachers' union

> but a strike would hurt all children in the public school system where over 250,000 are Puerto Rican. We are concerned about the effect of a school closing on Puerto Rican students who already experience a lack of instruction and inadequate facilities. We join the Association of Black Teachers and the Parents Association in accusing the Teachers' Union of extortion at the expense of our children. We resent the emphasis of the union in empowering teachers instead of promoting excellence in teaching. We will encourage school attendance on September 11.[53]

On September 27th, Ted Vélez's EHTC echoed the position taken by Héctor Vázquez on the matter of the teacher's strike. EHTC condemned the strike and offered praise for the teachers that dared cross the picket lines. The group also took the opportunity to reiterate its support for decentralization, for descriptive representation, and against school segregation. "Presently, East Harlem is divided in Districts 2 and 4. Such gerrymandering splits up the Puerto Rican population in the area so that they compose a minority in both districts and full attention is therefore not given to the needs of the Puerto Rican child."[54]

On October 8th, the Coalition for the Control of East Harlem Schools held a press conference to criticize the decision of the Board of Education suspending the governing board of the Ocean Hill-Brownsville school district. Speaking on behalf of the Coalition, Julio Morales, Program Director of EHTC, blasted the Board and the mayor, accusing the latter of capitulating to the demands of a "racist union" and charging the former with undermining the educational aspirations of the community. "We want a good education for our children," said Morales, "we want bilingual education and teachers that really care for Puerto Rican and black children. For that reason, our coalition supports the people of Brownsville."[55]

In November, at the conclusion of the strike, there was another protest outside the headquarters of the state education department involving about fifty Puerto Rican supporters of an ousted Puerto Rican principal; there were sit-ins at P.S. 144, 155, and 271, predominantly black and Puerto Rican schools, protesting the reassignment of their principals to other schools. There was more trouble on November 30th and December 2nd, but Puerto Ricans were not directly involved. The immediate outcome of these protests was the Board of Education's formal school decentralization proposal.

According to supporters of the striking teachers, this was not all that parents wanted. To many, the decentralization struggle was tainted by political agendas and racist attitudes. In Brooklyn, for example, in a letter dated December 2nd, a social studies teacher wrote to the group Comunidad Hispana Para Educacion [Hispanic Community for Education] (CHE), accusing one of CHE's members of promoting revolutionary change. She also made charges of anti-Semitism. She wrote: "On this past Wednesday, during the strike of students, a student in our school who is known to be a follower of Sonny Carson [a black leader known for his militancy], ran into the room of a Jewish teacher and cried out, "How many of you are Christians?" There have been several incidents of threats against white teachers."[56]

Such incidents were more than sporadic. When the mayor's office requested copies of all letters, complaints, reports, and literature involving racist appeals related to the strike, the Commission on Human Rights provided a total of eighty documents. The documents revealed a situation of reciprocal racial and ethnic hostility. Whites called blacks watermelon-eating pigs. Those who supported blacks were called nigger lovers. In an incident in the Bronx, a member of a Jewish congregation was attacked and beaten by a Puerto Rican youth. Another incident involved the beating of a black boy by a white teacher. After reviewing the documents, the mayor's office concluded that most incidents involved name-calling. More alarming than the reported violence was the unwillingness of the police to act as a neutral mediator, reportedly demonstrating partiality in favor of the striking teachers.[57]

In November, however, an incident at Seward Park High School, on the Lower East Side (on 350 Grand Street), showed that name-calling could not be dismissed lightly. Not only were the epithets disturbing but, also, in some cases they were the prelude to violence. Speaking on behalf of the school's faculty, Donald Morey wrote to Justice Bernard Botein, of the Apellate Division of the New York State Supreme Court, that on the evening of November 19, in a meeting held at the high school, "Puerto Rican militants and Black extremists [...] used threats and intimidation to cause fear in the hearts of the majority of whites present [...]. These threats and intimidations not only manifested anti-white hatred but also anti-Jewish hatred."

According to Morey, Puerto Ricans and blacks were heard saying things like: "They didn't burn enough of you dirty Jews in Germany. We'll finish the job here," and "Let's not buy Christman [sic] toys from the Jews," as well as calling whites "racist" and "pigs." During the meeting, one Julio Rosado assaulted Morey, breaking his nose and leaving him with bruises and cuts to the left eye. Rosado's brother was arrested for assaulting a policeman and for carrying a concealed weapon. The head of the local school board, Frances O'Brien, was dragged off the stage when she refused to give up her microphone and was allegedly bitten and her glasses broken. The President of the Parent's Association, Claire Kessler, was called "a mockie and a dirty bitch," and someone who came to her defense was assaulted. One of the parents summarized the proceedings thus: "We were there to hear about decentralization and instead got our third example of Local Community Control. Where will it all end?"[58]

In early November 1968, a group of Puerto Rican parents and teachers organized the Puerto Rican Inter-American Dynamic Educational Foundation, Inc. (PRIDE), to promote a boycott of the public schools until decentralization took effect. PRIDE wanted guarantees that the school system would not be disrupted again by a strike. In a letter written from the point of view of a student, PRIDE called for the boycott "until Lindsay, Donovan, Allen and Shanker decentralize all city schools, define the rights and duties of teachers, and promise that we will never be thrown out of school again."[59] Then, on November 18th, Mayor Lindsay announced that the strike was over. The announcement was made as Albert Shanker stood by his side. No representatives of the school district were present. In his statement the mayor said:

> We have learned that the decent majority of this and every other city must speak out sharply and forcefully against the spread of bigotry and rumor, or else that disease will spread across a city and imprison its citizens. This kind of disease must never again poison the people of New York. We have heard ugly words these past weeks. We have heard race against race, religion against religion. I hope this sorry hour will be over now. I hope we can return to a city where people believe in each other and trust each other.[60]

According to Herbert Oliver, the agreement between the mayor and the teacher's union was unfair. The day before, union members applauded the end of the conflict while decrying some of the terms negotiated by Shanker. "The strike will not end until you vote," said Shanker to union members gathered at Madison Square Garden.[61]

Lindsay's hope for a definitive conclusion to the teacher's strike remained unfulfilled for another three weeks, until the Board of Education finally came up with its school-decentralization proposal. The plan called for about thirty self-governing local districts, largely accountable to themselves. Nine anti-union activists were indicted on criminal charges. This ameliorated Albert Shanker's unhappiness with the decentralization plan, and a semblance of normality was achieved.[62]

•••

In the spring of 1968, protests in defense of the Search for Education, Elevation, and Knowledge (SEEK) program took place at City College, CUNY. The program was designed to recruit and assist college students from poor New York City neighborhoods. In early fall, Puerto Rican students organized a group by the name of Azabache. In November, the organization changed its name to Puerto Rican Students for Action (PRISA). It is likely that Puerto Rican students such as Iris Morales—who was a member of a black organization before becoming a founder of PRISA—Henry Arce, and Pablo Cruz participated in the 1968 protests. Previously, in 1967, two students who in all likelihood were Puerto Ricans, Pablo Torres and Gilbert Gutierrez, participated in actions promoting a SEEK student government.[63]

In January 1969, students again organized a series of actions, this time at Queens College, CUNY, demanding the continuation of the SEEK program.[64] On April 22nd, along with members of an African American student group, PRISA participated prominently in another protest at City College.[65] Their demands included that the student body at City College reflect the black and Puerto Rican population of New York City high schools; that students control the SEEK program; that blacks and Puerto Rican students receive a separate orientation upon entering the system; that a school of black and Puerto Rican studies be established; and that black and Puerto Rican history and Spanish be made a requirement for all education majors.

CUNY administrators were sympathetic but took no immediate action. Skeptical students continued and escalated their protests and, amidst a mounting crisis, negotiations were carried out leading to the adoption of "a special admissions program," whereby certain students would be allowed to be enrolled as City College freshmen: students from high schools in the Bronx and Manhattan that had less than the average proportion of college-bound graduates; those who resided in "poverty areas;" those who qualified for the SEEK program; and those who qualified for a special program called "100 Scholars."

This plan was decried by all the candidates running in the 1969 mayoral election as well as by Mayor Lindsay. Herman Badillo called it a quota system and argued that it would lead to a segregated college of inferior quality. Ironically, even some of the protesting students agreed with Badillo.[66] The college's Faculty Senate rejected the plan. In the end, on July 9th, the Board of Higher Education imposed a plan of its own that it had already projected to begin in 1975. Thus began open admissions at CUNY, hastened by the protests and demands of Puerto Rican and black students.

Poverty

As some Puerto Rican groups concerned themselves with issues as dissimilar as individual misconduct from community leaders, the decentralization of public schools, citizenship and homeland politics, a group of 25 Puerto Ricans added another issue to the mix in March 1967 when they picketed the offices of the Center for Community Progress claiming that the agency was not using War on Poverty Funds properly. The protestors also charged the agency's executive director Bill Nichols with discrimination against Puerto Rican employees.[67] The common denominator of all these issues was unequal treatment based on ethnic identity.

On August 31, 1967, about one hundred organizations protested in front of the Community Development Agency at 100 Church Street, alleging arbitrary decisions in the allocation of anti-poverty funds. The protesting organizations claimed they represented close to 175,000 poor people of all nationalities. The protest was organized by the Lower Manhattan Community Corporation. At the rally, participants held signs in Spanish that read "United Hispanic Movement" and "Protest for Displaced Programs." They demanded immediate action from the Anti-Poverty Municipal Council.[68]

On September 22nd, fifteen members of the Mott Haven Planning Committee were pictured in *El Diario-La Prensa* while they attended a hearing of the budget division of City Hall to lobby for housing, schools, parks, and daycare centers for the South Bronx.[69] That same day, the newspaper ran a story about El Grito del Barrio. This organization was active in the anti-poverty arena. The story was about a protest in which the group noted the "unfair distribution of anti-poverty funds" and demanded an immediate investigation of the matter.

The group acted as spokesperson for a coalition of twenty-one organizations under the umbrella of the East Harlem Planning Committee. The participants declared: "We submitted 105 requests and only 21 were funded. The Puerto Rican residents of East Harlem demand an investigation of the actions of the Planning Committee which clearly is in favor of the two anti-poverty organizations in this area that are the least effective. We refer to MEND [Massive Economic Neighborhood Development] and the East Harlem Tenants Council."[70]

The protestors that day were the Civic League Puerto Rican Gethsemani Community, Loyal Citizens Congress of America, Puerto Rican Leadership Alliance, Comité del Escudo de Puerto Rico [Committee for the Puerto Rican Coat of Arms], Black Action, 110th Mohegan Democratic Organization, Comité de Familias Necesitadas y Ancianos [Committee for Senior Citizens and Families], East Harlem Youth Association, El Grito Youth Movement, Metro-North Citizens Committee, Tenants Association, Building 201 Washington Houses, El Grito del Barrio, Arroyanos Ausentes, Asociación Cívica Arecibeña, NYC Amateur Sports Council, Aguilar Senior Citizens Seneca II, Aguilar Citizens for Community Action, Inc., East Harlem Vista, East Harlem Youth Task Force, and East Harlem Film Workshop. They had one thing in common: a Puerto Rican identity and claims structured by that identity.

A second protest took place on September 30th. Participants again objected to their exclusion from War on Poverty funds. They claimed that the leaders responsible for distributing funds made arbitrary funding decisions that led to improper allocation of resources. Some of the groups represented were the Asociación Cívica Arecibeña [Arecibo Civic Association], Puerto Rican Leadership Alliance, Arroyanos Ausentes [Arroyano Association], El Grito del Barrio [El Barrio's Lament], Asociación de Padres del Este de Harlem [East Harlem Parents Association], and Senecas II. They called their demonstration the "Crusade for the Poor."

On May 26, 1968, thousands of Puerto Ricans met in Central Park to participate in the Poor People's Movement march on Washington. This was an act of solidarity with blacks and an act of affirmation as well. According to the organizers, Puerto Rican problems were distinctive. Therefore, even though they planned to set up camp for fifty to 100 families near Resurrection City, they would do so at the end of their own march set to begin June 8th. Organizers included Gilberto Gerena Valentín, then director of the Puerto Rican Hispanic Affairs Commission, a branch of the New York City Civil Rights Commission; Joseph Monserrat; and Frank Espada, acting executive director of the Williamsburg Community Corporation.

Monserrat was the national coordinator of the planned march.[71] Even though Espada and Monserrat are not as recognized as Gerena Valentín as leaders of this movement, they were chair and vice-chair respectively of the Steering Committee that coordinated Puerto Rican participation in the campaign.[72] According to Gerena Valentín, Monserrat was "up to his neck in it. That cost him his job."[73] In June 1968, more than 5,000 Puerto Ricans reportedly marched on Washington as part of the Poor People's Campaign.

Riots: 1967-1968

The tenor of unfolding events involving Puerto Ricans in the city changed abruptly on July 23, 1967, when a riot erupted in El Barrio as a result of the shooting by the police of Reinaldo Rodríguez on the corner of 111th Street and Third Avenue. Disorder and violence prevailed for five days, forcing the intervention of the police's Tactical Patrol Force, a group also known as the "Riot Squadron." The rioters decried the brutality of the police, while community leaders expressed embarrassment for the rioters and looked for ways to end the violence. To that effect, on the evening of Monday, July 24th, Mayor Lindsay, concerned about the disturbances, met with a Puerto Rican delegation at Gracie Mansion.

Herman Badillo was sent by Lindsay to El Barrio to find out what the situation was and to report back to him. "It was disgraceful because Lindsay was allowing people to loot; he didn't want anybody arrested and anybody killed. I thought that was not the right thing to do but that's what was going on," said Badillo. On the ground, he helped diffuse the situation. In one instance, a group of policemen holding a boy for trying to steal from a jewelry store were surrounded by a menacing crowd. Badillo helped them by taking the boy with him so the cops could get away from the crowd.[74]

The police's Community Relations Bureau also responded to the crisis by establishing a presence on the scene to ascertain the facts and by communicating with community leaders to request their assistance. By Tuesday evening, the Bureau had received assurances that no further disturbances would occur. On the Sunday after the riots began, at a meeting sponsored by the Puerto Rican Bar Association, Bureau representatives breathed a sigh of relief after being told by participants that, in their judgment, the police had acted with restraint.[75]

Like all such disturbances, this one was a study in contrasts. In one photograph of the incidents, garbage cans are overturned in front of La Gran Parada Restaurant, located on Lexington Avenue between 111th and 112th Streets. Had it not been for the garbage strewn all over the street, by looking at the residents sitting by their apartment windows one would think it was a normal day in El Barrio. Another picture shows a young man being subdued by two policemen, one of them aggressively holding a baton; the man's forehead is covered in blood. A third picture shows a throng of children shouting, with arms lifted up in the air, clapping, smiling, looking across the intersection of Lexington and 111th Street, in front of an unperturbed policeman. The caption reads: RIOT OR PARTY?[76]

Commenting on the scene depicted in its front page, *El Diario-La Prensa* even suggested that the residents were actually out on the streets celebrating the victory of the Commonwealth formula in the plebiscite that had just been held in Puerto Rico without input from Puerto Ricans in the U.S. It is hard to tell whether this was a reflection of the confusion surrounding the incidents or cynicism on the part of the newspaper staff.[77] A fourth photograph shows a young man shouting into a bullhorn with a policeman by his side while some bystanders stare at him. Just by looking at the photo it is impossible to know what was going on: the caption explains that the man was exhorting the rioters, in Spanish, to go home.[78]

After five days of violence, the police arrested four men. Demonstrators tossing bottles, bricks, and beer cans managed to hit only three policemen who suffered minor injures to their heads or backs.[79] The hostilities ended with four Puerto Ricans dead. To many within the police, Puerto Ricans were simply *spics* and a good *spic* was a dead *spic*; so now there were four good Puerto Ricans in the city. According to the police, one of the casualties had occurred as a result of a broken neck and the other from a .22 caliber gunshot. The truth was that all were shot with police issue .38 caliber bullets.[80] Police action was reminiscent of the behavior of a legendary cop named

O'Hara who, according to popular lore, hit first and asked questions later; this time, *la jara*—the name for the police that Puerto Ricans had concocted as an anglicism of O'Hara—asked questions after shooting first.

Yet, according to an internal police department memo, at a meeting between police officials and community leaders on July 27, the performance of the police during the riots was commended while the conduct of the Spanish press was considered biased against the police. The memo also referred to an article published in *El Diario-La Prensa* on the same date, in which the police were praised for their "responsible and restrained action and for their overall attempts to work closely with the Spanish people in community programs." The article was penned by Victor Mangual, who was described in the memo as someone "who is not usually flattering to the police."[81]

The assessment of the riot by the *New York Times* is worth quoting at length:

> It is perhaps the ambivalent position of the Puerto Ricans coupled with the feeling that the city is a land of new hope, that made the four nights [sic] of disorder in East Harlem last week different from the desperate, nihilistic wrath of the negro riots.
>
> Triggered like most ghetto riots by a police incident—the killing of a knife-wielding Puerto Rican by an off-duty policeman—the violence was directed almost solely at the police. Windows were smashed but the looting was not as extensive as in some other cities; Mayor Lindsay's appearances were greeted with "Vivas," and white reporters for the most part could walk unpatrolled streets, often with bottle-throwing youths strolling protectively beside them.
>
> The police, particularly the elite Tactical Patrol Force who were described by youths as "savage dogs," were the targets, Puerto Ricans said, because of a long history of frictions. These stem from failure to understand Latin customs—like the crowds who gather nightly on sidewalks and stoops to drink beer and talk—from brutality on the part of some officers, contempt and slurs on the part of others, and from seeming indifference to real problems, often caused by inability to understand excited Spanish.[82]

Truth be told, the city actively worked to deflect the crisis and to avoid further violence. Religious processions were arranged. The climate was tense and confrontational but peaceful during these activities. The city found it hard to tolerate the burning of garbage on the streets, a form of protest that preceded the practice by the Young Lords in 1969, but nevertheless the response was not violent. Instead, the police arranged for sanitation trucks to do what they were supposed to do in the first place: pick up the garbage! This, according to Mayor Lindsay, "eased tempers."[83]

Shortly after the riots, Lindsay appointed Angel F. Rivera as first deputy director of the New York City Youth Board. This action was applauded by Edward Mercado in a letter to the mayor. Mercado, then a special projects coordinator at the State Commission for Human Rights, was one of the few Puerto Rican Republicans in the city. "I was in East Harlem during the riots," Mercado wrote, "and I saw Angel Rivera and Inspector Stephen Valle of the Police Department play major and effective roles in the quelling of the riots. Once again, I offer my congratulations."[84] Lindsay made the decision in August, and the appointment of Rivera became effective in September.

On July 21, 1968, in a section of the Bronx that was fifteen blocks north of the predominantly Puerto Rican Mott Haven neighborhood, a group of Puerto Rican youths went on a window-smashing and fire-bombing rampage that many suspected was in response to allegations that four Puerto Ricans who had recently been shot dead in Mott Haven had died at the hands of blacks. As a result, relations between blacks and Puerto Ricans in the Bronx reached a boiling point.[85] Also in July, civil disorder again rocked the community, this time in the Lower East Side. Puerto Ricans were seen hurling rocks at the police, protesting their presence in the neighborhood. As a result of these protests, Tactical Police Force Units were removed from the neighborhood.[86]

These incidents threatened to spiral into widespread violence, but Mayor Lindsay again walked the streets, confronted the restless crowds and told them, with enough passion to make himself credible, that they could either burn down their community in anger or use their energy to change it.[87] Martin Luther King, Jr. had been murdered in April, and the city was still on edge. His assassination was not, however, why Puerto Rican anger had spilled onto the streets in July 1968 and, despite expectations to the contrary, the city did not burn.

CHAPTER 4

RACISM CANNOT BE FOUGHT WITH SILK GLOVES

On February 17, 1970, about one hundred students took over Bronx Community College demanding that the administration stop sabotaging the bilingual education program. After five months of negotiations, the students decided that direct action was the only alternative left to force the administration to take their claims seriously.

Students also complained that college officials were unable to deal with the question of Puerto Rican identity and therefore could not relate to students properly. During the occupation, a second group of people picketed in front of the building, holding signs written in English and Spanish and waving Puerto Rican flags. Policemen stood by on alert while students chanted slogans and demands. "It is clear to us," said a spokesperson for the students, "that racism cannot be fought with silk gloves. We have been treated rudely and now we are treating them in kind."[1]

The proposition that inequality and oppression cannot be fought kindly can be easily misinterpreted. Did the students who took over Bronx Community College mean that racism had to be fought with violence? Their action did not seem to point in that direction. Their occupation was disruptive but not excessive. Why was it important to them that college administrators understand their identity as Puerto Ricans? To them, the assertion of Puertoricanness was an expressive as well as an instrumental tool, and just as the chronicle that follows suggests, it was a means to achieving a proper place within the society.

STRATEGIC ACTION
The fact that identity politics brings new issues to the forefront is not as important as the question whether mobilizing around those issues contributes to the reproduction of a legitimate political order or not. At face value, the attitude of Puerto Rican women in the city against the special treatment received by the 1970 Puerto Rican Miss Universe, discussed below, may seem trivial and unwarranted. But this was an example of Puerto Ricans relying on identity politics to broaden the scope of concerns about women. To be sure, this and other issues created conflict, but it was neither deeper than it had been previously nor unsolvable.

Organizational Activities
When Marisol Malaret obtained the Miss Universe title in 1970, she received the key to the city of New York from Mayor Lindsay. Many participants in the reception given to Malaret by public officials were unhappy, and some claimed to be "disgusted" by the event. Afterwards, a group of women met and concluded that the city needed an organization exclusively dedicated to promote and value the interests and contributions of Puerto Rican women.

On October 3, 1970, seven of them—María V. Rodríguez, Luz María Fonollosa, Felícita Lemus, Gonzálezita López, Virginia González, Dr. Amelia Hernández, and Irma Rosario—met at the Executive Hotel and the Puerto Rican Women's Association was born. Some of the work of the group was social-recreational, but some of it was advocacy-related, such as their work with female inmates at Rikers Island.[2]

In November 1970, in Brooklyn, Acción Hispana provided another example of the organizational dynamism of the community. The group was led by Esther Mendoza and Johnny Vélez in the Crown Heights section of Brooklyn. In only seven months, this group grew from one woman, Mendoza, knocking on doors, to a small core of ten members, and then to over 250 members serving over 15,000 residents. All of it with no budget and only access to free space for meetings provided by the Crown Heights Community Corporation. The group offered information and referral services, employment training, English instruction, and cultural activities, all on a volunteer basis. Mendoza was Puerto Rican, but the group served the community at large.[3]

In 1971, during a January meeting of another group, the Spanish Association of Women Voters, the director of Community Services of the Office of the Commonwealth discussed the workings of city government. Community Services was how the former community organization program was known in 1971, even though the new name did not reflect a change in rationale or objectives.[4] The meeting was later described as "fruitful and informative" but marred by low attendance. The Spanish Association held similar meetings every month.[5]

According to Manuel Casiano Jr., director of the Office of the Commonwealth, the community was "further back [in 1971] than 15 years ago. We have one state senator here," he said, "and two assemblymen; and that does not mean much in terms of power. We have no political or economic power. To a large extent this is our own fault." His explanation? The community's political leadership was inadequate and lacked the respect of influential Anglos.[6]

Puerto Ricans formed groups to pressure elected officials, sometimes working in coalition with other Hispanics. For example, in September 1971, the Puerto Rican Coordinating Committee for the Northeast was created to promote collaboration with Mexican-Americans. This group was headed by the president of the Puerto Rican Association for National Affairs, Dr. Francisco Trilla, and Frank Espada. Their aim was to achieve greater recognition of Hispanic needs.[7]

In October, a group of leaders in the South Bronx met to plan the organization of yet another community conference. The idea was to discuss the employment, education, housing, and health needs of Puerto Ricans. The conference took place in December at Junior High School Lola Rodríguez de Tió on 149th Street and St. Ann's Avenue in the Bronx. This was the first conference of its kind since 1967.[8]

The conference discussed issues such as housing, health, substance abuse, and drug trafficking. The chair of the conference was Ramón Vélez, at the time president of the Bronx Multi Services Center and member of the board of directors of the

Hunts Point Community Corporation. Vélez was also president of the National Association for Puerto Rican Affairs. The keynote speakers were Mayor Lindsay, Herman Badillo, and Bronx Borough President Robert Abrams.

Some wanted the conference to be held in Spanish in conformity with its goal of cultural preservation. Others wanted the proceedings to be in English with Spanish translation if necessary. Both sides acknowledged the importance of acculturation and saw the conference as a means to that end.[9] After a brief disagreement about the use of photographs of Puerto Rican leaders from the Bronx at the conference, the organizers agreed that the only one they would display would be that of Cándido de León, to whom the conference was dedicated in recognition of his recent appointment as president of Hostos Community College of the City University of New York.[10]

The conference proceedings were tense. Strict security measures had to be taken and at one point the police had to intervene to maintain order. The focus of the disturbance was the prevention of community and religious leader Louis Gigante from registering as a participant. Ramón Vélez told him he was not welcome because he was not Puerto Rican. "How do you know who is Puerto Rican and who is not here?," Gigante asked.

Gigante stayed for a while, but soon enough an organizer approached him accompanied by a policeman and asked him to leave. Gigante refused and was threatened with arrest. "This is not a Puerto Rican conference," he responded, "this is a closed event just for people who work for Ramón Vélez in anti-poverty programs." Vélez replied by accusing Gigante of trying to kill him: "I am in a state of fear for my life and that of my family. Father Gigante is in a state of political desperation. We kept him out of the conference because he wanted to disrupt the event."

Gigante dismissed the accusation as nonsense. Some Puerto Ricans also reacted with surprise and shame at the charges. Speaking about the conference later, Vélez claimed: "It was a complete success. The 700 participants demonstrated that Puerto Ricans in the Bronx are united to demand economic and political power."

The panel on politics rejected a proposal by the Puerto Rican Socialist Party to discuss the status of Puerto Rico but approved a motion also submitted by the socialists to push for the "fundamental change of the social structures of our society." The panel also proposed the following: 1) an end to discrimination against ex-convicts; 2) a redistricting process that would preserve the integrity of Puerto Rican communities; 3) a mass registration campaign; 4) and a rejection of Puerto Rican electoral candidates who challenged Puerto Rican incumbents, unless the incumbent was incompetent or dishonest.

Herman Badillo opened the proceedings by exhorting Puerto Ricans to help themselves rather than wait for help from politicians in New York or Washington. He was the emblematic Puerto Rican liberal even though it was on the basis of this idea that he redefined himself as an ex-liberal Republican thirty-five years later. In the end, it was not clear whether the multitude of resolutions, exhortations, and demands produced by the conference comprised an agenda for future lobbying or for self-help initiatives.[11] It was clear, however, that the ideological platform of the conference was identity politics.

...

In February 1972, Mayor Lindsay and Commissioner Eleanor Holmes Norton sent out invitations to what they called "a one-day think tank conference" on the issue of ethnic identity and conflict in the city. They recognized that the growth of ethnic consciousness and pride was a positive development but were also concerned about the possibility that racial and ethnic pride may translate into parochialism and extremism.[12] What is interesting here is that they viewed the pitfalls of identity politics as potential rather than inevitable. What theorists thinking about the relationship between liberalism and identity politics saw as an incompatibility, they saw as a surmountable challenge. If not, why bother organizing a conference to address a problem with no solution?

The conference was held on March 7th, and the panelists and participants included representatives of the Jewish, African American, Polish, Irish, Greek, Italian, Haitian, Japanese, Chinese, Hungarian, Ukrainian, Czechoslovakian, East Central Europe, and Puerto Rican communities.[13] In her opening remarks, Holmes Norton noted that "the documented experience of ethnic conflict arising out of such experiences as the poverty program ought to lead us to contemplate what might happen with the entry of the various other ethnic groups now seeking involvement in that and similar programs." The experience of conflict between blacks and Puerto Ricans over anti-poverty funds was sobering and should not serve as a model for further divisions and intolerance, she suggested.[14]

After the conference, the Commission on Human Rights followed up with a series of community dialogues in July to discuss how to address and/or prevent ethnic polarization and conflict.[15] A year after the conference, the Commission announced the formation of a Citywide Intergroup Coalition, an assembly of ethnic and racial groups throughout the city officially attached to the Commission. The Coalition was charged with the task of advising the Commission on how to promote unity within diversity.[16]

The Commission on Human Rights overlooked the question of intra-group relations. The task of representing the Puerto Rican community within the Coalition was assumed by Héctor Vázquez, executive director of the National Puerto Rican Forum. Was he capable of aggregating the interests of the Forum with the interests of ASPIRA, the PRCDP, the Hispanic Day Parade, the Puerto Rican Community Council of East Harlem, the Council of Puerto Rican and Hispanic Organizations of the Lower East Side, the Puerto Rican Bar Association, the National Association for Puerto Rican Affairs, and the Office of the Commonwealth of Puerto Rico, which was included along with these other agencies as another ethnic organization in the city's master list of ethnic groups?[17] The question was relevant to other groups as well, since virtually all ethnic communities in the city were represented by a multiplicity of institutions.

•••

On May 5, 1972, a meeting to finalize arrangements for a series of public hearings on discrimination against Puerto Ricans took place in the Brotherhood in Action building, located at 560 Seventh Avenue in Manhattan. At the meeting, participants would meet members of the Commission on Human Rights that would hear the testimony. Commission members were activists and community leaders. Among them were now Judge John Carro, former Assemblyman Gilberto Ramírez, anthropologist Edwin Seda Bonilla, Dr. Helen Rodríguez, and fabled lawyer, William Kunstler.[18]

The hearings were sponsored by a coalition of Puerto Rican organizations led by Gilberto Gerena Valentín and were scheduled to begin on May 15th.[19] "We support the objectives of these hearings," *El Diario-La Prensa* editorialized. "The time is now for not only serious soulsearching [sic] but for affirmative action. Wherever discrimination and exploitation directed at our people rears its ugly head it must be eliminated. Legitimate protests are not only a right but a responsibility of our citizens."[20]

During the hearings, Gilberto Gerena Valentín reiterated the position that the hearings were not a fact-finding mechanism but a forum to document discrimination against Puerto Ricans. The organizers had issued "people's subpoenas" to a number of public officials including Mayor Lindsay and Commissioner Amalia Betanzos.[21] Ironically, before any testimony was presented, a cry of discrimination by Puerto Ricans was heard in the Bronx from Tomás Forner. Forner claimed he had been arbitrarily removed from his position in the Board of Directors of a community corporation in the South Bronx by the President of the Board, José Serrano, in retaliation for running against Serrano for the position of district leader in Assembly District 75.[22]

Predictably, the hearings found that there was discrimination against Puerto Ricans. During the first day of testimony, the Rev. Rubén Darío Colón referred to the fact that the city employed only 200 Puerto Rican firefighters out of a workforce of 13,000 as evidence of discrimination. But more surprising than that was the statement of María Ortiz accusing the State Commission of Human Rights of discriminating against Puerto Ricans. Ironically, her charge was directed at two Hispanics within the Commission, Ruperto Ruiz, State Deputy Commissioner of Human Rights, and Florencio Linares, executive director of the city's Human Rights Commission. Ortiz also accused the State Department of Civil Service of making it impossible for Puerto Ricans to obtain employment in state and municipal agencies.[23]

During the hearings, not even the church was spared criticism. No one was surprised that participants would accuse the police of being prejudiced against Puerto Ricans. But the church too? According to State Senator Robert García, the Catholic Bishop and the Council of Protestant Churches were responsible for the lack of

Puerto Rican or Hispanic chaplains in city and state prisons. Rubén Darío Colón echoed García's charge, adding that the church was an accessory to the mistreatment of Puerto Rican inmates.

Testimony against the city's police force was dramatic because it was offered by Deputy Police Commissioner Luis Neco, on behalf of the Police Commissioner. Neco was the highest-ranking Puerto Rican officer within the Police Department. Another Puerto Rican police officer, Sargent Andrés Rivera, president of the Association of Hispanic Police Officers, declared that among the city's 300 female police officers not one was Puerto Rican and that only five of the 1,100 police detectives on the force were Puerto Rican.[24]

•••

In September, Puerto Rican students organized a national conference whose focus was independence for Puerto Rico. Were they distracted from paying attention to issues in New York? Did it matter? While the students were busy thinking about the island, a group from the Bronx simultaneously announced the formation of Puerto Ricans for Democratic Representation. "We are moved by the desire to promote the political advancement of our community," said the spokesperson of the group, Patricio Lausell, known in the Bronx for his civic and political involvement in the community.[25]

DEMAND-PROTEST

Do we lose a sense of shared moral and political purpose when we support or engage in identity politics? When Puerto Ricans focused on island issues, they risked not only becoming alienated from the political process in the city but also sowing discord among themselves and losing the center of their moral and political purpose, not so much in a ethical sense but in terms of their focus on urgent and more proximate issues. Substantively, however conflictive some of the issues that propelled their action were, they always raised liberal concerns: fair and equal treatment, individual freedom, freedom of expression, and equality of access to resources and opportunities.

Culebra

The issue of Culebra, an offshore island on Puerto Rico's west coast, twenty-one square miles in size, also known as the Spanish Virgin Island, had been the source of Puerto Rican mobilization in New York for a while. The U.S. military had taken over Culebra in 1901 to use for military practice, and by 1970 the consensus in Puerto Rico and New York was that it was time for the Navy to go.

Early in September 1970, Lin Espinosa, president of the Subcomité Neoyorquino Pro Rescate de Culebra [New York Subcommittee to Save Culebra], declared that the case of the Puerto Rican island was nearly solved because fifty senators out of fifty-two needed were in agreement that the U.S. Navy should cease military operations.[26] New York Gubernatorial candidate Arthur Goldberg joined another group, the Hands Off Culebra Association, in their petition to President Nixon to order a halt to military practice on the island. "There is no justification for using Culebra as target practice. A new site must be found," said Goldberg in a letter sent to Nixon.[27]

The solution offered by Congress and President Nixon in October to the Culebra issue was to request a study to be carried out by the Pentagon exploring alternatives to the use of the island by the U.S. Navy for its military exercises. The report needed to be submitted by the Pentagon by April of 1971.[28] The Pentagon was also asked to explore the possibility of asking the residents of Culebra to leave the island with due compensation, a proposal that generated widespread indignation in Puerto Rico. In Washington, D.C., Senator William Fulbright, Chair of the Foreign Relations Committee of the Senate, declared the proposal, authored by Congressman Charles Bennett, a Democrat from Florida, "arrogant" and "paternalistic."[29]

Another voice in the Culebra chorus was that of Senator Thomas Dodd from Connecticut. Dodd received a petition from Culebra's mayor, Ramón Feliciano, asking him to support a request for the cessation of military practice by the U.S. Navy on the island. Dodd replied that "the United States should not treat Puerto Ricans like colonial subjects." No other issue, he noted, had united Puerto Ricans as much as the Culebra case. He concluded that if Congress granted the Navy a larger portion of the island for target practice, it would only invigorate the pro-independence movement in Puerto Rico.[30]

On October 18th, the Comité Pro Defensa de Culebra de Brownsville [Brownsville Committee in Support of Culebra] held an assembly demanding the withdrawal of the U.S. Navy from the island. The assembly was in preparation for a march on Washington, D.C.[31] Earlier, the U.S. Senate had failed to approve a measure to retire the U.S. Navy from Culebra by January of 1976, choosing instead to limit the extent of military practice on the island.[32]

Despite the fiery and determined tone of the Comité Pro Defensa de Culebra de Brownsville, the proposed march on Washington, dubbed "Puerto Rican Unity Day," was not held as originally planned. Before cancelling the event, representatives of the group visited the offices of *El Diario-La Prensa* to request help publicizing the march, scheduled for November 21st. "The abuse suffered by Culebra on the part of the U.S. Navy is well-known, oppression, destruction of farms, and widespread terror," said Juan Feliciano and Lin Espinosa, to a reporter.

In a later statement, the organizing committee denounced "invisible pressures" on transportation providers to raise their fee so the organizers would not be able to afford the cost. The Committee had already heard from President Nixon that he was too busy and would not see their delegation. Speaking for the organizers, Gilberto Gerena Valentín promised that Puerto Ricans would eventually march on Washington to get the Navy out of Culebra. "The march has been postponed, not cancelled," he said, "We will use private cars, trucks, and even bicycles, we will walk down if necessary."[33]

In the end, a new set of buses was booked and, according to Gerena Valentín, one foggy morning on November 19, 1971, almost 5,000 Puerto Ricans descended into

Washington, D.C. to vent their grievance in picket lines in front of the Pentagon and the White House. "The activity was covered by the national press and several international wire services," recalled Gerena in his 2013 memoir.[34] But memory is tricky and one thing Gerena did not recall was that in April 1971 the Navy had already decided to leave the island; the only thing left to decide by then was when, but speaking to the *New York Times*, Secretary of Defense Melvin Laird indicated that bombardment of the island would cease by the end of the year and the relocation decision would be made sometime in 1972.[35]

In December 1972, Laird reversed himself, but his successor, Elliot Richardson, ordered the Navy to stop bombing the island by mid-1975. This decision, said the *New York Times*, "should settle the matter." Calling Culebra "the Caribbean mouse that roared," the *Times* declared Richardson's decision "a rare victory for human needs over military convenience."[36] And some victory it was: by 2005, 30 years after the Navy's departure, the island had become "a seasonal exile for scientists, business executives and other high-wattage Americans," who had the place mostly to themselves. According to one American resident, "the island isn't for everyone. There is no golf course, and the only tennis court doesn't even have a net."[37]

Why was a tiny off-shore island on the east coast of Puerto Rico of such concern to Puerto Ricans in New York? Was this not another distraction from more proximate issues? It was. But in the overall puzzle of Puerto Rican political mobilization, Culebra was one piece that distracted only those directly involved in the effort to get the U.S. Navy out of the island.

Education

In April 1971, in a decision that riled Puerto Ricans and others in the city, Community School Board 25 in Queens banned Piri Thomas' book *Down These Mean Streets* from the libraries of the schools in its district. The banning provoked a lawsuit from parents and teachers seeking the return of the book to the libraries on constitutional grounds.

On April 21st, Joseph Monserrat, speaking as a Board of Education member and as a Puerto Rican, condemned the action of the school board. On April 29th, the Queens Division of the American Jewish Congress also condemned the decision, lambasting the school board for not understanding "the dynamic nature of education in a democracy."

For its part, the lawyer for the Board of Education advised the Board to stay out of the fray in the absence of an expressed general policy from the Board concerning the maintenance of local school libraries. In June, the besieged school board voted to allow three copies of the book to be available only to the parents of children attending the schools involved in the issue.[38]

On May 2, 1972, a group of students took over the office of the President of Manhattan Community College demanding the renewal of the contract of Professor José Antonio Irizarry and the continuation of Puerto Rican studies at the college. The president of the college, Edgar Draper, met with the protesting students twice. But according to another member of the faculty, Américo Badillo, the future of Puerto Rican studies at the community college was uncertain. Badillo's contract expired in September, and he was afraid that a renewal would not be forthcoming, signaling the death of Puerto Rican studies. Students also complained about the dismissal of the coordinator of the Puerto Rican Studies Program, Migdalia de Jesús Torres. Torres had complained about drug trafficking on campus. The protestors also planned to file charges against a dean who had allegedly assaulted a female student.[39]

According to the police, such occupations were common; and therefore, they had no plans to intervene. However, the takeover was staged by about 200 students and was quite disruptive. In the end, the police arrested several participants who disrupted an on-the-air broadcast at WNET-Channel 13 to demand programming that presented a positive image of Puerto Ricans. This action was sponsored by the Puerto Rican Education Action Media Council in 1972 and contributed to the creation of the bilingual television program *Realidades*.[40]

At Hunter College, a group called the Committee to Save Our Studies registered a similar complaint. "The administration of Hunter has adopted a racist and paternalistic attitude towards Puerto Rican Studies," the Committee argued, using as an example the decision of the college to hire a non-Puerto Rican Hispanic to teach in the Department of Puerto Rican and Black Studies.[41] The hired faculty member was Ecuadorian professor Luis Rodríguez Abad.

A week after the Hunter College students registered their complaint, the groups Puertorriqueños Unidos [Puerto Ricans United] and the Sociedad Hostos [Hostos Society], took the President of the Board of Higher Education, Luis Quero Chiesa, hostage, demanding a meeting with Hunter College's President, Jaqueline Wexler. For his part Quero Chiesa declared that he was sympathetic to the students' demands but was not particularly pleased about being used as a bargaining chip.[42]

On May 11, *El Diario-La Prensa* published a story about discrimination of Puerto Rican students at Columbia University. "We have the support of the community board. President [William J.] McGill agreed to our demands but then he recanted," said the student leaders Emilio González and Juan López. According to González and López, McGill agreed to provide $3 million to black students for programs in Harlem but refused to grant $300 thousand for programs focused on Puerto Ricans. "This is unfair and discriminatory," they said. The students explained that they had occupied a university hall to highlight the urgency of their situation.[43]

Lincoln Hospital

An important community struggle early in 1970 centered around Lincoln Hospital in the Bronx. The issue of community control of the facility was long-standing. Now, there was a new twist with activists demanding *Puerto Rican* control. In response to a threat by Monserrate Flores, the Commissioner of Hospitals, Joseph V. Terenzio, obtained a court order to prevent a takeover of the hospital by Flores and his group. Flores demanded the appointment of a Puerto Rican physician—Antero Lacot—as hospital administrator at a meeting with the commissioner, which included Amalia Betanzos, representing Mayor Lindsay, and Herman Badillo, who was asked to be a "peacemaker."

The choice of Badillo to negotiate with Flores was odd; he and Flores had clashed on the question of voting rights in Puerto Rico for Puerto Ricans in New York, and in 1969 Flores was part of an anti-Badillo group that supported Lindsay when Badillo campaigned for mayor. The negotiation failed, and now Commissioner Terenzio had to openly fight Flores in court to prevent him from marching in and naming a hospital administrator—a symbolic but nevertheless disruptive possibility.[44]

Court order or not, about 200 Puerto Ricans gathered in front of the hospital on February 2nd, and about sixty went in and occupied the office of the administrator for two hours demanding the appointment of Dr. Lacot. One of the occupiers, Rafael Alvarado, calmly told the deputy administrator of the hospital that he, Alvarado, was now the "community-appointed" administrator. Commissioner Terenzio declared that Lacot was a talented physician but unqualified to manage the hospital. Terenzio offered Lacot a deputy administrator position in a different hospital so he could gain administrative experience but Lacot declined the offer.

The demonstrators and occupiers were orderly and polite. Nevertheless, twenty-one of them were arrested on charges of criminal trespass. They were released without bail and ordered to stand trial in March. Terenzio publicly reiterated what he had told Flores and his supporters privately: he wanted to appoint a Puerto Rican to manage the hospital and to plan the facility that was supposed to replace it. But in his view, Lacot just did not cut it. According to Terenzio, Flores and his group didn't really care whether a Puerto Rican was hired. What they really wanted was to control the choice.[45]

The man who in February was rejected as unqualified to run Lincoln Hospital, in March was selected to do so. With the endorsement of the Albert Einstein College of Medicine, where Lacot taught gynecology, obstetrics, preventive medicine, and community health, City Hall went over Terenzio's head and announced the appointment, insisting that it was not in any way related to the commissioner's resignation on February 18th. Lacot was to take over Lincoln Hospital after going through training in the city hospital system. The end of the training period more or less coincided with the actual departure of Terenzio, set for the end of May.[46]

Only six weeks into his tenure as administrator, Lacot confronted another occupation, this time staged by the Young Lords, who insisted on community control of the hospital. The Lords were a group of young Puerto Ricans who believed in independence for Puerto Rico but were not connected to Puerto Rican nationalist groups. They believed in socialism and liberation through armed struggle. Dr. Lacot was sympathetic to the Lords and agreed that there were problems at the hospital; but he and others wanted its programs to be supervised by staff physicians, not community activists. He believed that the "drama" staged by the Lords brought needed attention to the dire financial situation of the hospital, but he hoped they would leave soon, thank you very much. In the end, the occupation, which lasted twelve hours, was not entirely helpful, in his view, because workers were afterwards afraid to come to work, a situation the resource-starved hospital could not afford.[47]

Speaking on behalf of a broad array of community groups in the South Bronx, Monserrate Flores said that "in principle," these groups supported the Young Lords, whatever that may have meant. But it is not clear what the added value of their occupation was. Everyone agreed that the solution to the myriad problems at the hospital was the construction of the new facility. The occupation neither introduced nor changed that idea. The takeover was driven in part by concern with cutbacks in jobs and services but according to Dr. Lacot, cutbacks had never been an issue. In fact, the budget of the hospital for 1970-71 had increased by $260,000. The hospital had also been assigned a $300,000 supplementary allocation for adjustment to salaries negotiated with the hospital union.

Other demands by the Lords, such as setting up a grievance table and initiating a preventive medicine program, were moot because they had already been put in place or agreed to by the hospital on its own before the occupation. Some demands were nebulous, for example, "self-determination of all health services." Others were off the mark, for example, that funds to build the new hospital be allocated immediately; the construction delay was not due to fund-allocation issues but to an extension of time for the factory that occupied the site where the new hospital would be built to stay there.[48]

The concern of the Young Lords with cutbacks in services was ironic given that their occupation made staff reluctant to come to work. Two weeks after the takeover, twelve doctors threatened to resign, claiming continuing "harassment and intimidation" by the Young Lords and other groups. The director of pediatrics, Dr. Arnold Einhorn, declared that he was "probably on my way out too," because the daily presence of the Young Lords at the hospital created an intolerable work environment. Dr. Lacot begged to differ. No instances of harassment or intimidation had taken place in the hospital. There had been "disagreeable incidents," for sure, but nothing out of the ordinary.

Despite Dr. Lacot's assessment that the situation was "ordinary," the executive committee of the hospital board called an emergency meeting and wrote a memo to Lacot recommending the removal of the Young Lords and two other groups—the Health Revolutionary Unity Movement and Think Lincoln—from the premises due to their allegedly disruptive and threatening activities.[49] Upon receipt of the memo, Dr. Lacot met with the medical board and managed to appease its members. The complaining doctors backed off and agreed to give Lacot a chance to work things out with the protesters. Speaking on behalf of his colleagues, one of the doctors professed to care about patients and the community as much as the protesters; the doctors just had a different approach and attitude concerning how to provide services and did not appreciate being called "murderers" when anyone died at the hospital.[50]

In August, however, twenty-eight physicians and seventeen nurses from the obstetrics and gynecology staff walked off their jobs at the hospital, claiming intimidation and harassment by the Young Lords and the other groups. Hospital operations almost came to a halt. The Young Lords and their allies demanded the resignation of the chief of obstetrics and gynecology, Dr. Joseph Smith. At this point, even Dr. Lacot felt that the protesting groups had overstayed their welcome at the hospital.

Monserrate Flores called a meeting of the community advisory board and the board gave a vote of confidence to Dr. Smith and his staff. State Supreme Court Justice Arnold G. Fraiman served an injunction to the Young Lords and the other groups to cease and desist from interfering with patient care and medical services at the hospital. In an editorial, the *New York Times* called the Young Lords "a Puerto Rican imitation of the Black Panthers" and declared that it was high time to get them out of Lincoln, so that the climate of fear and conflict they had fostered could be dispelled.[51] Alas, Dr. Smith returned, but the doctors who walked out did not. At that point, one physician described working conditions at the hospital as "abominable." The hospital tried to, but it could not replace the missing doctors. The obstetrics unit was closed.[52]

In November, the crisis at the hospital took a new turn with the replacement of the chief of pediatrics Dr. Arnold Einhorn by Dr. Helen Rodríguez. Dr. Lacot had made the announcement anticipating that hiring a Puerto Rican doctor would go a long way in ameliorating and eventually overcoming the crisis. The dean of the Albert Einstein College of Medicine, Dr. Labe Scheinberg, who was ultimately responsible for staffing decisions at Lincoln Hospital, insisted that the reassignment of Einhorn to another facility only followed the disruption created by the Young Lords; it was not caused by their demands. This may or may have not been the case, but even before the intervention by the Lords, the hospital had publicly declared that it was looking for Puerto Rican personnel for top medical positions. Einhorn had just been threatened with bodily harm, and it seemed right at that point to remove him in order to protect him.[53]

A memorandum written by Dean Schienberg contradicted his public statement about the replacement of Einhorn. The memo read: "He is being replaced for political reasons. The Department finds it essential at this time to have a director of a different ethnic background." Upon learning this, two city councilmen, the American Jewish Congress, and the Civil Rights Division of the U.S. Department of Justice cried racism. The city's Commission on Human Rights reacted by opening up an investigation. A group of doctors from the hospital rejoined that the problem was not race but Dr. Einhorn's refusal to accept community-worker control of the pediatrics department. The real issue, according to this group, was the need to replace traditional practices of medicine, a need Dr. Einhorn did not recognize. The chief of the hospital's medical board, Dr. Elmer Foster, suggested keeping Dr. Einhorn as a condition of establishing a new Department of Community Medicine, headed by the newly hired Helen Rodríguez.[54]

The new department was demanded by Einhorn's antagonists in pediatrics. At this point, Mayor Lindsay intervened in the crisis, pledging that he would not tolerate decisions driven by racism. The compromise proposal did not seem to have much future, in part because none of its proponents were included in the negotiations initiated by top health officials following the replacement of Einhorn.[55] Instead, a compromise was negotiated with Dr. Einhorn: he would be reinstated, given a one-year sabbatical, but would not return to the hospital.[56]

In the end, Dr. Einhorn managed to spend a year in Paris at full-pay, while Helen Rodríguez and the Pediatrics Collective were left to serve 350,000 Puerto Ricans and blacks at an understaffed, decaying hospital fully in crisis. A facility that was still considered a "dump" by many employees and patients, that was "universally deplored as inadequate and obsolete," now displayed a banner that read "Bienvenidos Al Hospital Del Pueblo" [Welcome to the People's Hospital]. According to *New York Times* reporter, Harry Schwartz, the hospital "remained a battleground for contending forces, each striving for power and each conscious that the outcome may well set a model for ghetto medicine all over this country."[57]

Another irony of the crisis at Lincoln Hospital is that Dr. Einhorn was the architect of the community medicine model that, like Frankenstein's monster, got out of hand and ultimately turned against its creator. The turning point in the process took place when the doctors he hired organized as a collective behind his back and decided to establish relations with the Black Panthers and the Young Lords.

Dr. Einhorn was in favor of community participation in the process of medical care, but he would have nothing to do with groups that he considered radical and not representative of the community. His view of the Black Panthers was that they were racist. Dr. Einhorn was Jewish and had been an underground Nazi-fighter during World War II. The twelve-hour siege by the Young Lords in July was decisive for Dr. Einhorn.

At that point, the conflict became a full-fledged war, and Einhorn indicated that he would be damned if he was going to agree that a hospital should be run by the neighborhood instead of by professionally trained physicians. The head of the city's Health and Hospitals Corporation (HHC), Dr. Joseph T. English, summed up the situation as a conflict between "idealistic" and "battle fatigued" doctors. Speaking about the malcontents he declared: "I am sure that some of them are very well-trained physicians and socially responsible, but I've got a hunch that some of them are on the brink of irresponsibility."[58]

In May 1971, after reviewing Dr. Einhorn's case, the Synagogue Council of America concluded that his dismissal was not motivated by anti-Semitism. "It is in the interest of neither the Jewish community nor of the Black and Puerto Rican communities to allow themselves to be diverted by racial or religious divisiveness." The real issue, the Council noted, was the "scandalously inadequate" medical services at the hospital, which explained why some in the community had opted for radical solutions.[59]

The Human Rights Commission reached the same conclusion also in May: Einhorn was not fired because he was Jewish but because he was unable to bring a conflict involving the hospital administration, the pediatric staff, and members of the community to a quick resolution. The Commission acknowledged the involvement of radical militant groups in the controversy but concluded that both the Jewish and the Puerto Rican communities acted responsibly. "The majority of citizens in the South Bronx community surrounding Lincoln Hospital appear to understand that mere change in the ethnic background of personnel will not result in improved delivery of health services," the Commission concluded.

Even though the Commission favored community involvement in health care, it warned "The city does not need, cannot stand, and must do everything to avoid another decentralization battle of the kind that has shook the school system."[60] When the American Jewish Congress considered reviewing these findings, they were advised by one of their members that the reports of the Commission and of the Synagogue Council were credible and also that the Anti-Defamation League was in agreement that no anti-Semitism was present in the conflict.[61]

Prisoner Riot

Another example of disruptive conflict based on identity that served as a platform for advocacy for liberal values was the riot by inmates at the Queens House of Detention early in October 1970, protesting the conditions of their incarceration and demanding lower bails, speedier trials, and less overcrowding. This jail was built in 1884 to house 160 men, but it now held 338 inmates, the majority of whom were black and Puerto Rican. To safeguard the hostages taken by the inmates, Mayor Lindsay assembled a negotiating panel that included Deputy Mayor Michael Dontzin, Corrections Commissioner George F. McGrath, Herman Badillo, and Congresswoman Shirley Chisholm. The panel negotiated the release of the hostages in exchange for no reprisals against the inmates. But as soon as the prison was secured by the authorities, guards armed with ax handles, baseball bats, and riot sticks began to club the inmates so savagely that a photographer from the *Daily News* threw up at the sight of blood and crushed bones.

Three weeks after the beatings, the guards were exonerated and eight inmates were indicted for kidnapping, attempted larceny, and conspiracy. "The law is an outlaw," is how Jack Newfield characterized the situation in an article in the *Village Voice*. As a result, two committees were formed to defend the accused inmates: The Committee to Defend the Queens House of Detention Eight, sponsored by the First Presbyterian Church of Jamaica, Queens, and the Committee for Prison Justice, organized by the New York Urban Coalition. Manuel "Manny" Díaz, Jr. was the co-chair of the Committee for Prison Justice. Other supporters included Ted Vélez, from EHTC; Evelina Antonetty, from United Bronx Parents; Humberto Aponte and Frank Espada; Héctor Vázquez, from the Puerto Rican Forum; and Joseph Monserrat, from the Board of Education.[62]

Resource Allocations

In September 1970, the Council Against Poverty (CAP) announced to about a hundred representatives of Puerto Rican organizations that the days of PRCDP were numbered. The forecast was that by September 15th, 150 employees would be terminated and that the project itself, which had a budget of nearly $3 million distributed among over 100 organizations, would be closed by December 31. According to the participants in the meeting with CAP representatives, Puerto Ricans were not only underrepresented at the Council but neglected as well. African-Americans, who controlled the Council, were blamed, charged with indifference to the concerns of Puerto Ricans and as participants in a conspiracy to destroy a Puerto Rican institution.[63] Similar charges had been made a year earlier, prompting a demonstration by Puerto Ricans employed in agencies funded by the Council against Major Owens, head of the Community Development Agency (CDA), and David Billings, Jr., head of CAP.[64]

For this reason, George Rodríguez, president of the Project's board of directors, declared that the effort to destroy the PRCDP was longstanding. Referring to the Project's enemies he said: "We know who they are, and we will denounce them." Even though he did not name names or mentioned a specific group, everyone knew this was a reference to the African Americans in the Council and to Major Owens. His evidence of a conspiracy by blacks against Puerto Ricans was that black agencies faced only $60,000 in budget cuts while Puerto Rican groups were expected to shoulder an $800,000 reduction in funds.

Rodríguez intended to denounce his enemies at a protest before CDA on September 10th. Other Puerto Rican groups that stood to either lose funding or close altogether were the Puerto Rican Family Institute, whose record of service included providing help to over ten thousand families, and ASPIRA, which was instrumental in fostering access of Puerto Ricans to higher education. Also affected were the Congress of Puerto Rican Hometowns and the Children's Council. The protest was coordinated by a coalition that included the PRCDP, the Puerto Rican Family Institute, ASPIRA, the Hunts Point Multi-Service Agency, the Hunts Point Community Corporation and other community leaders from the Lower East Side.[65]

A separate coalition joined the fray, also claiming discrimination against Puerto Rican agencies. Speaking on behalf of the Frente Nacional Puertorriqueño [Puerto Rican National Front], Dr. María Bithorn and Jesús Irrizary demanded the intervention of Mayor Lindsay. The mayor was aiding and abetting a civil rights violation, they declared, by letting blacks and other groups take 90 percent of the positions in Model Cities agencies while Puerto Ricans had access to only 10 percent. In their view, Puerto Ricans deserved at least 50 percent of those positions. Another example of alleged discrimination given by Bithorn and Irizarry was a staff at the Model Cities General Office that was a mere one percent Puerto Rican. Lindsay, they claimed, was not only in violation of federal law but also of his Executive Order 22, signed August 24th. Bithorn and Irrizarry gave the mayor ten days to respond.[66]

"We fully realize that the cuts were made mandatory when Washington reduced the available funds," editorialized *El Diario-La Prensa*. But the cuts seemed to single out Puerto Rican agencies under the guise of technicalities—suggesting that Puerto Rican agencies did not offer assistance to other groups or that their executives had not done any fundraising of their own. Instead, the newspaper argued, cuts should have been made across the board to all participating organizations.[67] According to *El Diario-La Prensa*, the cuts were set in motion in 1969 through a mandate to participating agencies to phase out social services to people and replace them with technical assistance to community corporations. Because Puerto Rican groups had not complied with this "impossible mandate," they were now threatened—not for failure to fulfill their service mission but for failure to comply with what was considered a diversion of funds to agencies that were not qualified to service Puerto Ricans.[68]

On September 10th, close to one thousand demonstrators gathered at 349 Broadway to protest the cuts proposed by CDA. The rally was preceded by what *El Diario-La Prensa* described as a "gigantic motorcade" that paraded from the offices of the Model Cities Agency to the site of the demonstration. There was a moment of tension when a group of participants sat in the middle of the street, blocking traffic. This prompted the intervention of the police, and many feared that violence would break out. At a meeting with the director of CAP, the leaders of the demonstration were offered a six-month reprieve from the proposed cuts, which they rejected. The spokesperson for the participants, Raul Reyes, said that they would only accept a year's extension.[69]

Immediately after the demonstration and without any apparent motive, the police attacked the participants, pushing, shoving, slapping, and beating them with their nightsticks. Some participants were arrested. According to Monserrate Flores, the attack was unprovoked by the protesters. He demanded a full investigation by the police authorities.[70]

The controversy gave an opportunity for political candidates to score points with Puerto Ricans. According to the 1970 Democratic-Liberal gubernatorial candidate Arthur J. Goldberg, the proposed cuts were discriminatory and unfair. Puerto Ricans should be singled out for extra help rather than for reductions in assistance, Goldberg opined, because they were disproportionately affected by the problems of poverty. In his view, the community was doing well politically, but too many children dropped out of school, unemployment was excessive, infant mortality was grave, and they had the worst quality housing. "The Puerto Rican community can speak for itself," said Goldberg, "but it also needs and deserves help from friends and allies throughout the city to stop the proposed cuts. Any reduction in the poverty program against Puerto Ricans is discriminatory, iniquitous, and inconsiderate. The CDA must restore funding."[71]

Not to be left behind, Governor Nelson Rockefeller added his voice to those pleading for continued support for Puerto Ricans. "We need positive action, not promises," said the governor, "otherwise we will see the end of all the programs that assist the Hispanic community." The governor asked for continued support from federal officials in Washington and New York.[72] He also sent the director of the state's Office for Community Affairs, Jack Sable, to a meeting with representatives from the affected Puerto Rican agencies where Sable offered technical assistance and his advocacy on behalf of the agencies to ensure continued financial support. Sable also agreed to bring to the governor's attention the claim of insufficient Puerto Rican representation within CAP.[73]

•••

On September 15th and 19th, the city held special elections to select the Boards of Directors of eighteen of the twenty-five community corporations that controlled an average $63 million annually distributed to them by CAP. Of the twenty-five boards, Puerto Ricans were executive directors or presidents of ten throughout the city. "We could have more," editorialized *El Diario-La Prensa*. "We should have more members in the boards and more representatives in the Council Against Poverty. But we can't do it unless we go out and vote."[74]

On October 21st, Ramón Vélez stepped down from his post as executive director of the Hunts Point Multiservice Center, citing "constant and unfair pressure" against him and against the Center by city officials and officials from CAP. Vélez was suspected of questionable accounting and spending practices. One in particular involved a payment of $5,000 he received for "compensatory time." He claimed that those who wanted his ouster were "against the prosperity of Puerto Ricans and Hispanics. It is time for me to go back to the people," he declared. "I'm spending too much time in my office wasting time." His supporters included Assemblyman Armando Montano and Assembly candidate Louis Nine.[75]

Vélez was not alone in his sentiments against CAP. Just as he was stepping down from his post at the multi-service center, tensions between CAP and its clients were reported. The tensions were attributed to cutbacks in funding. Although the cutbacks did not affect all clients, which numbered over two million distributed throughout the twenty-six "poverty communities" of the city, the fear of a backlash was strong enough to make the chair of CAP complain to Mayor Lindsay about inadequate security at Council meetings. These meetings were open to the public and they did attract large numbers of concerned citizens. Inexplicably, however, Billings' complaint to the mayor was prompted by what he called an "unprecedented invasion of the [October 22] meeting by police" which resulted in the assault and arrest of a CDA staff member and the assault of Billings himself.[76]

•••

At the end of 1971, Angel Vega, from the Brotherhood of Arecibeños Campeche, chained himself to the doors of the South Bronx Community Corporation to protest the corporation's funding decisions. Claims concerning discrimination in the distribution of anti-poverty funds such as this were chronic. Vega also accused the corporation of sabotaging the records of the Brotherhood and appointing a black director to take away control of the organization from Puerto Ricans.[77] A bit earlier, in September, the news had been better: Cándido de León had become the first Puerto Rican college president in the United States when he assumed the helm of Hostos Community College. In November, Luis Quero Chiesa was elected to head the Higher Education Board, the ruling body of the City University of New York. This did not immediately compensate for inequities in resource allocation to Puerto Ricans but the appointments were promising.

A year later, on May 6th, a group of volunteers led by Amalia Betanzos known by the name "El Coquí," planned a voter registration marathon. This campaign was sponsored by the Office of the Commonwealth led by Nick Lugo, Jr., in cooperation with the Hispanic chapter of the League of Women Voters, radio station WBNX, *El Diario-La Prensa*, the Voters Legion, and the PRCDP, among other groups.[78] "As soon as Puerto Ricans get involved in the political process, they will become first-class citizens and our housing, education, and employment problems will be solved. Without political power nothing will be accomplished," said Betanzos.[79]

In other words, resource allocations were a function of political involvement, even if sometimes the allocations were just symbolic. To wit, at the end of the month, surrounded by forty-one prominent members of the community, including Betanzos and Gilberto Gerena Valentín, Mayor Lindsay declared May 28 to June 4, Puerto Rican Culture Week claiming that Puerto Rican intellectuals had achieved "a distinguished position in the cultural life of the city."[80] Piri Thomas, the Puerto Rican author whose work had been banned from public libraries in a community school district in Queens, was not invited.

CHAPTER 5
LIBERALS FOR JUSTICE AND PROGRESS

When Herman Badillo ran for the mayoral nomination in 1973, his candidacy received enthusiastic support from multiple quarters. At the community level, some offered him "services and political experience to run your campaign" and others offered money. From Puerto Rico, he was endorsed by the island's governor, who described him as a representative of "all who are liberals and for justice and progress."[1] In Washington, D.C., the Committee Pro-Badillo for Mayor of New York formed, under the leadership of Myrna Hernandez de Carter, to raise money for the campaign.[2]

What did his candidacy represent for community organizations? Not much. Badillo was never enthusiastic about War on Poverty resources—the staple of Puerto Rican institutional development during the 1960s—which he saw as bait for conflict between Puerto Ricans and blacks. In this regard, his role was not as significant as that played by the likes of Manuel "Manny" Díaz, Jr., or Toni Pantoja. As for identity politics, his run was interesting.

Badillo did not shy away from emphasizing his Puerto Rican background, although he always made it clear that he was not a typical figure—he was tall, a lawyer, could speak English well, and, even though he never made this explicit, he was white. He saw himself as a crossover candidate, appealing to Puerto Ricans as well as to Jews and blacks. Ultimately, the politics of his identity were subsumed under his liberal ideology and much like the chronicle below, he embodied the aspirations of justice and progress that the governor of Puerto Rico aptly associated with his campaign.

STRATEGIC ACTION
While the argument of this book is that identity politics and liberalism are compatible, there were some within the Puerto Rican community that saw it differently, although the issue was not addressed explicitly. The vignette below concerning education is one example. To some Puerto Ricans, identity politics was not a concern. To them the problems of the community went beyond the limitations of liberalism. Puerto Rican or not, anyone who experienced disadvantage could not expect solutions within the framework of liberal democracy. It is important to note this, even though the record suggests that this belief was not generalized within the community. To wit, the organizational activities chronicled below. These were not carried out explicitly under the banner of liberalism, but in practice they were expressions of identity politics in consonance with liberal democratic norms and values.

Education
In July 1973, the director of the newly established Center for Puerto Rican Studies along with a group of community leaders and educators reached out to the National

Institute of Education (NIE) to obtain funding for Puerto Rican projects, to secure staff appointments of Puerto Ricans at the Institute, and to exercise influence on educational research policy. On July 19, a meeting pursuant to these goals took place between NIE's director, Thomas K. Glennon, Jr. and some of the members of this group.[3]

Less than a year later, this effort ran into the ground. In a document titled "Statement of Puerto Rican Educators (A Response to the Multi-Cultural Education Task Force of the National Institute of Education)," Frank Bonilla and Josephine Nieves, from the Center for Puerto Rican Studies; Evelina Antonetty, from United Bronx Parents (UBP); María Josefa Canino, from Rutgers University; Mario Anglada, from ASPIRA; and Lourdes Miranda-King, from Universidad Boricua; among others, declared that NIE was incapable of addressing Puerto Rican needs in any meaningful way.[4] This is an amazing document that shows how convinced this group of intellectuals and activists was that within existing institutions no significant change could be accomplished, no resources could be marshaled, and no benefits could be obtained for Puerto Ricans. For them, anything short of systemic transformation was meaningless.

•••

In late August 1974, two years after filing suit demanding bilingual education in the city's public schools on behalf of ASPIRA, the Puerto Rican Legal Defense and Education Fund (PRLDEF) obtained a consent decree with the Board of Education establishing such programs.[5] The decree covered children with English-language deficits and required that the Board of Education provide them with intensive instruction in English, instruction in subject areas in Spanish, and instruction aimed at strengthening Spanish-language skills. Instructional materials had to be sensitive to, and reflective of the culture of, participant children; professionals in the program were required to be bilingual in English-Spanish. While the *New York Times* expressed dismay that it had taken litigation to establish a program dictated by common sense, the *New York Daily News* declared that English-only was a better policy. *El Diario-La Prensa* was jubilant, declaring the consent decree a "victory for bilingual education."[6] This was also a vindication of Maria Teresa Babín's idea of cultural citizenship, with language front and center in this form of identity politics.

Ironically, shortly after many proponents of bilingual education were removed from community school boards, bilingual education was scheduled to begin in the city. The consent decree won by ASPIRA was expected to be fully implemented by September 1975. However, according to Herbert Teitelbaum, legal director of PRLDEF, the subject of bilingual education continued to be mired in confusion and misrepresentation. Why was it so hard for everyone to understand that "bilingual" meant two languages—English *and* Spanish—not just Spanish? Why wasn't common knowledge already that whatever assimilation had ever occurred among previous immigrant populations, it was not just as a result of their school experience? "Ethnic tensions," Teitelbaum wrote in the *New York Times,* "are created and aggravated not by bilingual education but, on the contrary, by notions of language and cultural superiority that have formed a basis for much of the resistance to bilingual education."[7]

When the city began to offer bilingual education, Hispanics were 20 percent of all students in the city. It had been five years since PRLDEF had championed bilingual education. The initial court action took place in September 1970. In February 1973, the Board of Education was forced to respond to the court action after trying unsuccessfully to have the court reject ASPIRA's lawsuit. In 1974, the U.S. Supreme Court ruled in favor of the plaintiffs in the case of *Lau v. Nichols,* establishing the right to bilingual education, and PRLDEF requested a ruling on its lawsuit based on the precedent set by the Supreme Court case.

The city opposed PRLDEF's request. Upon consideration of evidence submitted by the parties, the court decreed in August 1974 that bilingual education was necessary in New York. Hispanic parents retained the right of their children not to participate in bilingual education programs. To some, the program promoted ethnic separatism and prevented assimilation. The teacher's union opposed bilingual programs as well, but its concern was that bilingual programs would bring unqualified teachers into the system. Defenders of the program argued that it was necessary not just for the sake of cultural pluralism but to improve educational attainment as well.[8]

During the summer of 1976, bilingual education was again in the news. A year after the beginning of implementation, the debate over its desirability was still intense. On the one hand, defenders like Awilda Orta, coordinator of programs in District 4 in El Barrio, argued that bilingual education had general academic value. On the other, opponents firmly believed that students would never learn English and that monolingual-English teachers would be fired. The fiscal crisis compounded the question by making investments in the program seem inappropriate at a time when money was scarce.

The Deputy Chancellor of the school system, Dr. Bernard Gifford, made matters worse by his ignorance. It was not clear to him whether bilingual education required bilingual or bicultural teachers. The program was also questioned because it emphasized Spanish instruction to the alleged detriment of Italian, Greek, French, and Chinese bilingual programs. Lost in this set of objections was the fact that Spanish-speakers were the largest linguistic minority in the city. In some places, like District 4, they were actually the majority. One key objection reflected the low level of broad acceptance and legitimacy of bilingual education. This was the belief that it was "a push for jobs and power rather than [an] educational vehicle to help the children." How could it be either one of those *without* the other? And why were jobs and power illegitimate? The irony of this argument was that it was embraced by administrators *and* teachers as well.[9]

On December 1975, PRLDEF took the Board of Education back to court, demanding a "show-cause" order. PRLDEF wanted to know why the Board was dragging its feet and not complying fully with the 1974 consent decree. A decision by the court was expected in September 1976.[10] By the end of 1976, a federal judge held

Chancellor Irving Anker in contempt of court for tolerating defiance of the consent decree, for letting implementation delays go unchallenged, and for evading his responsibility to carry out the terms of the agreement. PRLDEF celebrated, not knowing that little would change. The group could not have possibly guessed that, a year later, the Board would argue that it could not fully implement the consent decree because "the bilingual program makes desegregation impossible." The claim was declared preposterous by Dr. Kenneth B. Clark and Jorge Batista. Both were members of the New York State Board of Regents, which was pressuring the city both on bilingual education and desegregation. Batista was one of the lesser-known founders of PRLDEF and in 1976 its president and general legal counsel.[11]

In 1978, PRLDEF was actively involved in lobbying Congress to insure that the extension of the Elementary and Secondary Education Act included strong support for bilingual education. In this effort, the legal fund joined other Latino groups such as the Mexican American Political Association, the National Council of La Raza, the Mexican American Legal Defense and Education Fund, Chinese for Affirmative Action, the League of United Latin American Citizens, and ASPIRA.[12]

Electoral Politics
In May 1974, three hundred Hispanics opened the first Hispanic Democratic Club in Queens at a storefront in Corona to represent the will of some 200,000 Hispanic residents. The group was named United Hispanic American Democratic Club. Its headquarters were at 37-45 Junction Boulevard. The first slate of officers was installed on June 1, at a $50 a ticket dinner-dance at the Waldorf Astoria Hotel. According to Oscar Arce, the executive director of the organization, "Until now the politicians do not even know we exist." While this claim was hyperbolic and ignorant, its underlying rationale was legitimate: a demand for recognition and inclusion using difference as the starting point.

The officers of the club were businessmen and professionals; more than 80 percent of the club members were homeowners. The club originated in the 1973 Beame campaign. "We began meeting politically [and] we learned that when you work separately you don't accomplish much," said Alfredo Rey, president of the club. The club was pan-ethnic, with members from Argentina, Bolivia, Chile, Colombia, Cuba, Ecuador, El Salvador, Guatemala, Honduras, México, Nicaragua, Perú, Puerto Rico, Santo Domingo, Spain, and Venezuela. Their first activity was a voter registration campaign in twelve locations in Queens. They concentrated in Corona, which was estimated to have 50,000 Hispanic residents.[13]

In 1978, the Office of the Commonwealth of Puerto Rico resumed its efforts to register Puerto Rican voters in the city. In that year it sponsored and distributed short films encouraging Puerto Ricans to register and vote. Two of these films featured Herman Badillo and Robert García.[14] From 1978 through 1989, all agency work plans, with the sole exception of the plan for 1980-81, included a voter registration initiative. Two things stand out in these plans and subsequent reports: their ambitious goals and the absence of any indication that they were ever accomplished. At this point, monthly plans also start being brief, almost telegraphic and perfunctory, consisting mostly of statistical breakdowns of meetings held by month. The 1978-79 plan simply included voter registration as an objective.

In April 1979, there was an attempt by the leadership of the Office of the Commonwealth to promote Puerto Rican political participation by enlisting the assistance of the church. This was the idea of Félix Rodríguez "Bobby" Capó, the Puerto Rican singer and composer now turned government bureaucrat. At a meeting with Capó, various clergymen committed themselves to the task. In May, the effort was launched including the Cruzada Cívica del Voto [Civic Crusade for Voting] and Herman Badillo, among others. Hundreds of volunteers were recruited to meet the campaign's ambitious goal of registering over half a million voters. This number, however, must have been a misprint on the records because the Office of the Commonwealth's report for June notes that the campaign would hopefully produce 10,000 new voters—still a significant number but certainly considerably smaller and more realistic.[15]

Organizational Activities
In June 1973, the National Conference of Puerto Rican Women (NACOPRW), headquartered in Washington, D.C., held its first annual meeting in New York. At the conference five local women—Raquel Creitoff, Carmen Pérez, Gladys Rivera, Yolanda Sánchez, and Magdalena Torres—agreed to form a city chapter. The objective of this group was to promote equal rights and greater political participation of Puerto Rican women in the United States. It had three annual activities: a Three Kings Day event, a women's history month activity profiling Puerto Rican women in the city, and a voter registration campaign. Why didn't the members of NACOPRW simply join an established women's organization? They were women but also Puerto Rican, and it was this identity that propelled their effort.

•••

In August, the Office of the Commonwealth reported on an absence of voter registration activities due to a lack of staff. In September, the agency was declared ineffectual by its own sponsors. From September 1973 through February 1974, monthly reports make no reference to any registration activities at all. But agency supporters found relief in the existence of six hundred Puerto Rican self-help organizations in the city. These groups were considered an alternative to the government-sponsored office.[16] By the Office's own count, the number of Puerto Rican organizations throughout the city ranged between 217 and 469 during the period 1970-1972. These were substantial numbers even if somewhat inflated due to duplications and different ways of counting from year to year.[17] Despite inaccuracies in counting, the phenomenon of independent organizations substituting for the Commonwealth's office was real, even before 1973. On August 26, 1972, one such organization, the Puerto Rican Newspaper, Radio, and Television Society, Inc., requested the establishment of an East Harlem Branch of the Commission on Human Rights. The request was politely rejected by the city administration.[18]

The proliferation of groups could be used both in support of the argument that the Commonwealth Office was intent on controlling local organizations as well as against it. This issue recurred throughout the 1970s, especially regarding attempts by employees of the Office to win the presidency of the Puerto Rican Parade organization. "Just because I work for the Office does not mean the agency is interested in controlling the Parade or any local organization," said Wichy Santiago when objections were raised to his candidacy. "When Max Sanoguet, from the Puerto Rican Project, a government agency, ran last year no one said anything."[19] He probably was referring to the *government-funded* PRCDP. More important, the surge in organizational efforts was directly related to a strongly perceived need for *ethnic-based* organization.

For some reason, the staff at the Office of the Commonwealth's community organization program was compelled to make the following disclaimer in its 1974 annual report: "Our service does not seek to assume a paternalist attitude towards Puerto Rican organizations but rather to help them identify community problems and to stimulate them to use their resources to help themselves."[20] By 1974, outreach efforts by the Commonwealth Office directed at Puerto Rican organizations in the city were at an all-time low. Assuming that the reported number of persons contacted through community meetings is accurate, by 1974 the ability of the program to reach out to the community had decreased from its peak level of 68,072 persons contacted in fiscal year 1967-68 by 91 percent.[21]

• • •

On September 23rd, on the anniversary of El Grito de Lares, a group of Puerto Ricans gathered at the Hipocampo Club, on 2015 Jerome Avenue in the Bronx, to celebrate the nineteenth-century revolt against Spanish colonialism on the island by dancing away to the songs and rhythms of Ismael Miranda, Ray Barretto, Tony Rojas and his Orchestra, and several other artists.[22] Could it be said that their choice of activity meant that issues related to Puerto Rico were more important to them than local concerns? Perhaps. On the other hand, celebrating El Grito de Lares was a once-a-year event; it didn't say anything about the day-to-day activities of Puerto Rican organizations in New York. Further, Puerto Ricans were 13 percent of the citywide membership in community school boards. At this level of participation and decision-making, they were slightly overrepresented—Puerto Ricans were 10 percent of the city's population—although in places like Staten Island and Queens they had no representation at all.[23]

On October 23rd, the *Daily News* reported that New York City had been accused of violating the Voting Rights Act (VRA) by the U.S. Department of Justice for conducting elections only in English. The Department of Justice made the charge in a motion filed in U.S. District Court to re-open a 1971 voting rights case that sought to release New York, Bronx, and Kings counties from coverage by the VRA because of the elimination of literacy tests. In April 1972, the court agreed to release those counties from VRA coverage. But, according to the Department of Justice, English-only elections constituted a "test or device" that denied or abridged the right of Spanish-speaking citizens to vote. Therefore, in re-opening the 1971 case the Department was asking the court to rescind the 1972 judgment for the sake of the 425,850 Spanish-speaking voting-age citizens of the three counties.[24] The purpose of this suit was to re-authorize the application of the pre-clearance provision of the VRA to New York City.

Before this federal intervention, PRLDEF had initiated a court action, *Torres v. Sachs*, to strengthen the voting rights of Puerto Ricans in the city. In his opinion and order, Federal District Court Judge Charles E. Stewart, Jr., declared that even though the New York City Board of Elections agreed that bilingual ballots had to be available in all elections in the city and that there had to be Spanish-speaking inspectors in election districts having at least 5 percent Spanish-speaking voters, this was not sufficient to insure "full and effective voting rights" for the suing class.

Accordingly, before the U.S. Department of Justice case was resolved, he ordered the Board to comply with the previously agreed requirements in all future elections, plus to provide "conspicuous signs at all polling places and places of registration [...] indicating in Spanish that election officials are available to assist Spanish-speaking voters or registrants, and that bilingual printed materials are available; and [to] publicize elections in all media proportionately in a way that reflects the language characteristics of plaintiffs."[25] The court's order was delivered in July of 1974, almost a year after PRLDEF filed suit.

•••

On December 11th, a group of Puerto Ricans organized the New York chapter of the Puerto Rican Legal Institute. The mission of the chapter was to provide legal assistance in New York to Puerto Rican *independentistas* suffering political persecution or incarceration. In addition, the Institute intended to be active around important island issues. One issue that caught the immediate attention of the Institute was the proposal to establish a superport for oil tankers on Puerto Rico's west coast.[26] Three days later, the Special Committee on Decolonization at the United Nations issued a report reaffirming the inalienable right of the people of Puerto Rico to self-determination and independence. The Committee called on the United States government to refrain from any measures that could hinder the right of Puerto Ricans to exercise these rights. Of the 104 members of the committee only five voted against the report: the United States, Great Britain, Portugal, South Africa, and France.[27]

Even though forbidden to participate in partisan politics, community-based organizations nevertheless availed themselves of whatever resources politicians could broker for them. In April 1974, for example, Evelina Antonetty wrote in desperation to Commissioner of Manpower Lucille Rose, asking for help to maintain a seriously understaffed Youth and Drug Prevention Program at UBP. "Due to the recent budget cut [...] we have had to reduce our staff," she wrote. "This has resulted in absolute chaos since the number of youths that attend our center have [sic] increased [...]." The program was servicing 200 youths a day with a staff of four.[28]

At the same time that Antonetty was struggling to keep her program alive, she was also being asked to join a campaign against the establishment of a marine transfer station in the Hunts Point Peninsula. After considering the proposal for the station, Community Board 2 officials decided to oppose it. According to Teresa Morales, chairperson of the Board, the establishment of the transfer station "would seriously and adversely affect our community," and thus the Board wanted to enlist UBP as well as other community organizations in the effort to block its installation. Traffic problems, an overly strained street system, commercial traffic invading residential streets, and technically inferior facilities were some of the reasons prompting Community Board 2's opposition.[29]

•••

In November 1974, during the Regional Meeting of the Catholic Conference, held in Holyoke, Massachusetts, a group of delegates organized the Hispanic Youth Pastoral Council of the Northeastern United States. The Youth Council intended to promote a program of Hispanic youth leadership development within the Catholic Church, focused on sociology, economics, culture, and liberation theology. Migrant agricultural workers were identified as the group most in need of assistance.

The Council divided the region into four sectors: New England; the New York, Newark, and Patterson metro area; the Penn-Jersey area, including Pennsylvania, Trenton, and Camden; and the Capital area, comprising southern states in the Washington, D.C. area. In New York, Anthony Stevens Arroyo and Lourdes Torres were involved, Arroyo as an advisor and Torres as a student activist then associated with the Bronx group Naborí.[30]

While this could be seen as an effort by the Catholic Church to engage Puerto Ricans and Hispanics in social action, in actuality it was more an initiative from below, prompted by identity concerns that those involved thought the church had an obligation to address. The Council became a triennial conference that gave Hispanic Catholics a place to meet other like-minded people and an opportunity to spread a message of social justice within the Church.

By 1975, Lourdes Torres, whose involvement in Naborí stemmed from her dissatisfaction with the stance of the Church on issues such as divorce and homosexuality, as well as from her desire to nurture her Puerto Rican identity, was so disillusioned that the Youth Council was not enough to prevent her from leaving the Church to become, as she put it, "a revolutionary." Stevens Arroyo, who was the leading force behind Naborí, followed a similar path, leaving behind the priesthood for lay activism to promote his Catholic convictions.[31]

Nearly ten years later, the Youth Pastoral initiative was echoed by the Lower East Side Area Catholic Conference, a coalition of twenty-one Catholic parishes, in its effort to promote dialogue among religious officials and residents and to make the church more responsive to the everyday needs of parishioners.[32]

• • •

After the U.S. Civil Rights Commission published its report *Puerto Ricans in the United States, An Uncertain Future*, in 1976, Louis Núñez, who as deputy director of the Commission sponsored the report, called a meeting to discuss the report's implications. At that meeting, the participants decided to create a national policy advocacy organization.

On December 11th, a group of Puerto Rican leaders, the majority of them from New York, met in Washington, D.C. to discuss the formation of the new national organization. The meeting was convened by Luis Alvarez, executive director of the National Urban Fellows, and was held at the Gramercy Inn Hotel. Prominent participants were Amalia Betanzos, Manuel Bustelo, and Carmen Delgado Votaw. Among the guests were Frank Espada; Louis Núñez; and Juan Manuel García Passalacqua, a Puerto Rico-based journalist and political analyst; and William Pounds, from the White House Task Force. These persons had been elected to study the economy of Puerto Rico.[33] The organizational sponsors of the new group were ASPIRA, the National Puerto Rican Forum, PRLDEF, NCOPRW, the Latino Institute, and the Center for Puerto Rican Studies.[34]

The group convened as the National Puerto Rican Conference and initially its account at Banco Popular in New York City was held under that name. After much discussion, the meeting decided that the new group would be known as the National Puerto Rican Coalition (NPRC) and that it would be incorporated in Washington, D.C., rather than New York. Participants agreed that the organization should have a broad mission, including legislative and policy analysis, technical assistance to Puerto Rican communities throughout the United States, and lobbying. A national convention was planned for June 1978.

During the proceedings, Louis Núñez claimed that not much transpired that could be construed as positive follow-up after the publication of the Civil Rights Commission 1976 report. Similarly, it was not clear whether a Puerto Rican was being considered for the position of head of bilingual education at the federal Department of Health, Education, and Welfare—as the Department of Health and Human Services was known until 1978. After Amalia Betanzos reported that the conference's Urban Policy Task Force did not have a position paper due to poor attendance to task force meetings, the group proceeded to discuss President Carter's urban policy, focusing on the lack of resources available to address urban issues and the need for an urban policy that paid attention to Puerto Ricans.

The discussion then turned to youth issues. Participants were concerned that unemployed Puerto Rican youth could easily become part of an underclass. They also expressed concern that a law that directly affected Puerto Ricans—Public Law 94-311, which mandated the collection of social statistics by race and ethnicity—was not being enforced. In the midst of all this, Louis Núñez suggested that a letter be sent to the departments directly responsible for enforcing Public Law 94-311. Someone else recommended a study of Puerto Rican migration patterns. A study of the quality of services and service delivery by the Office of the Commonwealth was also suggested.

At this point, someone warned the participants that the list of tasks was growing beyond the capacity of the organization. Despite this, a subcommittee was formed to proceed with these studies. In addition, the group decided to write a position paper on bilingual education, to promote the organization of Puerto Rican youth, to push for presidential and judicial appointments, to form an advisory council on the issue of substance abuse, to study the status of Puerto Ricans on corporate boards, to raise funds, and to develop a public relations campaign. The organization had no staff so the responsibility to follow up on their agreements fell upon the Chairperson Pro Tempore, Luis Alvarez.

According to Josephine Nieves, the main weakness of NPRC was its dependence on federal monies. In her view, the group was not effective because in effect it eschewed advocacy in favor of lobbying. NPRC's program was also allegedly diluted by its attention to island issues. This was not contemplated in the original mission of the group. In 1988, Nieves thought that NPRC was ineffective and its work largely ceremonial. In her view, after ten years of existence, it was not clear what NPRC did or what it had accomplished. She could not say what potential the organization had, but she was convinced that it had "very little power."[35]

•••

At the end of 1977, bad news befell the community. PRCDP officials were accused of embezzlement. According to city controller Harrison Goldin, Project officials had authorized the use of $31,000 to pay for the personal debts of two employees. Claims of innocence, accusations, and counter-accusations flew back and forth wrapped in bureaucratic jargon. The treasurer of the organization, Johnny Meléndez, claimed that the charges were political, no more than a crude attempt to discredit Ramón Vélez, the former president of the Project's board.

Meléndez's defense rang hollow, as he was also president of the Hunts Point Community Corporation, another Vélez anti-poverty enterprise in the Bronx.[36] In 1978, Councilman Gilberto Gerena Valentín led a sit-in demanding the dismissal of the PRCDP's Board of Directors, halting the operations of the agency for a week. Shortly afterwards, the city took over the Project, charging misuse of millions of dollars.³⁷ According to Assemblyman Angelo Del Toro, an additional problem was that PRCDP was dominated by South Bronx organizations.³⁸

PRCDP funds were cut in July 1978. The press reported this on July 21st. Seven days later, Evelina Antonetty met with Carol Bellamy. The meeting was arranged by Yolanda Sánchez, from the Puerto Rican Association for Community Affairs. The meeting was part of a tour of East Harlem, but Sánchez thought it was important for Antonetty to meet Bellamy to advocate for PRCDP.³⁹

On October 31st, a group of PRCDP Board members resolved that Luis Cardona be appointed by CDA as interim overseer of PRCDP. They recommended that Cardona be given full management authority over PRCDP and the authority for him to act as the organization's legal agent as well. On November 21st, Haskell Ward, commissioner of CDA, approved this request, instructing Cardona to direct the operations of PRCDP without relating to its Board in any way. Cardona was instructed to report to Russell Francione, from CDA's staff, instead.⁴⁰

According to Josephine Nieves, the conflict at PRCDP was essentially over who would control the Board of Directors. Part of the conflict concerned whether institutional development would serve as a means for individual advancement or as a mechanism for change, for improving the welfare of the community. In Nieves's view, some "people viewed the opportunities in these agencies as job opportunities, they were not viewed as mechanisms for radical change in any way."⁴¹ But it was difficult to actually use the resources of community agencies for political purposes since they were forbidden to do so by law. In November 1978, for example, Evelina Antonetty was told in no uncertain terms that CDA regulations "specifically prohibit the participation of program personnel during working hours or the use of program resources at any time in support of partisan political activities."⁴² Identity politics could be played but not on the federal government's dime.

In March 1979, the fate of PRCDP was sealed by Haskell Ward. Ward was appointed by Mayor Koch to run the city's anti-poverty programs, against the advice and preferences of most of his staff and black leaders. Privately, Assemblyman José Serrano agreed that PRCDP had to be closed, but in public he joined Herman Badillo in denouncing the closing. On his own, Badillo attacked Ward in *El Diario-La Prensa*, calling him negligent and incompetent. When Koch took both Badillo and Serrano to task they pleaded innocent—Badillo claimed he was just playing the role of indignant Puerto Rican, and Serrano alleged that he had not been asked his opinion; he was assumed to agree with Badillo by *El Diario* because at the time the working assumption was that all Puerto Rican politicians were proxies of Herman Badillo.⁴³

After concluding its contract with the PRCDP, the CDA decided to support the creation of an alternative citywide organization to provide technical assistance and training to Puerto Ricans. CDA's plan envisioned a group deeply rooted in the community, with a governing body fully representative of socioeconomically disadvantaged Puerto Ricans. According to tne CDA, "a complicating factor is that the Puerto

Rican community resides throughout the city in mixed residential patterns with all other groups. This factor mitigates against the conduct of public elections for a board of directors for the organization." Thus, an appointed committee was charged to select the governing body.

Among those invited to serve on the committee were Manuel "Manny" Díaz, Jr., Evelina Antonetty, Francisco Trilla, and now Supreme Court Justice John Carro. In addition to sixteen representatives from community-based organizations, the committee was instructed to select six representatives from the private sector to serve as board members. The three Puerto Rican members of the City Council were invited by CDA to sit on the selection committee, and they were expected to join the governing board as well.

One interesting requirement of CDA's plan was the exclusion from participation in the governing body of the proposed organization of any group or individual member of PRCDP's Board of Directors that had served between February 1974 and February 1979.[44] State elected officials were also excluded, a condition that was duly noted and protested by Assemblyman Angelo Del Toro.[45]

DEMAND-PROTEST
There is no reason why conflict based on identity politics should be considered damaging and undesirable in general or a priori. Motives, circumstances, and the specific actions that define conflict must always be taken into account. Conflict driven by racism and prejudice, police brutality, or unequal treatment, as is the case of the two accounts that follow, is damaging and undesirable by definition. It should not be surprising that in the two cases chronicled below, the latter kind of conflict prompted a response that brought to the fore the identity that motivated the conflict. Educational struggles were politicized along ethnic lines and police targeted Puerto Ricans. Political action along identity lines, emphasizing the rights of Puerto Ricans as a group, logically followed.

Education
Around March 1973, Schools Chancellor Harvey Scribner, faced intense pressures to summarily fire Puerto Rican superintendent Luis Fuentes. He did not budge, insisting that Fuentes was entitled to due process. To fire him, Scribner argued, charges had to be formally presented, evidence had to support the charges, and Fuentes had to have the opportunity to defend himself.[46] The fact that Scribner was at that point a lame-duck Chancellor took away some weight from his defense of Fuentes; the enemies of Fuentes simply needed to wait Scribner out until his contract was due in June. After that they could resume their attack.

In May, the conflict over control of School District 1 in the Lower East Side was rekindled with the celebration of a new round of elections. This time, the positions on the community school board would be allotted proportionally, due to the charge from minority parents that the voting system used in May 1973 favored white residents. In the contest, the UFT-backed slate proposed strong classroom discipline, English-centered instruction, and central control of hiring and promotion decisions. The so-called Por Los Niños [For the Children] slate, was in favor of community control, bilingual education, and more Spanish- and Chinese-speaking teachers.

The undeclared leaders of the slates were Albert Shanker, the head of UFT, and Luis Fuentes, District 1's superintendent, respectively. The irony of this conflict, which gained national attention, was that it pitted Jews against Puerto Ricans in almost the same way that the Irish had been against the Jews when the latter were the community's newcomers.[47] Fuentes in particular was charged with racism, poor moral character, tolerance of criminal behavior in the schools, and favoritism in hiring. The Por Los Niños slate lost. It was small consolation that the UFT now had a majority of one instead of three votes, as Fuentes was nevertheless on his way out.[48]

Fuentes' ouster effectively began in 1974 when the Board voted to remove one of his supporters from the governing body in June.[49] The key argument of the ousted member was that the Board could not expel her without going through the central Board of Education. Yet to be a member of a local Board it was necessary to have a child in school, which she did not, and this was the ostensible reason for the expulsion. The real reason was that the expelled member was a supporter of Fuentes. By August, the Board renewed its effort to get rid of Fuentes directly, by alleging insubordination and mismanagement. His suspension in October 1973 had provoked a twenty-school boycott that kept 11,000 students out of the classroom for several days.[50] But in 1974 Fuentes did not survive the challenge to his incumbency.

In May 1975, his specter continued to haunt School District 1 in the Lower East Side. He had been suspended for a year and his contract was due to expire on July 30th. Before the school board elections, his future was uncertain. What was not uncertain was the raw animosity that prevailed against him and his supporters in the district among the pro-UFT majority on the district's board. When it became known that the election had reaffirmed their control of the district, this faction was jubilant, knowing that now they would be able to get rid of Fuentes, once and for all. Fuentes accused the UFT of running a racist campaign. Yet, in District 7 in the Bronx, the majority of Puerto Rican winners were endorsed by the union. The same was true in districts in Manhattan and Brooklyn. Albert Shanker summed up the issue thus: "I think it would be much more democratic for the Mayor or the central board to appoint [school board members]."[51]

•••

In 1975, on the issue of bilingual education, the Board of Education was forced to promote change. On the issue of desegregation, it was pressured to keep the status quo. This was evident when the Board proposed a zoning plan that would move white students in Brooklyn from a predominantly white school to one where minority students were 33 percent of the student body. At a public meeting of the Board, angry parents told Board members to "stop shuffling students around and to preserve the concept of the neighborhood school." Protesters outside the building chanted, "We need a Board of Education, not a Board of Transportation." The minority members of the Board—African American Isaiah Robinson and Puerto Rican Joseph Monserrat—were shouted down by the audience several times. Protesters emphasized that their concern was not racial but in effect they were all white, and were against moving their kids to an integrated school.[52]

Police Brutality

In May 1973, Puerto Ricans in the uptown Manhattan neighborhood of Morningside picketed the 24th Precinct police station demanding a solution to the mysterious killing and mutilation of an eleven-year-old Puerto Rican boy. Three similar deaths had been reported in the area during the previous eighteen months, and the police were charged with indifference.[53] By then, almost three years had passed since the police had been warned by the Rand Institute of New York City that the recruitment of more Puerto Ricans and blacks to the police force was both desirable and necessary. The Institute's 117-page report had been ignored.[54]

In February 1979, an incident that had all the markings of a police brutality case rocked the community in the Bronx. It happened at a bar known as "Mr. G." on 181st Street, in the vicinity of police precinct 46. According to *El Diario-La Prensa*, the incident involved two Puerto Ricans—Domingo Morales and Manuel Martínez—both Bronx residents. For reasons unknown, the two got into a fight and while at it, policeman Kevin Durkin intervened by simply shooting them. A few days after being shot, both died. Neither one was carrying a weapon at the time, nor did they have criminal records.[55] A highly decorated policeman, Durkin was charged with attempted murder.[56]

In this, Puerto Ricans fared no better than blacks but in the case of blacks, there was at least an acknowledgement on the part of City Hall that race relations in New York were at an all-time low and the mayor took time and spent energy trying to address the situation. Ed Koch, however, only grudgingly accepted responsibility. In fact, his attitude was that blacks had a problem with whites and whites had a problem with blacks and he was caught in the middle, as if his administration was a powerless bystander.[57]

On August 22, 1979, the community became incensed when the police shot to death Brooklyn resident Luis Baez. The Black and Latino Coalition Against Police Brutality, which was formed in the wake of Baez's murder, turned him into the lead symbol of its campaign against government-sanctioned racial violence. "There is nothing that can excuse five fully armed policemen shooting 24 times at a small, unarmed, mentally ill man whom they had already surrounded," reads an undated Coalition document. And further, "Luis Baez was killed because he was a Puerto Rican, and Latinos like blacks and other oppressed people are always expendable in this society rooted in national oppression and racism." At a demonstration protesting the killing, 3,000 participants marched under heavy rain. Two signs stood out among the crowd. In retrospect they seem hyperbolic but at the time they must have felt self-evident: "POLICE: HIRED KILLERS FOR THE SYSTEM" and "KKK & PBA: DIFFERENT NAME BUT SAME GAME."[58]

Lincoln Hospital

In November 1976, Lincoln Hospital was again the site of intense political theater. Elite conflict mixed with collective action. The city's Health and Hospitals Corporation (HHC) appeared to have appointed Julio César Galarcé only to placate community demands and was now ready to get rid of him. An opportunity to do so came up after three patients lost their lives due to lack of proper attention at the hospital. For their part, Puerto Rican political leaders were at each other's throats over the issue.

While Dr. Rafael Izquierdo accused HHC of using the hospital as a political football, Herman Badillo accused Galarcé of being incompetent. Izquierdo supported Galarcé and joined community protests over his firing. Badillo called the protesters barbarians for taking their protest inside the hospital and cheered the firing of Galarcé as well as the dismissal of Ramón Vélez as president of the hospital's community advisory board. "The hospital should provide health care to Puerto Ricans without being used as a political club by a discredited leader such as Vélez," said Badillo.[59]

Ethnic identity was certainly an adhesive, a rallying point in the struggle against racialization and for redress of grievances and the provision of services. But clearly, as the clash between Badillo and Izquierdo demonstrated, it did not guarantee solidarity or agreement between co-ethnics. This was perhaps the best antidote to the hardening of boundaries, to the entrenchment of narrow and partial judgments, and to the oppression of individuals that identity politics allegedly made inevitable.

Save Hostos

Discussing the Save Hostos campaign is the perfect way to conclude this chapter because the campaign so neatly fits within its opening theme. No other issue between 1973 and 1979 better exemplified the blend of liberalism and identity politics for the sake of social justice. The participants in this battle were not all Puerto Rican, but it was a battle where the latter were protagonists and beneficiaries and one that illustrated how a simple demand of access to higher education could be one with deep implications for equality and social justice in the city.

Hostos Community College, originally known as Community College Number Eight, was the product of mass mobilization, militant action, and organized lobbying. It was an institutional development fully set within the parameters of the mainstream educational system as well as a good example of the preeminence of identity politics over the self-sufficiency ideal articulated by Antonia Pantoja in 1989. When the college opened its doors to students in 1970, media and computer-based instruction was innovative and almost seemed revolutionary. Remedial education and bilingual education were acceptable for a time, until fiscal retrenchment in the mid-1970s reared its ugly head, taking in its wake free tuition and open admissions, along with reductions in the resources available for both programs and staff that were critically needed by Puerto Ricans and blacks.[60]

It was in this context of financial precariousness that the Board of Higher Education decided that it was best to close the college, thus prompting a battle for the college's survival that began in 1973 and lasted through 1978.[61] One important difference between Hostos and other community colleges was that it was established not just as a consequence of open admissions but to be a vehicle for descriptive representation for Puerto Ricans and other Hispanics in the South Bronx. The name of the college itself, Eugenio María de Hostos, a tribute to the well-known writer, educator, and anti-colonial activist from the island, made Puerto Ricans want to enroll. The ethnic composition of the college also contributed to the vehemence with which Puerto Ricans rallied to its rescue. The fact that the college was committed to bilingualism also helped cement its identity as a college named after a Puerto Rican for Puerto Ricans.

The movement to save the college began innocuously in the fall of 1973, as a private meeting between a student and Professor Gerald Meyer to discuss ways of improving the college's facilities. From there, demands were articulated through mass mobilization. On April 3, 1974, a large group of students and faculty rallied in front of the offices of the Board of Higher Education. This prompted a meeting between students, faculty, and members of the Board who reacted with surprise, claiming no prior knowledge of any special needs at Hostos. Other acts included a march through the Grand Concourse up to Third Avenue in May, with a stop at Congressman Herman Badillo's office, and a trip to Albany on May 29th to lobby the state legislature, where two busloads of students and faculty rallied on the steps of the Capitol Building.

While the movement was initially successful in getting support for a new facility, the fate of the college came back into question during the 1975 fiscal crisis. Hostos was one of the three colleges targeted for closure by Mayor Abraham Beame. Even though closure actually meant that Hostos would be absorbed by Bronx Community College, the reaction to the proposal was negative. A campaign that included letter writing, petitioning, and community outreach was organized by the faculty union. A voter registration campaign was also organized to put pressure on elected officials with constituents who were Hostos students. In March 1976, Deputy Mayor John Zuccotti was presented with a petition to save Hostos with twenty thousand signatures, while a large contingent of students and faculty stepped out of eight buses and circled City Hall demanding action to keep Hostos as a separate entity. What began as a meeting between a student and a faculty member in 1973 had developed into a multi-member coalition publicly challenging a discriminatory decision.

The Board of Higher Education ignored the movement and, with the objection of only its Puerto Rican and African American members, adopted a resolution to effect the proposed merger. This was met with strong resistance, including a massive public demonstration in front of the offices of the Emergency Control Board in Manhattan, involving close to three thousand people. In the end, militancy, lobbying, and good press coverage saved Hostos but only after the state legislature passed legislation that gave Governor Carey the budget he wanted for CUNY in exchange for the preservation of Medgar Evers and Hostos community colleges. Once the Board of Higher Education saw the writing on the wall, it voted to rescind the resolution calling for the dissolution of Hostos.

Hostos was the only bilingual college in the city and had the largest percentage of Puerto Rican and Latino students in CUNY. For a time its degrees were anchored in the liberal arts and its pedagogy, which eschewed grades and promoted individualized advancement, was innovative. It is not entirely clear whether these features were fairly quickly rejected because they were unconventional or because they were associated with the personality of its chief proponent, Hostos' president Cándido de León. The coalition that saved the college could do nothing about the configuration of its programs, some of which were closed after the integrity of the college was secured, or about the size of its faculty which decreased just as the number of Spanish-dominant students increased.

The battle to save the college, which continued after 1976 and through 1978 as the battle *for* the college, brought together individuals from the faculty, from the student body, and from the community. After the college was saved, the coalition that came together to battle for the college emphasized equality of funding and of the provision of services. They united as members of organizations such as the Professional Staff Congress, the Student Government Organization, the Veteran's Club, the Puerto Rican Students Association, the Dominican Club, the Federation of Puerto Rican University Socialist Students, The Latin American Students Club, and the Black Student Union, among others.

In his account of the Save Hostos campaign, Gerald Meyer concluded that "the students often felt genuine loyalty to these clubs which represented core elements of their identities."[62] The battle to save and develop Hostos was an example of identity politics played out under the rubric of important liberal values: autonomy, choice, and equality. It was a battle that enjoined *de facto* liberals in a *de facto* campaign for justice and progress.

CHAPTER 6

THE MOST SERIOUS PROBLEM

In January 1980, the Office of the Commonwealth of Puerto Rico was part of a committee organized by Mayor Koch's administration to conduct a public relations campaign to encourage citizens to participate in the census count. The committee included representatives from business, labor unions, churches, and private agencies. The task of the Office was to highlight the importance of the count to community leaders who in turn would relay the message more widely.[1]

It is interesting that as late as 1980, City Hall still considered the Office of the Commonwealth as the go-to umbrella institution when it was necessary to reach out to community institutions. This made sense for several reasons. In spite of the fact that the Congress of [Puerto Rican] Hometowns was a citywide federation, it was not as prominent, and its leadership had a history of conflictive relations with city officials. Other groups, like the National Association for Puerto Rican Civil Rights or United Bronx Parents, to name just two examples, did not have the resources or the inclination to serve as liaison between City Hall and other organizations. And then there were organizations like the Puerto Rican Community Development Project that were unreliable.

As the chronicle below suggests, however, community institutions were robust, if at times also riddled with conflict. In 1980, Commonwealth Office director Bobby Capó declared discrimination in housing "the most serious problem Puerto Ricans have in the city." This chapter suggests that the focus of community action lay elsewhere.[2]

STRATEGIC ACTION

If one of the sins of identity politics is parochialism, it is hard to see how Puerto Ricans were guilty. The scope of Puerto Rican organizational action was often national and its focus on issues comprehensive. This was sometimes a weakness because efforts were diluted, but it did not reflect an insular, narrow-minded approach to political action. Whenever it was necessary, Puerto Rican groups worked in coalition with other organizations that reflected a broad spectrum of racial and ethnic participants in New York City politics.

Organizational Activities

In April 1981, the founding convention of the National Congress for Puerto Rican Rights (NCPRR), held in Philadelphia, had a satellite meeting in New York at the Paul Robeson School in the Bronx. In addition to the Committee Against Fort Apache (see below), the long list of endorsers of the event included noted musician Ray Barretto, Frank Bonilla, Councilman Gilberto Gerena Valentín, Pablo "Yoruba" Guzmán, Evelina Antonetty, and Nick Sánchez. Among the groups and institutions supporting the convention were the musical group Conjunto Libre, the New Rican Village Club, the Black and Latino Coalition Against Police Brutality, El Comite MINP, The Puerto Rican Educators Association, and the Hispanic Labor Committee of NYC of the Central Labor Council.[3]

According to the documents of the convention, more than five hundred Puerto Ricans gathered at the Paul Robeson School to attend workshops, discuss a program of action, and to establish the Congress as a national organization. The keynote speech in New York was offered by Juan González—of Young Lords fame but now a reporter for the *Philadelphia Daily News*. In his analysis, González credited the radical movements of the 1960s with the progress experienced by the "significant professional sector [that had] developed in our community." At the same time, he continued, "we are suffering as never before in the history of our migration to the United States." According to González, blacks had built the NAACP and the Urban League, Jews the American Jewish Congress, and Italians the National Italian Civil Rights League. Now it was the turn of Puerto Ricans to follow in their footsteps and build their own national organization to defend the democratic rights of the community.[4]

As for the political orientation of the group, the activist, anti-establishment attitude of the 1960s was evident in the resolution adopted by the convention concerning political activity. The emphasis was on grassroots, mass membership, and on independence from political parties and government agencies.[5] Discursively, the group sounded not just militant but also radical.

The Congress set a hugely ambitious agenda for itself. It is difficult to understand how its leaders came to the conclusion that the newly formed organization could marshal the energy, time, and resources to cover the areas of law, politics, culture, housing, education, economic development, labor, social services, youth, health, women, mass media, senior citizens, and Puerto Rico. The group's agenda for the period 1981-85 lists no less than fifty-six issues requiring twice the number of actions and activities. In the area of politics alone, the list included developing a program of action based on a study of the community, the creation of a task force to provide training to NCPRR chapters on voter registration, the development of a national voter registration campaign, the creation of an information center in Washington, D.C., the development of a campaign in solidarity with El Salvador, Nicaragua, and other Latin American countries, the support of a march on Washington for jobs and peace, the oversight of bilingual provisions of the Voting Rights Act, and participation in the campaign in support of Puerto Rican political prisoners.[6]

One important feature of NCPRR is the fact that three of its national chairs were women: Frances Cerpa, Diana Caballero, and Lourdes Torres. The status of women was a concern that occupied much of the Congress's time, energy, and resources, no doubt in part because of the conviction among some of its female leaders that when it came to the gender question the enemy was both within as well as without. In theory, radical men were all for equality, but practice was a different matter.[7] In this area, the work of the Congress focused on educational activities—film showings, forums, and workshops.[8]

Another important feature, which in fact distinguished NCPRR from groups such as NPRC, PRLDEF, or the National Puerto Rican Forum, was its dual emphasis on identity and self-sufficiency. This allowed the group to "speak forcefully and openly against government or societal policies that hold back Puerto Rican progress." The Congress assumed that because its member organizations were community-based they exerted "influence on the thinking of fellow Puerto Ricans in their communities." This assumption led the organization to believe it had political legitimacy.

At the same time, the Congress saw itself not as a mere representative of Puerto Ricans at the mass-level but rather as a trustee whose responsibility was twofold—to provide its members with the "broader perspective of how national and state government policies directly impact upon their constituencies" and to give them instructions on how to respond to those policies.[9] This was an interesting combination of democratic orientation and elitist behavior—from the left.

In June, the organization of the New York chapter of NCPRR began in earnest. The first meeting held in the city took place at John Jay College, CUNY, on June 23rd. A second meeting was held in the same location on July 14th to discuss models of organization, select a coordinating committee, identify areas of work, set a division of labor, and select chairs and vice chairs for each work area identified.[10] The first meeting of the coordinating committee took place on August 26th, also at the college. The organizing goals of the chapter were:

> to bring together progressive Puerto Rican-Latino activists and organizations on a community and city-wide level, and thereby institutionalize (not bureaucratize) our struggle for human and civil rights and to direct this organized coalition toward real political empowerment: the political control of the centers of economic, cultural and social power in our communities.

To do this, the group proposed to develop a list of key contacts—activists and organizations citywide—invite them to a community forum and then have them attend membership meetings every three months to discuss the situation in their communities.[11]

The NCPRR in New York focused on four major areas. The labor task force consisted of union organizers, and it published the newsletter *Obrero Boricua*. The women's task force did work on reproductive rights of Puerto Rican women. The education task force comprised community school board members and activists in the educational system. NCPRR members participated in the New York Coalition for Bilingual Education, which included Puerto Ricans, Haitians, Italians, and Asians.

The higher education task force intended to organize Puerto Rican college students. It was also involved in the Puerto Rican Council of Higher Education.

The New York chapter also brought together community-based organizations such as the Puerto Rican Association for Community Action, Latinos United for Political Action, UBP, EHTC, Padres Unidos, the Center for Puerto Rican Studies, the Hispanic Organization of Park Slope, Ramitas de Borinquen, and ASPIRA.[12]

Even though NCPRR emerged as an organization with a focus on Puerto Ricans in the United States, it could not stay away from island issues. One of the first actions of the group concerned a student strike at the University of Puerto Rico (UPR). During the strike, students were subject to mass dismissals and harassment by the police force. "We consider such actions gross violations of the civil and human rights of the student body, teachers and employees of the university," wrote NCPRR's president Juan González to Enrique Irizarry, president of the University's Council of Higher Education.

Speaking on behalf of NCPRR, González demanded the start of negotiations between students and university officials, the removal of the police force from the campus, and an end to all sanctions against participants in the strike: "Failure on your part to act to resolve the crisis and end further confrontation will be reported to our membership, and will necessarily require actions here in the United States directed to the proper authorities or complaints to international bodies such as the United Nations or Amnesty International."[13]

At the end of 1981, NCPRR had an opportunity to develop a working relation with the National Puerto Rican Coalition (NPRC). The record shows that one NPRC board member, Isidoro Rodríguez, was eager to help in the organization of NCPRR, and the Congress was quite pleased that NPRC was adopting an aggressive lobbying role in Washington.[14] Despite this, strong feelings against the Coalition surfaced during its December conference.

Rodríguez happened to also be a member of a group that called itself "Los Cuarenta," and during the December conference the group denounced the Coalition as an elitist and undemocratic group. These charges were answered by the Coalition by clarifying that the December conference was not a membership meeting. At that point, board members of NPRC had been selected by and from within the nucleus of its founders, but the group's intention was to expand its membership base at the conference and from the resulting pool elect a new board in 1982, according to clearly spelled out nomination and election procedures.[15]

This explanation did not impress Juan González, who attended the conference, and he echoed Rodríguez's view. "We were disappointed and disgruntled that at a time when our community is facing such desperate economic and social conditions, so little was said by conference organizers of the fundamental reasons for our current situation, of who is responsible and of the methods necessary to rectify our situation," he said afterwards.[16] But it is puzzling that González would be disappointed by what was not said by conference organizers given that he was a panelist along with César Perales, Enrique Arroyo, and Luis Cabán, all Congress members. Why didn't any of them provide the analysis that was needed?[17]

In any event, NCPRR members threatened to disrupt the December conference and, through what Juan González called "an excellent combination of plenary-floor tactics and negotiating," they forced the Coalition to admit six new members to their board of directors and were able to pass resolutions that the Coalition would not have adopted otherwise. "They may not agree with us," said González in a report to NCPRR board members, "but they must respect us." During the last day of the conference, NCPRR members organized a "grassroots" meeting with Hispanic residents in D.C., which González called "the final success." The meeting drew about twenty people.[18]

Activities by NCPRR in New York up to March 1982 included continuing support for the striking students at UPR, housing campaigns in the Lower East Side, organizing in support of bilingual education, and a reproductive rights campaign in the Bronx.[19] This work continued through the end of the year. The activities in support of UPR students took place between December 1981 and January 1982 and consisted of a forum and two rallies. The group also participated in a rally commemorating International Women's Day on March 7, 1982, and on March 13th, the chapter held a seminar for housing organizers which attracted one hundred participants.[20]

In April, the Congress established the National Bilingual Education Task Force with Diana Caballero, from New York City, and Félix Ruiz, from New Jersey, as co-chairs.[21] On April 26th, Caballero testified in opposition to Senate Bill 2002 on bilingual education. According to Caballero, if approved, the bill would have "a dramatically devastating effect on the linguistic, academic, cultural and social development of Puerto Rican children" by limiting participation in bilingual programs to one year. "By officially sanctioning a return to the 'sink or swim' treatment, it is in essence implementing a policy of educational and cultural genocide [...] under the pseudonym of English 'immersion' programs," she concluded.[22]

Two days later, the Congress began its involvement in electoral politics with a meeting held at John Jay College to discuss electoral activities in other cities, the situation in New York, different approaches to participation, and the relationship of the Congress to a Conference on Puerto Rican Political Strategies for the 1980s scheduled for May 8th at Hunter College.[23] Concerning electoral politics, the Congress proposed to focus on issues and programs of action rather than personalities. Coalitions were preferred, but the group emphasized that "we don't want to dominate nor be dominated."[24]

In 1982, the New York chapter of NCPRR worked to establish a state-level assembly with representatives from the city, Rochester, Long Island, Newburgh and New Paltz. Meetings began in August. By mid-September a State Assembly Coordinating Committee had set November 5-6 for the state assembly to take place at SUNY, New Paltz.[25] By October, the organization was working in Long Island.[26]

The SUNY, New Paltz, assembly actually met on November 13th, sponsored by UBP, Nassau County Hispanic Foundation, La Voz Latina of Haverstraw, NY; Fuerza Estudiantil Latina of SUNY, New Paltz; the Center for Puerto Rican Studies, the Citywide Housing Coalition from New York City, and the Puerto Rican Association of Community Affairs.[27]

The officers of the assembly were Enio Carrión, president; Dámaso Seda, vice-president; Olga Díaz, vice-president; Kathy Andrade, secretary-treasurer; Edwin Espaillat, recording secretary; and Víctor López, sergeant of arms. The Executive Board consisted of Eddie Pérez, Héctor Torres, Dennis Rivera, José Soler, and Juan Laboriel. Listed as trustees were Rafael Cordero, Lydia Ramos, and Elma Cintrón. The main objective of the assembly was to unite and coordinate the efforts of Puerto Rican community, labor, student, professional, artistic, social, and political organizations in the state, to share information and technical assistance, and to mobilize around issues when necessary. The by-laws of the assembly noted that preserving the language and culture of Puerto Ricans would be a priority, as well as efforts to end discrimination against Puerto Ricans and to achieve equality. The assembly was also committed to the goal of unity among minorities and workers struggling to secure their democratic rights.[28]

At the end of October 1982, NCPRR came out against the candidacy of Lew Lehrman for Governor. "This man is no friend of the Puerto Rican community. We urge all Puerto Ricans and all New York State residents who believe in economic and social justice and equality to reject Lew Lehrman and the politics of America's wealthy elite." According to NCPRR, Lehrman was nothing but a millionaire candidate who had spent $8 million to buy his way to the governorship. His credentials as a Reagan advisor did nothing to help him with the group. The group estimated that his policy agenda, which included cuts in employment and training programs, the elimination of affirmative action, the minimum-wage, and child labor laws, was clearly inimical not just to Puerto Rican interests but to the interests of all New Yorkers.[29]

NCPRR regarded itself as the only Puerto Rican organization with the potential to effectively defend the democratic rights of Puerto Ricans in the United States. The conditions needed to perform this role were a full-time staff, offices, and a public presence based on complete financial independence. NPRC was considered "the rallying point for the moderate and conservative Puerto Rican leadership." It was seen as a group that "scurried" around seeking foundation and corporate support. According to NCPRR, this did not allow it to be an effective advocate.[30]

The feature that NCPRR valued the most was its umbrella character. Identity was the basis for organization but only as a point of departure. Only an organization with a mix of identitarianism and ecumenical values could bring about the unity of all Puerto Ricans. If this meant working with individuals and groups that were "strategic enemies of our community and the labor movement," so be it. Those who were dishonest and opportunist would expose themselves through their deeds. "In the process, some will cause discord and confusion, may even capture control of local chapters or state councils before their real attitudes or intentions become clear. But [...] that is the price we must pay to build a genuinely mass organization, the price we must pay to convince the broad masses of active concerned Puerto Ricans [...] that we are building a democratic organization."[31]

The issue of bilingual education was a means toward effective advocacy. On this, a recognized NCPRR leader wrote:

> The National Bilingual Education Task Force has won the respect of many parents, educators and the community in general not only for its consistency and militancy but because of its grassroots focus and multi-faceted approach, which has united individuals and organizations to fight on all fronts. The TF has helped to give people a sense that there is a broader struggle taking place to save bilingual education and has attempted to unite all the scattered, but strong, local efforts.[32]

The rationale for bilingual education programs was laid out by NCPRR as more than just a language issue. Bilingual education was fundamentally a political issue for Puerto Ricans because it provided tools that protected Puerto Rican children from being victimized as Spanish speakers and as Puerto Ricans. Bilingual education deserved support not just because:

> research proves that it's a viable program, no matter how true this is; but because it's a democratic right. [...] Bilingual education is a political issue because we are talking about the survival of our community and about a struggle against linguistic and cultural genocide by the U.S. It is a fundamental right for every national group to raise and educate its children in its own image and language. [...] Language helps to maintain our ties of identity and a sense of group strength, solidarity and security.[33]

In 1984, the New York chapter of NCPRR decided to actively participate in the electoral process to defeat the reelection bid of Mayor Edward Koch in 1985. Why oust Koch? Because of the distressing poverty experienced by Puerto Ricans and other minorities, the masses of homeless people freezing to death on city streets, because of the lack of health services for poor people, an educational system in shambles, massive unemployment, a crumbling mass transit system, rampant racism, and widespread political corruption. "Our people can ill afford four more years of Koch in City Hall," wrote Zoilo Torres, co-chair of the chapter.[34]

By 1984, NCPRR had come to the conclusion that it needed a new direction after failing to meet the goals of its work plan for the period March 1983 through March 1984. Problems included combining substantive and menial work, which made meetings unproductive, a drastic decrease in membership, lack of direction from leaders, lack of a central office, unproductive task forces, and personality conflicts between the chair and co-chair of the chapter. A lack of consistency concerning the practice of collective leadership was also acknowledged. Interestingly, members thought they were not able to do much because they had done too much:

Externally, we have also been confronted with problems which has [sic] taken us away from working on the development of the chapter such as the State Council Crisis, organizing for the National Convention and other major events, demonstrations and pickets necessary to respond to important issues which effect [sic] our community, and many other particular but critical problems.[35]

Nevertheless, at an April retreat, the leadership of the New York City chapter ignored its own findings by recommending a course of action that only perpetuated their state of overreach. According to their plan, task forces would be not only developed but also expanded and their individual activities increased. The chapter would be present "at all activities of the Puerto Rican community," more outreach would be conducted, more leadership development seminars would be organized, and more committees would be created to work on membership, recruitment, and financial issues. And all of this despite the fact that the chapter did not have office space, a telephone, or a filing system to keep track of its records.[36]

By 1985, a crisis loomed large at NCPRR. A 1983 internal report had already raised very serious issues regarding the organizational development of the organization. By 1983 the group was still "amateurish" in its organizing, the quality of its literature and planning for activities was "uneven"; finances, planning, monitoring, fundraising, and accounting were "sharp failures"; and beyond three states there was no growth in membership.[37] According to another document from 1985, the goals set for 1983 had not been accomplished. "We have not created a national movement nor a strong organization," the document reads, "the central contradiction appears to be an inability to balance core development with mass development and this has caused membership to be diluted."[38]

•••

Early in 1985, the October 1984 agreement between the Coors beer company and an ad-hoc coalition of Hispanic organizations, which included the National Puerto Rican Coalition (NPRC) became the subject of a brief controversy in New York. The agreement with Coors—which promised to be beneficial to members of this coalition—was modeled after one between the same company and a coalition of African American organizations. According to Louis Núñez, executive director of NPRC, the Coors agreement was "a landmark in developing a new relationship between our community and Corporate America and further represents a major advocacy effort on our part on behalf of our community." Why? Because after this agreement, Puerto Rican groups would be in a position to obtain further concessions from American corporations rather than just complain about corporate neglect. Coors made a commitment to hire Hispanics at all levels within the company, to make annual contributions to Hispanic organizations amounting to no less than $500,000, to use Hispanic banks, and to target the community for partnerships and distributorships, among other things.[39]

On December 1984, Angelo Falcón, from the Institute for Puerto Rican Policy, had written a letter to Núñez, objecting to a clause in the agreement that Falcón understood required the members of the ad-hoc coalition to act as a "political buffer" between the company and the Hispanic community.[40] The clause read:

Each member of the Coalition agrees to cooperate with Coors, including appointing an organization officer to address ongoing issues and potential political and social difficulties that may occur in the national scene regarding Coors and its products over the life of the agreement.[41]

Falcón circulated his letter to the press, and in January 1985, Juan González wrote about the agreement in the *Daily News* declaring that Latino groups had sold out the community for "a glass of beer."[42]

Falcón's accusation prompted a series of letters and memos that revealed that the leaders of the ad-hoc coalition, as well as the liaison from Coors, had decided it was best for Hispanics to negotiate directly with Coors rather than through an African American/Latino coalition. From Coors, the National Manager for Community Relations, Frank Solís, argued that to address the specific needs of each community, separate agreements were necessary.[43] According to the president of National Image, Inc., Anabelle Jaramillo, the coalition had not pursued an alliance with blacks, specifically with the NAACP because, in her view, the NAACP had "never thought to include Hispanics in their efforts to establish relationships with Corporate America."[44] The clause that led to the "buffer" claim was ambiguous. Nevertheless, at this point that claim had been lost in the shuffle.

The exchange prompted by Falcón's letter revealed another interesting feature of the agreement process. This had to do with the power relationships between the participant Hispanic organizations. The lead in the Coors process had been taken by Mexican American organizations. Puerto Ricans were represented by NPRC. No Puerto Rican group from New York had been invited to participate. The League of United Latin American Citizens (LULAC) allegedly refused to sign the agreement because it was not allowed to sign separately from the ad-hoc coalition. Publicly, LULAC claimed that their withdrawal was because the terms of the agreement were not satisfactory.[45]

In a letter to Anabelle Jaramillo, Falcón argued that "the six national Latino organizations that signed the Coors agreement have set an irresponsible and dangerous precedent for Puerto Ricans and other Latinos." Why? He took this stance based on: 1) his inference that the National Puerto Rican Coalition had participated without being fully informed; 2) his conclusion that the explanation of LULAC's withdrawal was not consistent; and 3) his feeling that the Hispanic agreement did not seem as generous as the black agreement. His main contention, based on the clause cited above, was that Coors had managed to turn the participating Latino organizations into its "political buffers" within the community.

This interpretation was as unconfirmed as the clause was vague, but according to Falcón, from his reading of the agreement it followed that Latino organizations had agreed to act as political commissars for Coors. "Cooperation, to me, is a two way street and I will expect support from Coors in addition to giving support," wrote Annabelle Jaramillo in response to Falcón's interpretation. For his part, Frank Solís clarified that "the agreement is a moral commitment and not a legal document."[46]

DEMAND-PROTEST

One important criticism of identity politics is that it subverts the boundaries between what is appropriately political and what is not. Language is one issue where this question often comes up. The Puerto Rican answer was that language was not a private matter. To the contrary, just like distorted representations of Puertoricanness in the media, language was a political issue at heart. Bilingualism expanded the boundaries of the public arena and was a tool that enabled cultural citizenship, that is, the practice of membership from the vantage point of difference. This concept of citizenship was not exclusionary; it was a point of departure for cooperation and collaboration with other groups; and further, it did not make its adherents blindly loyal to individuals simply because of their group membership. The section below buttresses this argument with illustrations from several campaigns. It also notes the irony in the focus of attention of some expressions of identity politics.

Education

On June 2, 1982, the chancellor of the New York City public school system, Frank Macchiarola, issued a memo to all school principals telling them to advise parents of limited English proficiency students of their option to choose or refuse bilingual education for their children. The week of June 7th, parents picketed in front of the Board of Education protesting the letters. Letters, telegrams, and phone calls to the Board urged Macchiarola to stop violating the 1974 ASPIRA consent decree. On June 16th, PRLDEF delivered a letter to the chancellor also urging him to stop the distribution of his memo.[47]

On September 30th, Macchiarola finally responded to PRLDEF, stating that "experience has demonstrated that some of the students scoring in the 10-20 percentile on the LAB [Language Assessment Battery] test have acquired a degree of competence in English and may be best served by a general education program with instruction in English as a second language." To the NCPRR, this was yet another attack on bilingual programs.[48] In the end, they were not eliminated, thanks in part to the actions of PRLDEF and NCPRR.

In November, PRLDEF filed suit on behalf of ASPIRA and others charging the Board of Education with violations to the consent decree of 1974 establishing and governing bilingual programs in the city. In its suit, PRLDEF accused Chancellor Frank Macchiarola of violating the decree by instructing school superintendents to inform parents that "their children could better learn in the monolingual English classes than in the bilingual classes." PRLDEF asked the court to issue a restraining order to stop the chancellor from issuing those instructions. On December 7th, Federal District Judge Robert Carter affirmed the currency of the consent decree and the Board's obligation to comply with its terms and to consult with PRLDEF regarding any changes. On that day, more than five hundred educators, community leaders, and children picketed the central offices of the Board of Education in Brooklyn to show their support for bilingual education and to condemn the actions of Macchiarola.[49]

This protest was organized by the New York Coalition for Bilingual Education, which included NCPRR, as well as the Asociación Comunal de Dominicanos Progresistas, the Puerto Rican Educators Association, ASPIRA of America and ASPIRA of New York, UBP, Parent Advocates for Bilingual Education, United Parents Association, People's Educators, the New York State Association for Bilingual Education, students and faculty from the City University of New York, and parents and students from school districts throughout the city.[50] A meeting between PRLDEF attorneys, the city's corporation counsel, and lawyers for the Board of Education was set for December 15th to settle the dispute. But Judge Carter was clear that if a satisfactory settlement was not reached, PRLDEF was free to return to court.[51]

On May 26, 1983, the New York Coalition for Bilingual Education, headed by NCPRR members Diana Caballero and Luis O. Reyes, called for a community speak-out in support of bilingual education in the city to be held on June 15th at CUNY's Graduate Center on 33 West 42nd Street. The purpose of the speak-out was to collect success stories on bilingual education and to publish and disseminate the proceedings widely.[52] In a letter announcing the hearing, coordinators Caballero and Reyes wrote: "We want testimony to be presented by all those who want to be heard—by parents, students, educators, community representatives and others who want to share their success stories with the rest of the community." But the purpose was not just to celebrate. Problems and recommendations for improvement were also expected so that a full picture of bilingual education programs could be presented to school board members and the schools chancellor.[53] One thing they surely did not want to hear was anything proffered from the Heritage Foundation. There, Robert E. Rossier had described bilingual education as "training for the ghetto."[54]

Following the blueprint laid out by Diana Caballero in her summary and workplan for 1983, presented to the Bilingual Education Task Force of NCPRR, the Puerto Rican/Latino Education Roundtable was formed in 1983 by a coalition of community organizations, educators, and activists. It focused its work on various issues such as community empowerment, bilingual education/bilingual special education, adult literacy, and Latino political representation. One important area of activity was in opposition to the English Only movement's attempt to make English the official language of the state of New York. Throughout the second half of the 1980s, the Roundtable worked tirelessly to promote bilingualism in New York as part of the Committee for a Multilingual New York and on its own.

Fort Apache

In March 1980, an advertisement for the movie *Fort Apache, The Bronx* in *Variety* read: "A chilling and tough movie about the South Bronx, a 40 block area with the highest crime rate in New York. Youth gangs, winos, junkies, pimps, hookers, maniacs, cop killers and the embattled 41st precinct, just hanging in there."[55] This representation of the South Bronx prompted the formation of a coalition of groups that included United Tremont Trades, UBP, Black United Front, Black and Latino Coalition Against Police Brutality, Coalition in Defense of Puerto Rican and Hispanic Rights, Union of Patriotic Puerto Ricans, New Rican Village, and the New Alliance Party. Participants met for the first time on March 5th, at Lincoln Hospital in the Bronx and named their coalition the Committee Against Fort Apache (CAFA). CAFA tried to stop production of the movie but failed. Rallies and demonstrations were similarly powerless to stop the release or the showing of the film.[56]

The protests against Fort Apache were earnest and sustained. In an April 11th editorial, *El Diario-La Prensa* called for a boycott of the film and asked all elected officials to speak out against it. This plea was rejected by the New York City Council. Governor Hugh Carey's office reacted with surprise and disappointment at the attacks. "The tax dollars are very beneficial," declared Thea Sklover, speaking for the Governor.[57] The first elected official to condemn the film was Congressman Robert García, who denounced it as "racist and dehumanizing."[58] He was joined by the Reverend Neil Connolly, from the Archdiocese of New York, who expressed "outrage at Time-Life Films for continuing to beat the drums of racism and classism for the price of a dollar."[59] Adding his voice to the criticism was Thomas J. Walker, the retired captain of the 41st precinct and author of the book *Fort Apache*, who charged the producers with plagiarizing his work to create a racist film.[60]

Between April 12th and 22nd, the coalition mobilized about 125 people, of which over thirty testified, to a public hearing called by councilman Gilberto Gerena Valentín; it co-sponsored with New Rican Village a three-day Stop Fort Apache Cultural Arts Festival, held at Soundscape, at 500 West 52nd Street. Participants were treated to the poetry of Americo Casiano, Gylan Kain, and Pedro Pietri, and the music of Libre and Friends, Rafael Cortijo, Hilton Ruiz, Dave Valentín, and Ray Barretto. CAFA also brought about eighty people to the Joint Disease Hospital in Harlem to disrupt a filming sequence; only the presence of a large contingent of policemen at the scene prevented CAFA from interrupting the proceedings.

At the end of April, Hispanic policemen expressed their unhappiness with the film. The Hispanic Society of City Police Officers called it "one-dimensional" and "slanted" in its view of Hispanics and blacks. The President of the Society, Frank Miranda, decried the fact that "unsavory characteristics of a tiny segment" would stand as representative of the whole community.[61]

During the month of May the campaign intensified. On May 1st, in a letter addressed to CAFA, a group of Puerto Rican academics and professionals declared that "the production and dissemination of such film, in any form or version, would be detrimental to individual and community health."[62] This sentiment was not shared by Judge Thomas Sinclair, who found no evidence of wrongful conduct or irreparable harm in the film. He proceeded to dismiss a CAFA lawsuit, charging the plaintiffs with building a case on ideology and speculation.[63] On May 7th, CAFA held a demonstration outside Studio 54 during a dinner organized by the mayor's office in charge of film promotion. On May 15th, the City Council's Committee on General Welfare broke the council's silence by passing a resolution calling the film racist and heeding *El Diario-La Prensa*'s call for a boycott. The following day more than 100 people mobilized by CAFA disrupted filming at 162nd Street and Westchester Avenue.

The month's activities culminated with two marches. On May 20th, more than 100 people marched throughout the 41st precinct chanting "No se Necesita, Película Racista" [We Don't Need this Racist Film].[64] In a press conference held in front of the 41st precinct headquarters, Congressman García condemned the film as a symbol of "everything that is wrong with this country" and called for its boycott.[65] Four days later, CAFA organized a march from the offices of UBP at 156th Street to Hunts Point Park on 163rd. Nineteen groups, as well as the Catholic Vicariate of the Bronx and Planning Boards 1, 2, 4 and 6, sponsored this event. The sponsors also included black, Dominican, and Chicano organizations.[66]

On June 6th, the New York affiliate of the American Jewish Committee condemned the film. In a letter sent to the director, producer, and lead actor of the film, Arthur Kimmelfield and Haskell Lazare objected to the depiction of policemen as cruel and dishonest and of Puerto Ricans as drug addicts, pimps, and prostitutes. Kimmelfield and Lazare requested a revision of the script to substitute positive for negative images.[67]

Fort Apache was released in 1981. Puerto Ricans continued their campaign against the movie. By then CAFA claimed the membership of over seventy organizations in New York, Philadelphia, New Jersey, Los Angeles, Chicago, and Boston. According to the *New York Times* film critic, Vincent Canby, the movie was acted with conviction, was entertaining, accurate, and surely fated to be a hit.[68] The reaction from Mayor Koch was interesting. "I saw a fascinating film in terms of excitement," he said, "but a racist film in the following way: There was not one Puerto Rican personality that was without some major character defect."[69] In a letter to Norman Levy, President of 20th Century Fox Entertainment, Congressman William H. Gray, III, wrote: "I am told that this film leaves viewers with the overwhelming impression that the South

Bronx is populated by 200,000 transvestites, prostitutes, drug addicts, maniacs, and cop killers, who are all Puerto Rican."[70]

On February 9th, the Committee on General Welfare of the New York City Council acted again on the issue by voting five to two to censure *Fort Apache* in a resolution sponsored by councilman Gerena Valentín. The opponents of the resolution were Robert Steingut, D-Brooklyn, who had not seen the film and did not think the Council should sponsor censorship, and Ruth Messinger, D-Manhattan, who offered no explanation for her vote.[71] According to Nat Hentoff, the resolution threatened to make New York City "the nation's paradigm of virtuous censorship—a source of inspiration for all who would enlist the state in the squashing of films, books, and other materials subversive of the public good."[72]

In March, CAFA decided to dissolve as an organization. Its members voted unanimously to endorse and participate in the April 25-26 National Puerto Rican Convention that gave birth to the NCPRR in Philadelphia. The work of CAFA would continue through a Media Task Force within NCPRR. *Fort Apache* provided an opportunity for this when on November 13, 1983, like Dracula rising from the grave, the movie came back to haunt Puerto Ricans in the city. This time NBC planned to show the film nationwide that Sunday evening. "We are demanding that NBC not show this racist movie," reads an announcement of a "Day of Unity & Pride" to be held in front of the NBC building on the afternoon of the scheduled showing. The goal of the event was to "make a public statement that the Puerto Rican and Black communities reject the racist stereotypes of 'Fort Apache' and to set a framework within which the movie must be analyzed—if it is shown."[73] NCPRR took the opportunity to participate in a protest rally cum cultural celebration against the broadcasting. The celebration part of the event was meant to emphasize the positive aspects of Puerto Rican culture and heritage.

Lincoln Hospital

In November 1980, news came of the appointment of Antonio Silva as chief of Obstetrics and Gynecology at Lincoln Hospital in the Bronx. Silva was head of family planning in Puerto Rico from 1974 to 1977 and in that capacity was responsible for a program of massive sterilization of women.

This caused an uproar among Puerto Rican activists, who promptly organized the Bronx Coalition Against Sterilization Abuse to stop what they believed would be the beginning of a genocidal campaign of massive sterilization of Puerto Rican women in the Bronx. The Bronx Coalition included the Coalition in Defense of Puerto Rican and Hispanic Rights, The Committee for Abortion Rights and Against Sterilization Abuse, St. Ann's Church, led by the Rev. David García; The Rev. Neil Connolly, Catholic Vicar for the South Bronx; Councilman Gerena Valentín; UBP; United Tremont Trades; the Medical Committee for Human Rights; the Civic Committee in Support of Puerto Rican POWs; and the Puerto Rican Socialist Party.[74]

In a letter dated November 21st, Neil Connolly protested Silva's appointment. "With Lincoln making valiant efforts to build up the trust of the community it seems counterproductive to appoint a man who was formerly assistant Secretary of the Family Planning Agency of Puerto Rico. We know of the thousands of sterilizations that took place while Dr. Silva worked for that agency. How can anyone who participated in such a massive campaign engender confidence in the South Bronx community?"[75]

The claim of genocide by the Bronx Coalition may have been exaggerated—from January 1 to June 30, 1980, eighty-seven sterilizations were conducted at the hospital.[76] This was about fifteen per month or one every two days. But even such an active program was not vigorous enough to wipe out the reproductive capacity of Puerto Ricans residing in the U.S. Nevertheless, concerns with abuse and improprieties were legitimate.

On November 25th, Joseph Cintrón, executive director of Lincoln Hospital, admitted that the hospital's sterilization program did not always conform to legal requirements governing the procedure. Problems included the hospital's lack of compliance with surgery and post-surgery counseling schedules, with dates being forged to meet the legal requirement; improperly signed documents (in 67 percent of cases); lack of attention to the linguistic needs of patients—consent forms in English given to non-English-speaking patients and failure to provide interpreters—and physicians signing consent forms as their own witnesses.[77]

At Lincoln Hospital, abortions had been banned in 1979 in disregard of Koch's policy to use Medicaid funds to pay for them, the state's permissive approach to the procedure, and Planned Parenthood's claim that there was a "crying need" for them among the poor, particularly Puerto Ricans.[78] In that context, a mass sterilization program did not quite make sense, unless it was an alternative to abortion because it could not be so readily equated with the taking of a human life.

On January 28, 1982, the saga of Antonio Silva at Lincoln Hospital continued with a petition demanding his dismissal signed by a group of community leaders. These included the Rev. Peter Encenado, Secretary of the Association of Hispanic Clergy; Assemblyman Armando Montano; and Fernando Oliver, state president of the National Coalition Against Drug Abuse. The latter group sponsored a demonstration in front of Lincoln Hospital on February 6th.[79] This was almost a year after the Bronx Coalition Against Sterilization Abuse had first protested against Silva at a forum at St. Ann's Church in the Bronx. The forum took place on February 21, 1981, and it was followed by a massive demonstration in front of Lincoln Hospital in June demanding his dismissal.[80]

The fight against Silva proved to be an uphill battle. On February 22nd, the Bronx Coalition Against Sterilization Abuse met to discuss how to meet its goal. On March 11th, the group met again to formalize a new plan of action.[81] By the end of April, the Bronx Coalition was still struggling after a resolution introduced by Gerena Valentín at the City Council demanding an investigation of Silva's activities at Lincoln Hospital was tabled for "future consideration." In the resolution, Gerena Valentín referred to Silva as "morally unqualified to hold his present post."[82]

On June 9th, the Bronx Coalition had another public meeting to educate the community on sterilization abuse but now in the publicity materials distributed by the group the percentage of women that had been sterilized in Puerto Rico was said to be 40 percent, rather than the widely publicized 35 percent, and 5 percent of Puerto Rican men were included among the victims.[83] One source notes that subsequent to Silva's recruitment, the sterilization rates of low-income Puerto Rican women in the Bronx increased.[84] Thus, after all the "vehement" protests by Puerto Ricans and other groups, Dr. Silva was removed from his position.[85]

March on Washington

On August 27, 1983, thousands marched on Washington to commemorate the 20th anniversary of the 1963 March on Washington to demand jobs, peace, and freedom. The march was sponsored by an array of figures and organizations led by The American Friends Service Committee, The National Organization of Women, the NAACP, the Martin Luther King, Jr. Center for Non-Violent Social Change, and the Southern Christian Leadership Conference. In New York it was coordinated by Cleveland Robinson, from District 65 UAW, Assemblyman José Rivera from the Bronx, and by the Rev. David García from the Lower East Side. From NCPRR, Lourdes Torres, Zoilo Torres, and Dennis Rivera were involved—Torres to coordinate transportation, Zoilo to draft a political statement, and Rivera to produce a leaflet and a press work plan.

In a post-march analysis, Juan González claimed that the rally was an exercise in democracy and a signal to the powers-that-be that the civil rights agenda of the 1960s was unfinished. Was the march less effective, less powerful than its predecessor? Not according to González. In 1983, the women's movement was stronger, the presence of labor was more evident, and Puerto Ricans and other Latinos played a larger role. The march was a symbol of maturity rather than weakness, he concluded.[86]

According to Hector Villafañe, from NCPRR's Executive Committee, NCPRR mobilized about 500 Puerto Ricans who were close to half of the Latino presence at the march. His assessment of the march was not as glowing as González's. The communication between local, state, and national representatives of NCPRR was deficient, and this prevented a more accurate account of participants. People marched, but not everyone understood why Puerto Rican participation was necessary. And the organization underestimated how much work it would take to have a successful presence in the event. Making sure that Puerto Rican issues were recognized on the basis of equality was a "gigantic struggle." Villafañe concluded that the long-term political benefits of participation were not clear but that the national recognition gained by the NCPRR was worthy of the effort.[87] In all likelihood both González and Villafañe were right.

Vieques

In May 1980, the Club Cívico Hijos de Vieques (Sons of Vieques Civic Club) and the National Association for Puerto Rican Civil Rights were two of the many organizations sponsoring a march and rally in Washington, D.C. on May 17th against the presence of the U.S. Navy on the island of Vieques. In addition, solidarity committees in Boston, Bridgeport, Camden, Hartford, Lorain, Newark, Philadelphia, Rochester, Trenton, and Vineland were mobilizing Puerto Ricans to the march. The demands of participants included a cessation of repression against activists supporting the Vieques cause, an investigation of the death while in jail in Tallahassee, Florida, of Puerto Rican activist Angel Rodríguez Cristóbal, and the return of land occupied by the U.S. Navy to Vieques's residents.[88]

On the appointed date, more than 25,000 Puerto Ricans and their supporters from New York, Philadelphia, Boston, and other northeastern cities congregated in front of the White House. According to Juan Ramos, press coordinator for the activity, the rally would be followed by hundreds of Puerto Ricans from the United States descending upon Vieques to stage an on-site protest. "This will be the first time that Puerto Ricans in the United States rally behind an island issue beyond party lines," declared Torres.[89] It had not happened before; and this would not be the last time.

In August 1985 two studies found that Puerto Ricans in the city had a higher rate of mental illness than other ethnic groups, that 20 percent of Puerto Rican deaths among those between 15 and 44 years of age and born on the island were the result of drug and alcohol abuse, and that Puerto Ricans in New York were "a people in poverty and a community in crisis."[90] One of the studies had been carried out by Governor Cuomo's Advisory Committee for Hispanic Affairs, the other by the Association of Puerto Rican Executive Directors (APRED).

Then, in October, reportedly the only thing that Puerto Ricans in the city talked and worried about was the death of several hundred compatriots and the fate of thousands others that had been left homeless by a tropical storm on the island. A Puerto Rican with relatives in the town of Aguadilla declared to the *New York Times* that the storm had "touched everybody in El Barrio. Everybody wants to manifest their support for those who are suffering."[91] Mayor Koch urged New Yorkers to help Puerto Rico and designated Ramón Vélez—the same Ramón Vélez that he had previously called a poverty pimp—as coordinator of the city's relief effort. According to the *Times*, some Puerto Ricans flew to the island just to find out what may have happened to relatives and friends.

On December, Mayor Koch turned his attention back to Puerto Ricans in the city in part prompted by the August study by APRED. At the association's annual conference the mayor announced that the city would establish a $1 million job-training program to help Hispanics with an emphasis on Puerto Ricans since they were, in his words, "at the bottom of the economic ladder."[92]

While the issue of Vieques and the aftermath of a storm in Puerto Rico managed to grab the attention of thousands of Puerto Ricans, the news about widespread mental illness, poverty, and disadvantage among Puerto Ricans in New York came and went, with some attention paid to these issues by Mayor Koch but without a ripple being felt in the community at large. Why did 25,000 march in Washington in support of Vieques? And why was a tropical storm in Puerto Rico the cause of mass concern while poverty, mental illness, alcoholism, drug abuse, and premature death in El Barrio hardly registered? Identity politics was clearly at work here, but the contrast in the focus of attention of Puerto Ricans as a community to certain issues as opposed to others was not without its ironies.

CHAPTER 7
THE EYES AND EARS OF THE COMMUNITY

In February 1986, NCPRR clashed with Mayor Koch on the matter of Hispanic representation within the Board of Education. "I have selected the two people whom I think can best serve," wrote Koch to the Coalition for Latino Representation on the Board of Education, of which NCPRR was a prominent member. "It is totally unfair on your part to suggest that the Hispanic community is not represented [...] when the number one person in terms of authority is the Chancellor who happens to be Hispanic." But the mayor wanted to have it both ways—appeasing his critics by referring to descriptive representation on the Board, while claiming to make his appointments only on the basis of qualifications. "I believe there should be a greater diversity on the Board, which I have advocated not on the basis of race, religion or sex but rather on expertise."[1]

The issue of representation within the Board of Education was one of the many that Puerto Rican organizations and their allies tackled during the second half of the 1980s. Their antagonism with Mayor Koch was predicated on an irony: Koch was popular among Hispanics. Hispanics were poor, overcrowded in the public schools, lacking in affordable housing, and unemployed at a relatively high rate but, according to Hispanic supporters, the mayor was working hard to overcome these problems. In 1987, he appointed Lillian Barrios-Paoli to head the Department of Employment. This was touted as a sign of responsiveness and from the mayor's office Luis Miranda vowed to keep up the good work. "My office is and will continue to be the eyes and ears of the Hispanic community," Miranda declared, "I can assure you that we are listening to what it has to say."[2]

STRATEGIC ACTION

Identity politics is often rejected because it allegedly champions causes that impose unfair burdens to the majority of citizens in any given society. On the other hand, politicians often respond to claims based on individual behavior—such as voting—that reflects a collective response to electoral appeals. In those types of situations, identity politics is both embraced—for example, when it entails electoral support—and rejected—when it requires rewards for support of that kind. Identity politics is not always fair-minded, but even its outrageous expressions never occur in a vacuum, and they are often the product of equally outrageous reductions of a given group to a set of negative attributes.

Organizational Activities

In March 1986, in testimony regarding the mayor's Commission on Hispanic Concerns, established in October 1985, the Institute for Puerto Rican Policy (IPRP) questioned the legitimacy of the Commission and the consultation process it initiated.

Koch established the Commission in the aftermath of his re-election, in which 80 percent of the Puerto Rican/Hispanic vote had been for him. "I want to do something special for Hispanics," the mayor-elect declared after realizing that the level of Hispanic support—mostly Puerto Rican voters—was so high. The consultation arranged by the Commission consisted of five hearings from March 19 through April 16, 1986, one in each of the city's boroughs. But according to IPRP, "If the man this Commission is supposed to be advising does not hear our community when it tries to speak to him directly on a subject of deep concern to Latinos [...] then he makes these hearings and this Commission a mockery."[3]

After criticizing Koch, IPRP also decried the alleged transformation of Governor Mario Cuomo's Advisory Committee for Hispanic Affairs into his "Hispanic re-election committee." Cuomo's Committee had also conducted hearings to identify Hispanic concerns but, according to IPRP, it had accomplished nothing other than to give the impression that something was being done to serve Hispanics. Similarly, Koch's Commission was blasted for merely heightening the community's expectations and providing the mayor with a photo opportunity with Hispanics.[4]

On December 5, 1986, the executive director of Mayor Koch's Commission on Hispanic Concerns, Dennis deLeon, announced that a report would be handed to the mayor the next day. "Many people will be surprised when they read the document," said deLeon, in reference to those who did not believe that the Commission could in any way be critical of the mayor and a true advocate of the community.[5]

The report, however, was Hispanic boilerplate: requests for more representation in city government, more representation at the Board of Education, a Hispanic office of economic development, more low-income housing, and professional development programs for Hispanics. It would have been hard to find anyone surprised by the contents of the document. Yet, boilerplate or not, the report presented a profile of a highly disadvantaged community, poorly represented or completely ignored, with a 62 percent school dropout rate, and in dire need of services—one estimate suggested that 43 percent of welfare recipients in the city were Hispanic.[6]

When Mayor Koch was asked for a reaction his reply was: "I read it and I have no further comment."[7] But he did comment by forcefully rejecting the idea of a Hispanic appointment to the Board of Education. One city commissioner said that the report was a positive contribution but full of unaffordable recommendations.[8] Koch instructed his commissioners not to go out of their way to do anything. If something could be done on the cheap that was fine, but otherwise, the directive was "if it costs too much, never mind."

In an editorial, *El Diario-La Prensa* expressed its disappointment with the mayoral reaction: "Unfortunately the mayor could not even wait until the press conference which he held to announce the report was over to begin to say no." Koch indicated that only if the state legislature agreed to increase the size of the Board of Education to fifteen members, would he be able to appoint a Hispanic. No one understood the mayor's logic and he did not explain. The paper concluded that there was only one obstacle left in the Commission's way: the mayor.[9]

• • •

By the end of September 1986, an offensive remark was protested by NCPRR. This time, the Prime Minister of Japan was quoted as saying that "the presence of blacks, Puerto Ricans and Mexicans has lowered the level of intelligence in the U.S." "We are not surprised that President Reagan and his administration have not condemned Nakasone's remarks," declared NCPRR in a press release. "Evidence strongly suggests that they agree with the racial purity theory upon which these remarks are based." According to NCPRR, Nakasone's remarks and Reagan's silence were two additional good reasons for Puerto Ricans in New York to join Puerto Ricans from across the nation in a march planned for October 4th in Washington, D.C.[10]

According to journalist Carlos Alberto Montaner, Nakasone's statement was a "perfect political hara-kiri." In Montaner's view, Nakasone was only partially correct. Blacks and Puerto Ricans could not be faulted for the problems of the American industrial economy because "the presence of blacks and Latinos in that economic sector is not significant enough to determine the quantity and quality of production. By the middle of the XXI Century Nakasone may be proven right." Why? Because by then, more than half the population would be of Latin American, Asian, or African origin and these groups did not have the European attitudes and values that had made America a successful country. "This is not racism," said Montaner, "but common sense."[11]

Behind the press conferences and the militant postures of NCPRR, a number of difficulties confronted the organization in 1987. During the previous six years of activity, efforts to build a statewide organization were described by the Board of Directors as fruitless. Discussions on strategy were abstract and did not consider ways and means for implementation. The Board was also "fractionalized and in a cold war among its members." Nevertheless, the Executive Committee of the Board stated that during the previous two years the organization had made "great strides." Yet, after six years of activity, its primary organizational goals were "institutionalizing the NCPRR through a bold yet realistic plan for raising funds for full-time staff" and "conducting a mature debate on electoral politics."[12] These goals were not only vague and difficult to measure, but, also, did not suggest an upward trajectory since 1980.

As of April 1989, NCPRR's New York chapter could count on six local committees, three task forces, and sixteen member organizations to do outreach for mobilization to the fifth national convention to be held in Boston from May 26th to May 28th. Some member organizations were loosely structured groups staffed by NCPRR members. By the chapter's own admission, a significant number of members in the city were inactive at the time. No wonder then that the convention mobilization goal for the city was a mere 250 people.[13]

Organizational outlandishness—or identity politics run amok—was embodied best in the National Association for the Advancement of the Hispanic American People of African Origin, Inc., led by erstwhile political operator Julio Sabater, now known as Oggun Nike. In a letter sent to Judge Frank Torres, Sabater lamented the destruction of ancient black civilizations by the "children of the devil," that is, white people; he railed against the "anti-God, anti-human, anti-American, anti-Democratic-racist so-called American way of life; accused "Asians, Arabs, Hebrews and Jewish people" of resenting black people; and warned that "the children of the devil will never share with us, on a voluntary basis, their economic and political powers." Sabater informed Torres that it was

> the highest priority of our organization to find the proper mathematical equation which will put us, the black people, back in to our God-given role by the creator of our Universe (to be the catalistic force of his master plan-global-comprehensive-developmental-process), so that our planet can become again an eternal and harmonious operating system.[14]

The reach and influence of this organization was in all likelihood nil, but it provided perfect testimony to the fact that nothing was absent in the organizational life of the community. Oggun Nike was a rare case. It was unknown to most people except Frank Torres and Sabater, so his pronouncement made no waves.

DEMAND-PROTEST

Is it true that under identity politics each group has a set of interests that is exclusive of the group and must be served regardless of the social and/or political costs that doing so may entail? Puerto Rican interests were specific but not out of the ordinary. They required descriptive representation but not at the expense of credentials and qualification. Puerto Rican demands reflected a desire to preserve their language and receive fair treatment in society. In other words, their demands, even if made on the basis of a collective identity, were always anchored on individual experiences and did not require anything beyond adherence to liberal norms—democratic inclusion, non-discrimination, and equality of respect.

Education

On January 14, 1986, Angelo Falcón wrote Mayor Koch on behalf of IPRP a five-page letter taking him to task for "removing all Black and Latino representation from the Board [of Education] unilaterally," for telling Latinos that "we don't count," and for adding "insult to injury by implying [...] that when minority considerations are taken into account [...] this precludes competence and leadership as criteria."[15] The following day, the executive director of ASPIRA, Angelo González, wrote to Koch, also protesting the replacement of Miguel Martínez with Richard Beattie at the Board. According to González, this decision left "over 600,000 minority children [...] without any Latino representation."[16] Koch's response to Falcón and indirectly to González, was swift and unequivocal: "I don't withdraw a word of what I said. This administration will not play race, religious or sex games. This administration will be judged on performance regarding the delivery of services and having an open administration without discrimination being allowed."[17]

What Koch considered openness, others saw as exclusion; lack of discrimination translated as lack of Latino representation. This prompted the formation of the Coalition for Latino Representation on the Board of Education, a group comprised of the Asociación Comunal de Dominicanos Progresistas, ASPIRA of New York, Concerned Parents of Brooklyn, the Center for Puerto Rican Studies at CUNY, Educadores del Pueblo [People's Educators], El Puente de Brooklyn, NCPRR NYC Chapter, the Puerto Rican Association for Community Affairs, PRLDEF, the Puerto Rican/Latino Education Roundtable, and UBP. Among other things, the Coalition demanded that the mayor rescind one of his appointments to the Board to fill the vacancy with a Latino.[18]

During debates on ethnic representation, Koch was consistent in his double standard: rejecting what he called "race games" while promising racial representation. He was also consistently more supportive of blacks than Puerto Ricans. In 1977, he promised a group of black leaders that he would appoint "more blacks to high positions in the administration" than Wagner, Lindsay, and Beame combined. He was alarmed when he realized that he had committed himself to make 27 percent of his top administrators African American. Then, in 1984, he boasted that he had reached that mark in 1983.[19] Nothing comparable was ever promised to, or done for, Puerto Ricans.

In August, the national director of the Office of the Commonwealth of Puerto Rico, Nydia Velázquez, added her voice to the chorus of critics of the mayor's approach to representation in the Board of Education. Velázquez questioned the lack of Hispanic representation in a Board that was supposed to manage a school system in which 35 percent of the student body was Puerto Rican and Hispanic. In his reply to Velázquez, which was offered through his first deputy mayor, Stanley Brezenoff, Koch stuck to his guns: Board members would not be appointed on the basis of race, religion, or sex but solely on qualifications. Brezenoff reiterated Koch's promise to accept nominations from a screening committee or nominating panel if the state legislature approved a bill enlarging the Board.[20]

On October 10, 1987, the Puerto Rican Educators Association (PREA) held a forum with five candidates for the position of chancellor of the public schools.[21] In addition to PREA, a whole range of individuals and groups worried about this issue gathered under the umbrella of the Puerto Rican-Latino Education Roundtable led by Diana Caballero. Another coalition led by APRED, chaired by Elba Montalvo and Elizabeth Colón as executive director, also demanded the inclusion of Puerto Ricans/Latinos to the Board's screening committee.[22] The president of the Board of Education, Robert Wagner, Jr., publicly agreed that not only should incumbent chancellor

Nathan Quiñones be replaced by a Hispanic but, also, that the Board should have an additional Hispanic member. "Yet, we do not want to repeat the conflict created during the appointment of Anthony Alvarado four years ago. This could discourage qualified candidates," Wagner said.[23] The last Hispanic to serve on the Board, Miguel O. Martínez, had resigned in 1986. Political pressure came also from Assemblyman José Serrano who warned the Board about being in a weak position the next time state funds were requested if the body had no Hispanic representation.[24]

At a meeting with Wagner, Diana Caballero, Elizabeth Colón and Luis Reyes, and Julia Rivera from ASPIRA, demanded more representation within the search committee and suggested several names. At that point, the only Puerto Rican member of the committee was Víctor Marrero, then a member of the Board of Regents of the State University of New York.[25] Wagner was sympathetic and supportive and promised to take their plea directly to the mayor and borough presidents.[26] A few days later, the Board of Education announced the appointment of Dr. Albert Bowker, from CUNY, to head the advisory panel that would assist the Board in its search for a new chancellor. The panel included two Puerto Ricans, as the coalition demanded: Marrero and William Díaz, from the Ford Foundation.[27]

In October and November 1987, the Board of Education process gave community activists an opportunity to vent their frustration with Puerto Rican elected officials and to insist on Puerto Rican representation on the Board. At a forum in October, Angelo Falcón criticized elected officials for failing to press mayor Koch on the issue. During a testy exchange with State Senator Israel Ruiz, Jr., Falcón was asked if any of the organizations that were critical of Puerto Rican elected officials had ever actually asked for help. Falcón ignored the question by saying that if elected officials did not take a position on their own they failed as leaders.[28]

As it turned out, Assemblyman José Serrano had been pressuring Koch to insure Hispanic representation on the Board of Education. When Falcón was confronted with this fact, he admitted he did not know about it but refused to take back his criticism.[29] For his part, Luis Reyes threatened to go on a hunger strike if the Board did not appoint a Hispanic as a member.[30] On November 19, 1968, similar protests had come from the Hispanic community, and had resulted in a demonstration. "Twenty years later we are still asking for the same thing. You cannot call that progress," said Luis Garden Acosta, executive director of El Puente, a Brooklyn-based organization.[31]

Two days later, Garden Acosta announced that he would join Reyes. El Puente was part of the coalition demanding Hispanic representation. The coalition wanted an appointment within ten days of a planned demonstration before the Board on November 19th. This was a significant date because it marked the third anniversary of the death of noted education advocate and community leader Evelina Antonetty. Antonetty had moved to El Barrio as a small girl in 1933. She helped establish Head Start, child-care, and bilingual education programs. Her most important contribution was the establishment of United Bronx Parents.[32]

On November 1st, *New York Newsday* revealed that the Board of Education intended to produce a short list of twelve candidates from a pool of thirty-eight contenders. According to the paper, the majority of the applicants were black or Hispanic. In a related story, the *New York Times* revealed that Puerto Rican Hernán Lafontaine was among the list. But of the seven mentioned as being closely reviewed, none was Hispanic.[33]

On November 19th, the coalition for Hispanic representation held its demonstration with about one thousand participants. In a fiery address, Luis Garden Acosta reduced the conflict to racism and announced that the promised hunger strike would begin in ten days dubbing it "a hunger for education, a hunger for justice and a hunger for love."[34] On his way to New York from an immigration conference in California, Assemblyman José Rivera announced he would join the hunger strike.[35]

At the rally, other prominent supporters of the demand for Hispanic representation were Andrew Stein, president of the city council; David Dinkins, Manhattan borough president; Claire Shulman, Queens borough president; Howard Golden, Brooklyn borough president; and state legislators Olga Méndez, José Serrano, Roger Green, and Israel Ruiz, Jr.[36]

Then, when Koch asked Richard Beattie to resign in order to appoint Amalia Betanzos to the Board of Education, he was accused of caving in to the demands of Hispanic militants. The *New York Times* wrote that, with a school system in which 34 percent of the students were Hispanic, "The Mayor has been under persistent pressure from the Hispanic community, which makes up one of his most solid blocks of support, to appoint a Hispanic board member."[37] Of all the responsibilities of members of the Board of Education, choosing a Schools Chancellor was the most important. Betanzos' appointment was considered critical to the achievement of descriptive representation in that position, even though within the Board she would be a minority of one. In her own view, however, the new chancellor to be appointed should be "someone energetic, charismatic and a good administrator."[38]

Responding to the criticism of the remarks of her group that the appointment of Betanzos was illegitimate, Diana Caballero wrote: "We had broad support from Latino parents, our elderly, students, teachers, community groups, as well as unions, African-Americans, Asians, Haitians, Jews, Italians, church groups, some good government advocacy groups, four borough presidents, the city council presidents, and a good number of white, African-American, and Latino legislators." Betanzos attributed her appointment to "the very active and effective involvement of the Hispanic community in New York City." But her appointment was seen as a questionable victory. "Betanzos may be capable. But she was not on our list of potential appointees," said Caballero. The fear was that as a political ally of Koch, Betanzos would not be able to stand up to him if necessary.[39]

In any event, what was interesting about this process was how Koch did a complete turnabout on the issue of ethnic representation. The year before, he was adamant that his administration would not play racial, religious, or sex games. He insisted that his appointments were based solely on qualifications. Now, he explicitly promised to ask Beattie to step down in order to replace him with a Hispanic appointee. Similarly, while in 1986, the idea of enlarging the Board was presented as a mechanism to allow for general input on candidates, now it was presented by Koch as a way to appoint a Hispanic.[40] Where had all the principled talk about qualifications and against identity politics gone?

On December 30th, Assemblyman Roger Green called for a halt to the deliberations for the chancellorship due to the fact that, in his view, none of the candidates had the experience or qualifications to do the job. According to Green, none of the candidates supported initiatives focused on the needs of black, Asian, and Latino students who were 70 percent of the student population. His statement was endorsed by key black and Puerto Rican legislators and by the members of the Black and Puerto Rican legislative caucus.[41] In the end, the Board of Education appointed Richard R. Green, the first African American chancellor of the city's public school system.

• • •

According to a Board of Education report from 1988, Hispanic students were 29 percent of the total in high schools but 39 percent of all dropouts and 31 percent of dropouts from high school. Ironically, the 39 percent figure provided some consolation because in 1983, ASPIRA had estimated the rate at 60 percent.[42] Nevertheless, this was a troubling situation that Chancellor Green did not think required special attention. According to Joseph Pacheco, vice president of PREA, Green had a "shoulder-shrugging attitude" towards Hispanic problems. From ASPIRA, in coded language, Luis Reyes charged that the chancellor seemed to believe he was above criticism because he was black. After some pressure, Green relented, acknowledged the gravity of the Hispanic situation and grudgingly appointed Dolores M. Fernández as his deputy for instruction. It had taken heated meetings at the Board of Education and protests from Puerto Ricans for Green to change his attitude. Green, however, did not get much of a break because Fernández was unsatisfactory to many Puerto Ricans. The reason for this was that she was Spanish, a difference that was probably meaningless to Green.[43]

Language
In July 1986, the advocacy group U.S. English seemed poised to succeed in declaring English the official language of California, after gathering over a million signatures on a petition to put a proposal for it on the November 1986 ballot. The organization was also campaigning in Alabama, Florida, Idaho, Iowa, Kansas, Maryland, Massachusetts, Missouri, New Hampshire, New Jersey, New York, Washington, and Wisconsin. In New York City, however, the movement did not seem able to make headway. The executive director of ASPIRA, Angelo González, nevertheless, expressed

caution and resolution: "We'll have to be prepared to engage these people, just as we engaged the opponents of bilingual education."[44]

On November 11, *El Diario-La Prensa* published a story on efforts at the state assembly to pass a resolution declaring New York a multilingual state. This was part of the initiative led by Assemblyman José Rivera to provide funding for bilingual education programs, including $30 million for ESL instruction. "Bilingualism is a democratic right," the resolution read. "We seek to put a stop to discrimination against linguistic minorities," said Rivera, while suggesting that the desire of U.S. English to make English the official language of the nation was "racist, absolutist, and reactionary."[45] Rivera's initiative was suggested by the group Latinos United for Political Action (LUPA), and it had the support of the Black and Puerto Rican Legislative Caucus.[46]

Also in November, California voters confirmed the July prediction about making English the official language of the state, by approving Proposition 63. This emboldened U.S. English to push for a similar measure in New York; their plan was to start early in 1987. Even though supporters of the English Only movement were weak in New York, the California decision was considered a boost that could invigorate English Only ranks in the state. "That seed will not grow," predicted Schools Chancellor Nathan Quiñones, but because of the zealotry of English Only members, he thought it was important to pay close attention to its intentions and actions.[47]

Angelo González had said as much back in July, but this time the need to prepare to contend with U.S. English was a sure thing. To that effect, Assemblyman José Serrano called for a meeting of Hispanic, Italian, and Chinese community leaders interested in the issue, to be held on November 12th.[48] At Serrano's meeting, participants agreed to form a coalition to fight and defeat U.S. English in New York. Leading the coalition were Joseph Monserrat, former president of the Board of Education; Celia Chong, from the Chinese-American Progressive Association; and Joseph Scelsa, from the Italian American Institute at New York University.

Serrano promised that his office as well as that of Assemblymen Angelo del Toro, José Rivera, and of Senator Olga Méndez, would not allow any resolution or legislation favoring U.S. English. For her part, Nydia Velázquez, from the Commonwealth Office, offered the support of the Governor of Puerto Rico, Rafael Hernández Colón.[49] *El Diario-La Prensa* joined the protesters, warning its readers that the real agenda of U.S. English was to eliminate bilingual education, Spanish-language ballots, interpreters in emergency rooms, and bilingual 911 operators.[50]

In 1987, a bill introduced in 1985 by Assemblyman William Paxon advocating English-only in New York State was still pending. Then came the challenge of bill S-901 introduced on January 22, 1987, by Senator John Marchi, Republican from Staten Island, at the state legislature, to amend the state constitution to make English the official language of New York.

On February 19, the Committee for a Multilingual New York, a coalition that included ASPIRA, The Puerto Rican/Latino Roundtable, NCPRR, PRLDEF, LUPA, the

Chinese American Progressive Association, Local 1199, and the State Association on Bilingual Education, among others, held a rally and demonstration in front of Senator Marchi's law practice at 2 Wall Street in Manhattan. The protest was poorly organized and attended by about one hundred people.

Despite this, Miguel Pérez wrote in his column on the *Daily News*: "For every person [in attendance], there are hundreds who will wish they could be there. And maybe they will, at the next demonstration, when their leadership really gets its act together."[51] This inauspicious beginning notwithstanding, bill S-901 was defeated in Albany. Opposition included not just prominent legislators but Governor Mario Cuomo himself. On May 13th, José Serrano gleefully declared to *El Diario-La Prensa*, "U.S. English is dead." The assembly's committee on education, over which Serrano presided, killed both the Paxon and Marchi bills.[52]

On October 6, 1988, the New York City Council passed resolution 1474 denouncing the English Only movement and declaring New York City a multilingual, multicultural city. By the end of October, U.S. English was decapitated, with the resignations of its Chairman John Tanton, its President Linda Chávez, and prominent board member Walter Cronkite, over an inflammatory memo written by Tanton in 1986 describing Hispanics as promiscuous and a threat to the separation of church and state because of their Catholicism.

A contributor to U.S. English advocated for the forced sterilization of minority women and Tanton also claimed that Hispanics were naturally inclined to commit crime.[53] Responding to Chávez's description of Tanton's memo as "repugnant," the Committee for a Multilingual New York declared: "Where was she two years ago? How is it possible to believe that she has only learned of the real aims of U.S. English just last month after working with Tanton every day for 2 years?"[54]

The implication was that Chávez was just as much of a racist as Tanton and had reacted only after being exposed. Of course, the Committee was entitled to this assumption, but it was interesting that they did not also question the integrity of Walter Cronkite, who resigned under the same circumstances as Chávez. Also at the end of October, the Committee for a Multilingual New York sponsored a rally in support of Marlín Segarra, an attorney who had been fired from her job at Artha Management allegedly for refusing to comply with a workplace English-only rule.[55] Segarra's firing suggested that New York had yet to be a place where language diversity was seen as a real asset.

In February 1989, in Suffolk County, which had the largest Hispanic population outside New York, U.S. English rose from the grave to put fear in the hearts of all Spanish speakers in and outside the county. A bill at the county legislature proposed to require English-only in all governmental operations and transactions and explicitly made human rights abuses under the law exempt from being investigated or accounted for. Supporters of the bill acknowledged their desire to eliminate bilingual programs and Hispanics responded by calling them racists. Proponents saw the bill as a tool of assimilation, and opponents believed it was intended to deny county services to residents whose only "disqualification" was not being fluent in English. Fortunately, County Executive Patrick G. Halpin saw the proposal as divisive and unnecessary and vowed to veto the bill if it was approved by the legislature.

The response of citizens was divided but vigorous. No issue had generated as much mail and phone calls in the previous ten years. Ironically, even moribund U.S. English did not want the breath of life that Suffolk County was offering the movement in New York. After the Tanton debacle, why would they want to be associated with legislation that equated opposition to English-only with being un-American or with supporters of the legislation who told opponents to just go back to their home countries?[56]

Back in May 1987, the Committee for a Multilingual New York, which was led by members of NCPRR, thought that the defeat of bills proposing English-only for New York in that year's legislative session was temporary.[57] The legislation proposed in Suffolk County proved the Committee right. The Committee thus declared: "In 1987 we traveled 200 miles to Philadelphia when U.S. English had its first convention. Now they are right in our backyard and we must let them know that their politics are NOT welcome and that we are prepared to fight back."[58]

On March 18th, NCPRR addressed the issue of English-only by organizing a regional conference on the U.S. English movement at the Community Service Society in New York. At this strategy conference, representatives from Connecticut, New Jersey, and Philadelphia joined their New York colleagues to assess the impact of the movement on the Puerto Rican community and to develop an action agenda against future English-Only initiatives.[59] NCPRR was not alone in this. On September 26, the Community Service Society also held a conference on the English-Only movement with presentations by representatives from NCPRR, MALDEF, and the Chinese Progressive Association of New York.[60] Then, on October 20th, Hostos Community College held a forum on English-only. Speakers included the chancellor of CUNY, Joseph Murphy, and Assemblyman José Serrano.[61]

On July 25, 1989, APRED publicly condemned the attack of the U.S. English movement on bilingual education: "The U.S. English position on Bilingual Education is blatantly anti-Hispanic, anti-immigrant, and serves no purpose other than to inflame passions and create mass hysteria," said Elizabeth Colón in a press release. APRED promised to conduct a vigorous campaign to secure the adoption of the State Department of Education Bilingual Policy Paper and Action Plan, which sought to strengthen bilingual education programs and services for students in need.[62] By then, the English Only movement was dead in New York.

Police Brutality
On January 2, 1987, *El Diario-La Prensa* published an editorial decrying police brutality against Puerto Ricans, citing the case of Evelyn Rivera and her friends. According to Rivera, on her way home from a wedding, one of her friends was assaulted by a gang of black youth. As Rivera and others intervened, a transit police officer appeared, only to

make matters worse. The police officer refused to hear Rivera and ordered her and her friends to shut up. Then several cops arrived on the scene and dealt with the agitation by holding Rivera and beating her up. Rivera and her friends were then charged with resisting arrest and possession of dangerous weapons. According to the victims, the "weapon" was a beer can. "Unfortunately, the story is not unfamiliar," said the editorial. "There are too many reports of police brutality, particularly in cases which involve Hispanics and other minorities. And there are too few cases ever resolved."[63]

In February 1987, PRLDEF joined *El Diario-La Prensa* and Progress, Inc., in denouncing the assault of Rivera and her friends. In a press release, PRLDEF added that the victims had been called "spics" and "dykes" by the police. The incident was explained as part of a context of economic and racial divisions and discrimination promoted by the policies of the Reagan and Koch administrations. In the city, Mayor Koch was blamed for ignoring Latinos. His proposal to provide additional funds to the Commission on Human Rights was deemed "too little and too late."[64]

At some point during the day of January 30, 1988, in Brooklyn, Dominican Juan Rodríguez began banging violently on the doors of several of his neighbors. The reason for this behavior was not known at the time, but Rodríguez's neighbors did know he had a history of mental illness. Rather than confront him, they called the police. To subdue him, four policemen used force and Rodríguez died while in police custody. According to José Luis Morín, Rodríguez was beaten by the police in his own apartment. In his report, the city's medical examiner noted that Rodríguez's death was caused by a variety of factors including "blunt force injuries." Others were not so clinical in their descriptions, declaring that Rodríguez had been "savagely beaten to death by four policemen from the 83rd Precinct in Brooklyn. Juan Rodríguez, a 40-year-old Latino, father of three, died for being Latino."[65]

This was not an isolated case. According to NCPRR member Richie Pérez, there was a pattern of abuse that resulted in serious injury or death for at least seven Latinos—mostly Dominican and Puerto Rican—in only two years.[66] Something had to be done about it. Thus, NCPRR joined a coalition of churches, labor, and civil rights organizations to demand statewide legislation enhancing penalties for racially motivated violence and for a special prosecutor to handle such cases.[67]

On April 12, 1988, the Latino Coalition for Racial Justice acted on the Rodríguez case by staging a small protest before City Hall. According to Howard Jordan, a coalition member, Brooklyn's District Attorney, Elizabeth Holtzman, was simply dragging her feet on the case. A spokesman for Holtzman denied the charges, claiming that this was a sensitive case that required diligence rather than speed. This did not mollify the protesters who promised to return to City Hall on April 21st, this time in the hundreds. "We will shut down City Hall," said Jordan.[68] On April 21st, the City Hall demonstration took place with about 200 participants. While the Coalition managed to block the main entrance for twenty minutes, this did not shut down city government; Mayor Koch and others entered the building through side doors.[69]

By August, the police officers involved in the Juan Rodríguez incident were still on duty, the grand jury charged with investigating his death had not issued a report, and the mayor continued his vow of silence on the case.[70] This prompted another demonstration at City Hall, organized by the Latino Coalition for Racial Justice on September 8th. At this demonstration, participants called attention to another killing: on May 29th, a Dominican by the name of Modesto Ruiz was shot by a policeman in his own taxi-cab. A grand jury exonerated the policeman, but the Coalition was not convinced of the cop's innocence, given that Ruiz was a father of six with no criminal record and no history of problems with the police. The slogan of the demonstrators was "Alcalde Koch no Mientas Más, Los Asesinos te Gustan Más" [Mayor Koch, don't lie; you do like murderous cops].[71]

Perhaps it was time to pay heed to a 1986 municipal report that suggested that the city's police department needed to increase the number of Hispanic and black recruits. The Association of Hispanic Police Officers could not agree more. For years the group had been pushing for more Hispanic recruits with an emphasis on bilingual officers. In a section about ethnic representation, the report noted euphemistically that "underrepresentation is not only unfair, but it also affects the quality of services."[72]

Race

On June 1, 1986, about thirty members of NCPRR marched on the Puerto Rican Day Parade to publicize an October march on Washington. Then, on June 14th, the NCPRR again marched from Harlem to Central Park, this time as part of a demonstration against apartheid, sponsored by the Anti-Apartheid Coordinating Council of New York. NCPRR was part of a contingent from the group Latinos for a Free South Africa. "Latinos whose cultural diversity includes our substantial African ancestry understand that South African liberation is an essential element of a comprehensive and total human liberation," reads the press release of the NYC Chapter of the organization.[73]

Incidents of racial violence in the Bronx in June and July led NCPRR to call for an ecumenical procession to denounce the attacks and to demand social justice. The call was answered by Assemblyman José Serrano but, after a meeting with Mayor Koch, Serrano and assembly candidate Roberto Ramírez denounced NCPRR as a fringe, leftwing organization. Serrano and Ramírez suggested that the incidents were criminal rather than racial. Yet the victims of the June attack were Puerto Rican and black and the perpetrators were white. Similarly, the July attackers were a white mob and their targets were two Puerto Rican youths—Pedro Molina and Ramón Rivera.[74]

In August, a group of Puerto Ricans speaking on behalf of Educadores del Pueblo in the Bronx, distributed an open letter to the community condemning the racial attacks against Molina and Rivera; these had occurred in the Belmont area of the borough. Molina suffered a fractured skull and broken jaw while Rivera had an arm broken and was bitten three times. In retaliation, two Yugoslavian youths were subsequently attacked. "As long as there is racial inequality," Educadores del Pueblo wrote, "true democracy and respect for human beings will never exist in the United States." They concluded their letter with an appeal: "Young Puerto Ricans, brothers, Italians and Yugoslavians are not your enemies; Young Italians and Yugoslavians, Puerto Ricans are not your enemies; our enemies, who have destroyed our minds with their lies, drugs, and political corruption, laugh at us in their luxury suites while we kill each other out of ignorance thanks to their Machiavellian or rather diabolic schemes. Let us come together for a better community."[75]

In response to the Molina and Rivera incident, LUPA asserted the right of Puerto Ricans to defend themselves against harassment, intimidation, and physical assault. The Coalition for Racial Justice organized a march for racial harmony scheduled for August 9th. The march was cancelled at the urging of Assemblyman José Rivera. According to Rivera, his Racial Violence Hotline had been flooded with calls threatening bodily harm and death to the participants in the march. The organizers also received notice that the Belmont community was in no mood for any kind of demonstration in their neighborhood.

The fact that the older brother of one of Molina's and Rivera's attackers was the police officer accused of beating another Puerto Rican in the same neighborhood, persuaded the organizers that they could not count on police protection. According to Howard Jordan, from LUPA, racial violence would end only if a new Latino, black, and progressive political movement developed to provide a new leadership dedicated to the preservation of individual liberties.[76] Cleveland Robinson, Secretary Treasurer of District 65 of the United Auto Workers, also condemned the violence and declared "there must be no area in this city where one can not walk, live or work because of race or ethnicity."[77]

In late September, the Parents Association of P.S. 16 formed a coalition dubbed United Parents Against the Wall (UPAW) to protest the construction by the school board of a wall intended to separate Puerto Rican and Jewish students. The construction of the wall was demanded by Hasidic parents. On September 27th, UPAW held a march from the school to the residence of the rabbi of the petitioning Hasidic group. There they protested the construction of the wall and demanded racial and ethnic integration in the school. ASPIRA supported the demonstration.[78]

On December 19, 1986, Puerto Rican George Torres and Dominican Rafael González were attacked in Howard Beach, Queens, with bats by over a dozen of whites yelling "get out of here, you dirty Hispanics." Torres and González had just attended a meeting at a local church and were attacked around 10:00 pm. Seeking refuge in a nearby cafeteria, they were told to leave because no Hispanics were wanted there. When the police finally arrived, Torres and González were told that the attack was their own fault because they should not have been in the neighborhood.[79]

A week later, two white youth were identified by the police as suspects in the attack against Torres and González. One of them, Joseph Aprea, was identified by González as the instigator of the attack. Very early that same morning, a local baker had reported a threat to his business from a black group. At 3:55 am a caller told him: "Merry Christmas, this is the Black Liberation Army," and hung up. Ten minutes later the phone rang again and the baker was told: "We are going to blow up your place tomorrow at 2 pm."[80]

"Koch is responsible," said Richie Pérez from the Coalition for Racial Justice, because he failed to use all the resources available to him to clearly stand against racism. Meanwhile, the mayor and Schools Chancellor Nathan Quiñones, announced the creation of a program to instill tolerance of ethnic diversity in the city. To Pérez this was not good enough: "the authorities always wait until someone gets killed to then pretend they are doing something," he said.[81] To appease the community, Koch personally called and met with Torres and González in his City Hall office.[82] While calling for the creation of a national commission to campaign against racism, Koch also told reporters that it was not necessary to have another Kerner-type commission declaring the existence of two societies irremediably divided by race. "I do not believe that to be true," said Koch.[83]

Incidents similar to the one in Howard Beach had occurred in 1985 in the Graves End section of Brooklyn and in the Belmont section of the Bronx. These were just incidents; what happened in Howard Beach was a crime.[84] Tensions continued to escalate. On December 25, 1986, three Hispanics were shot at from a moving vehicle while they walked down 28th Street and 24th Avenue in Astoria, Queens. Rolando Romero, one of the pedestrians, took a bullet to his knee. Earlier during the day, a caller to *El Diario-La Prensa* reported that a group of Hispanics were insulted and threatened with a gun by a white man just because they were speaking in Spanish. The group fled the scene and filed a complaint with the police.[85] On December 28th, a group of blacks and Hispanics, numbering five thousand according to one report, marched through the streets of Howard Beach to protest the incidents and what they considered an attempt on the part of the authorities to deny their racial nature.[86]

As a black police officer recalling an incident in 1969 indicated, it was futile to deny that the neighborhood of Howard Beach was a bastion of racial prejudice. He said:

One day we received a call from a home concerning a possible heart attack. My partner, who was white, and I arrived at the scene and looking at my partner, the lady of the house told him that only he could come in. My partner refused to go in without me and the woman calmly responded that she would wait for the ambulance. I could not believe that she was willing to risk her husband's life before allowing a black man in her house.[87]

But it was not necessary to go back to 1969 or even 1985 to illustrate the existence of racism in Howard Beach. The day of the December 1986 march, about one hundred white residents proffered insults to the participants. When Mayor Koch made an appearance at the Lady of Grace Church to appeal for racial harmony, the parishioners shouted him out, angry at the suggestion that there was any racism in

Howard Beach.[88] In her *El Diario-La Prensa* column of December 29th, Rossana Rosado offered anecdotes that illustrated the widespread nature of prejudice, from an Italian taxi driver who claimed that blacks belonged in the sewers, to a Dominican mother who disliked her daughter's Puerto Rican boyfriend because of his kinky hair, to Hispanics who decried white racism at the same time that they claimed that blacks wanted to take over the whole city.[89]

On January 14, 1987, PRLDEF and NCPRR demanded the appointment of a special prosecutor to investigate the 1986 attacks on George Torres and Rafael González. News reports in 1987 placed the attack in Ozone Park, Queens, and offered new details such as the alleged comments of a man driving by who allegedly pointed a gun at Torres and González shouting "You dirty spics, I am going to blow your heads off," and of one police officer who allegedly told Torres: "You spics come here and make us look bad, you are troublemakers." PRLDEF also reported on five additional racial attacks on Hispanics.[90]

These incidents jibed perfectly with the January declaration by Progress, Inc., that "racial and ethnic antagonism has unfortunately become part of everyday life in New York City ever since large waves of immigrants began reaching the city's shores more than 200 years ago."[91] Progress, Inc. also noted that:

> the base cause of racial violence are [sic] underlying feelings of distrust and suspicion of other races and cultures, accentuated by stereotyped images whites, blacks and Hispanics have of each other's behavior. Racial violence is just one manifestation of larger social ills—poverty in minority communities and xenophobic attitudes.[92]

Race relations in the city were getting worse and according to a poll conducted by *New York Newsday*, 44 percent of whites, blacks, and Hispanics agreed.[93]

CHAPTER 8
WE ARE ALL LIBERALS NOW

The activities of Puerto Rican community organizations during the 1960s, '70s, and '80s around issues related to education, electoral involvement, health, island concerns, police brutality, and resource allocations, provide evidence of the mainstream-oriented, liberal character of Puerto Rican political participation in New York City. How so? Those battles, as well as the one waged against the English Only movement, were fought on the basis of group identity but for the sake of individual rights. As a group, Puerto Ricans were not an abstraction but a community of individuals with distinct personalities and backgrounds, bound together by a common history and a sense of shared culture, but also by disadvantage, unequal treatment, and the feeling of vulnerability that attends processes of racialization.

While identity politics blends individuality and community, racialization dismisses and denigrates them. This point is sometimes lost on scholars who condemn racialization *and* identity politics. Liberalism in the abstract is supposed to be all about individuality and autonomy while identity politics allegedly melts all traces of individuality in the cauldron of community. In the world of real politics, however, these distinctions become fuzzy if not altogether irrelevant. Puerto Rican mobilizations in support of bilingual education and for the democratization of community school boards took place inspired by a commitment to liberal democratic values: choice, integration, civic duty, and equal participation. The previous narrative shows how Puerto Ricans were clearly inspired by these values in a practical sense and therefore how instead of melting the solidity of liberalism into the air of group identity they brought the two together in practice.

Some of the activities undertaken by Puerto Rican groups such as the National Congress for Puerto Rican Rights (NCPRR) felt radical in nature, and some of the group's pronouncements had a semblance of radicalism. In retrospect, it is apparent how the discourse and style of these groups and the nature of their demands fit within a liberal democratic framework. When Puerto Ricans organized NCPRR, they were to the left of ASPIRA, the Puerto Rican Forum, and the National Puerto Rican Coalition, but they all wanted the same thing: first-class citizenship. When the Office of the Commonwealth created its community organization program, it promoted both self-sufficiency and identity politics. These approaches, however, were affirmative and did not promote segregation or a separatist sentiment.

At this point, Puerto Rican studies scholars may wonder why the Congress of Puerto Rican Hometowns has been so conspicuously absent from the preceding account. The Congress was organized in 1956, modeled after the service provision system of the American Labor Party, and it included in its organizational mission the defense of the civil and human rights of Puerto Ricans in the city. Its precursors were social and cultural clubs organized around Puerto Rican identity but not active in politics. As the Congress developed, it expanded the scope of its activities from the purely socio-cultural to the provision of services. During the 1960s and '70s, it relied on funding from the Puerto Rican Community Development Project to pay for office supplies and support staff. And it was during this period that the Congress was a player in the fight against literacy requirements for voting, against police brutality, and against discrimination of Puerto Ricans in the labor market.

In his 2013 memoir, Gilberto Gerena Valentín claimed that the Congress, of which he was the leader, was "the vital force" behind the creation of groups such as the National Association for Civil Rights, the Puerto Rican Parade, and the Puerto Rican Folk Festival. Gerena Valentín also claimed that the Congress was the determining factor in the electoral and bureaucratic fortunes of leading Puerto Rican figures such as Herman Badillo and John Carro.[1] However, the record does not support Gerena Valentín's claims: the Congress provided important services to Puerto Ricans in the city, especially new arrivals, and it was active in key community struggles, but the claim that no other group was as important and as militant in the defense of Puerto Rican interests in the city as the Congress is not credible. Gerena was right, however, when he conceded that by the 1970s, the Congress had lost the prominence it once had within the Puerto Rican community in New York.

CONTEXT OF IDENTITY POLITICS
The Puerto Rican community-based activities and collective action documented during the three decades between 1960 and 1990, took place in the larger context of a long history of Puerto Rican political participation in the city. During the Great Depression, young Puerto Ricans like Manuel "Manny" Díaz, Jr., participated by helping the "ladies" of the Democratic Party carry turkeys from Sheep Meadows to the East Side Line to distribute them among Democratic voters indebted to the Irish-controlled machine. In 1937, Oscar García Rivera was elected to represent a Manhattan district in the State Assembly and later on, during the 1950s, Puerto Ricans elected representatives in increasing numbers. According to Nick Lugo, a South Bronx Puerto Rican entrepreneur, political activism in the community emerged at a moment of transition, when East Harlem was saturated demographically, pushing Puerto Ricans out into the Bronx. In his view, early elected officials such as García Rivera had no real power base in the community; they were creatures of the political machine.[2] This is a dubious claim, and García Rivera is not a good example because he was elected without support from the Democratic Party and was defeated in 1940 by party regular Hulan Jack by a margin of over 3,000 votes.[3]

According to Manuel "Manny" Díaz, Jr., in East Harlem Italians gave Puerto Ricans "enough crumbs" to elect Tony Méndez as the first Puerto Rican Democratic Party district leader and Carlos M. Ríos as the first Puerto Rican councilman. They were creatures of the political machine, but they also had supporters within the community. To Díaz, however, Méndez and Ríos represented the "infantile" stage of Puerto Rican politics in the city; a politics whose three institutional pillars were the Office of the Commonwealth of Puerto Rico, the Congress of Puerto Rican Hometowns led by Gilberto Gerena Valentín, and the Puerto Rican Forum.[4] But this claim is also incorrect because this triumvirate was only the most visible and prominent set of a larger array of community groups that gave Puerto Rican politics its energy and drive. Here I have sought to emphasize this point by deliberately focusing on actions by community groups that at one time or another made a contribution.

During the period covered in this book, first *El Diario de Nueva York* and later *El Diario-La Prensa* routinely encouraged Puerto Ricans and other Hispanics to vote. Typically, editorials would endorse candidates and/or explain why a vote in support of a particular proposition, bond issue, or amendment was necessary. These editorials were published in English and Spanish. Sometimes editorials commended the efforts of individuals, many of them women, who went beyond the call of duty to exercise their voting rights. One example was that of nine women and four men who, after being denied their right to register, spent one full day making their case before the Board of Elections with the assistance of their pro-bono lawyers Herman Badillo and Assemblyman José Ramos López.[5]

Prequel to the 1960s

What did community-based activities and collective action look like before the 1960s? Bernardo Vega refers to the Alianza Puertorriqueña, the Club Latinoamericano, and the Club Betances as the leaders of an initiative to form a federation named Liga Puertorriqueña in 1922. The Asociación Nacionalista was also active, but it was quick to alienate Puerto Rican working-class leaders for reasons that Vega does not specify;[6] in all likelihood, the reason was political: Puerto Rican workers were interested in labor issues in New York, and the Asociación thought that anything unrelated to the cause of independence for Puerto Rico was a waste of time.

The Alianza Obrera was one working-class group that fell into the useless category established by the Asociación Nacionalista since it was only interested in promoting the unionization of Puerto Rican workers and to advocate for their interests as a group, independently of political affiliation.[7] And then there was the Puerto Rican Brotherhood of America, established in 1923 and described by Vega as "the most important organization in the life of Puerto Ricans in New York in those days [...]."[8] Virginia Sánchez Korrol also refers to this group as "one of the most significant organizations of the period [1920s]," and although the group did not consider itself political, identity politics was clearly the framework for its agenda.[9]

In his study of the Puerto Rican community in New York in the 1930s, Lawrence Chenault highlighted the work of groups such as the Union Settlement, on East 104th Street, and of the Puerto Rican Service Center of New York, on 103W 110th Street. The Puerto Rican Service Center, "while yet young and doing only a small amount of case work," Chenault noted, "often intercedes for the unfortunate Puerto Rican family with charity organizations or relief agencies."[10] On 114th Street and Seventh Avenue, the Church of Nuestra Señora de la Medalla Milagrosa stood out among the various small Catholic and Protestant churches that doubled as places of worship and acculturation.

Chenault makes reference to an August 30, 1936, ten thousand-strong demonstration promoted by Congressman Vito Marcantonio, explicitly concerned with the colonial subordination of Puerto Rico to the U.S. For a period of three hours, Puerto Ricans paraded through the streets of Lower Harlem chanting "Free Puerto Rico" and "Down with Yankee Imperialism."

But it is not clear whether this period was any different from the 1960s and '70s when anti-colonial activity was frequent and often massive but nevertheless not representative of the politics of the community. Chenault himself provided a clue that to some extent dispels this lack of clarity when he wrote that "The unfortunate Puerto Rican on relief usually becomes a member of the Workers Alliance," a Communist Party-sponsored organization with a Spanish-speaking branch located at 27-29 West 115th Street, where "unemployed workers and ruined small-businessmen" sought assistance.

At the same time, he noted that "between the two major political parties, the Puerto Rican is almost without exception Democratic."[11] And at the Alliance one could find even people like Oscar García Rivera—a progressive Republican—who used it as a point of contact with his constituents.[12] Thus, on the one hand, there were anti-colonial marches, but, on the other, Democratic Party affiliation was routine, even if practical needs were met by using resources provided by fronts of the Communist Party.

If identity politics is correlated with interest representation, before the 1960s the designation of "first Puerto Rican elected to Congress" must go to Italian-American Vito Marcantonio. Even though he formally represented a slice of the city, he was the one politician with a citywide Puerto Rican constituency. As Manuel "Manny" Díaz, Jr. put it, he was a "solid citizen" when it came to defending the interests of the community. His association with Puerto Ricans was highlighted unkindly by the local press, which accused him of enticing "destitute and ill" Puerto Ricans to come to New York "with gold promises," for political purposes.[13]

By 1949, when Marcantonio ran unsuccessfully for mayor, the erstwhile friendly government of Puerto Rico, joined forces with Marcantonio's detractors to accuse him of exacerbating the so-called "Puerto Rican Problem" in the city—a media creation that turned Puerto Ricans into scapegoats for a variety or urban ills. Ironically, a by-product of this campaign was to facilitate the emergence of the Office of the Commonwealth of Puerto Rico as the leading community institution of Puerto Ricans in New York.[14]

In the early 1960s, Puerto Ricans were kept abreast of the details of electoral races both in New York and Puerto Rico by radio station WWRL, known as La Voz Hispana.[15] The connection between New York and Puerto Rico intensified during electoral periods. In 1960, for example, the volume of letters sent by Puerto Ricans on the island to Puerto Ricans in New York and vice versa was larger than usual as island residents, and migrants encouraged each other to vote, in this particular election year, for Kennedy in New York and for the pro-statehood party on the island.[16]

At this point, most Puerto Ricans in New York did not pay attention to affairs in Puerto Rico in order to promote any particular form of status; the colonial question was not a concern. And as this book shows, the connection was also alive at the community level beyond electoral matters in strategic and demand-protest collective action around issues such as the presence of the U.S. Navy on the islands of Culebra and Vieques.

In the electoral arena, Puerto Ricans worried about pressures to vote in a certain way and about discrimination—in registering and at the voting booth. During the 1960 election, some complained to the attorney general that members of the Democratic Party had warned them that if they voted Republican they would lose their welfare benefits. The attorney general reassured them that the days of votes-for-favors, favors-for-votes were over.[17]

Claims of discrimination were brought to the attention of Mayor Robert Wagner by a group of Puerto Rican leaders that included Herman Badillo and others that are not as well known, such as Celia Vice, Faustino Luis García (who ran for Congress in 1960), Joseph Erazo, Jorge L. Gómez, and the two immediate successors of García Rivera, Assemblymen Felipe N. Torres and José Ramos López. During his meeting with this group, Wagner agreed to place voting machines in public schools to teach Puerto Ricans how to vote and to assign Spanish-speaking policemen and poll workers to districts with large concentrations of Puerto Rican voters.[18]

Many Puerto Ricans ran for office with support from the Liberal Party. But in 1960, this third party was not much more than an appendage of the Tammany Hall organization, blindly endorsing any candidate proposed by Democratic Party boss Carmine De Sapio in exchange for patronage. According to *El Diario de Nueva York*, this could change if the party took advantage of the struggle between reformers and regulars within the Democratic Party to set itself as an independent political force. To do this, the party needed to stop being a "yes man" organization and to start running its own candidates.[19]

Judging by the number of Puerto Rican candidates the party supported during the 1960s, forty-two altogether, this advice was heeded. Nevertheless, social clubs, more so than political parties, provided the organizational basis for Puerto Rican political participation during the 1960s. In the context of party decomposition, community organizations that picked up the slack always focused on Puerto Rican identity as their driving force. Entrepreneurs such as Nick Lugo, Sr., also played an important role; O. Roy Chalk, the owner of *El Diario*, gave Herman Badillo a $10,000 campaign contribution when Badillo ran for Bronx Borough President in 1965. The money was funneled to the campaign through Lugo's travel agency.[20]

In November 1960, *El Diario de Nueva York* reported the appointment of Manuel Ramos as assistant district attorney in the Bronx. While there was rejoicing about the appointment within the community, reporter Gonzalo Jusino was quick to remind his readers that Ramos was simply replacing Bart Ortiz who was appointed before him. Ortiz' appointment was the real accomplishment, whereas Ramos had just kept the position in Puerto Rican hands.[21] But how significant was this? Not very much, according to Puerto Rican Republicans. The office of Manhattan's borough president had a staff of four thousand, and only one employee was Puerto Rican, they claimed. Why? Because "the Democrats who run the city would not even allow Hispanics to sweep the streets."[22]

Puerto Rican Republicans also protested the fact that of five thousand firemen in the city not one was Hispanic.[23] These claims are plausible, but it is difficult to ascertain their accuracy. What's interesting is that within the Puerto Rican community, there were some who believed Puerto Rican voters should support the Republican Party as the only one that "respects our culture and dignity." They also believed that Puerto Ricans should vote for all Puerto Rican candidates no matter what, thus giving pride of place to ethnicity as the key proxy for voting decisions.[24] In the context of Democratic Party politics at least, ethnicity was a key factor for voter behavior.

The Kennedy administration named several Puerto Ricans to positions of relative importance. Chief among them was Teodoro Moscoso, from Puerto Rico, who was tapped to head the Alliance for Progress. Herman Badillo was asked to join the President's Committee on Juvenile Delinquency and Youth Crime, and also from New York, Paul Torres was designated postal representative; Pedro San Juan was named assistant chief of protocol in the Department of State.[25] These were not the type of appointments that could be used to promote policies that generate mass upward mobility, but they belied the notion that Democrats would not consider Puerto Ricans even as street sweepers. Of course, that claim is a straw man and therefore refuting it is easy. During the 1960s, thirty-one Puerto Ricans ran for office as Democrats; not an overwhelming number but certainly not nothing.

The point here, however, is that as important as participation was along partisan and electoral lines, the community level was also rich in terms of numbers and action. The contours of the preceding historical collage should make this apparent. And, as noted in the introduction, the pattern had precedents.

IDENTITY POLITICS AND LIBERALISM FROM THE GROUND UP

The Office of the Commonwealth of Puerto Rico in New York has been characterized as inefficient, with little power and little will to help Puerto Ricans in the city.[26] But it is inappropriate to think that a mere division of an island agency could comprehensively manage Puerto Rican life in New York City, offset "negative discriminatory public opinion," insulate Puerto Ricans from the impact of market failures in housing, education and health, place them in high-wage manufacturing jobs when most migrants had "unskilled working-class backgrounds," and ameliorate the impact of deindustrialization in the Northeast.[27] Was the Migration Division inefficient because it was not able to do these things?

To answer YES to this question would suggest a perspective that sees the forest but misses the trees: what the Migration Division could do, it did fairly well. Thus, in the early 1960s, the Division was the preeminent Puerto Rican institution in New York City. This was the case, in part, because it provided real services to the community and also because of a "lack of vigorous competition from other groups." Michael Lapp's dictum that the agency was *for* Puerto Ricans but not *of* them, also misses the point because the focus of the agency was intrinsic to the identity of its main constituency.[28]

According to John Carro, when Joseph Monserrat took over the Office from Manuel Cabranes he put it on the map.[29] Monserrat was dynamic and effective. Puerto Rican New Yorkers clashed with him because allegedly he would not provide opportunities for community leaders such as Carro, Frank Bonilla, or Antonia Pantoja to come into their own. "Joe could not be Mr. Be All to the community," said Judge Carro in 1988.[30] And that's one reason why agencies like the Puerto Rican Forum were created, to provide a vehicle for the leadership who felt stifled by Monserrat. It is important to note this because it reveals one important motive behind community institutional development initiatives that is rarely acknowledged.

Yet, Monserrat was actually interested in developing leaders from the community—he was a mentor of Robert García, who ran unsuccessfully for the State Assembly in 1965 and was elected to the State Senate in 1967 after Eugene Rodríguez was barred from occupying his seat. What was irking about Monserrat was not indifference to Puerto Rican issues and needs or an unwillingness to promote local organization and talent but that he wanted to carry out good works only on his own terms. Some felt that Monserrat's ties to the government of Puerto Rico limited his ability to be more militant in his defense of New York Puerto Ricans. In Joseph Erazo's view, Monserrat was too diplomatic whereas Erazo "didn't give a damn. We had to fight whoever it was that was abusing our people."[31]

Carro and his colleagues had a different strategy for empowerment. To them, the most promising approach was to place Puerto Ricans in key positions within government where they could influence fiscal, housing, and educational policy. "We began with the idea that education was the most important [area] to us," said Carro years later.[32] Ultimately, however, they were all driven by identity politics no matter what their strategy or political style.

The Migration Division was eventually overshadowed by the myriad new organizations that emerged during the 1960s and beyond. This growth is indicated by the fact that by 1969 the Division only assisted other organizations rather than individuals. The eclipse of the Division by then is suggested by the contraction of one of its main projects—its annual voter registration campaign was reduced to providing office space for one day to enroll voters. Also, during the latter part of the year, there was no staff available for community organization.[33] This occurred over a short period of time, almost as quickly as Antonia Pantoja's goal of self-sufficiency was overshadowed by identity politics.

As the Division waned, The Forum, ASPIRA, and a host of new organizations waxed; in that process, the liberal orientation of Puerto Rican community-based collective action expanded by embodying, in practice, the value of public reason. In other words, Puerto Ricans were willing to play by the rules of the game provided they were applied equally to all. In practice, they also embodied the value of moral learning, that is, they acted not just on the basis of what was acceptable to them. And this they did by promoting the common interest through the promotion of group interests, by breaking through the boundary between the public and the private, and by challenging the myth of state neutrality, among other things.

The 1984 campaign of NCPRR against Mayor Koch is a good example of identity politics serving as a tool for the promotion of collective goods—which is another way in which public reason and moral learning unfold in practice. When NCPRR blasted Koch, blaming him and his policies for Puerto Rican poverty, for homelessness in the city, for rampant racism, corruption, and lack of adequate health services, their language always added the concerns of other minorities to the plight of Puerto Ricans. In other words, the message the organization sent was that its members—and the Puerto Rican community at-large—were in it not just for themselves but for the sake of all similarly situated citizens.

If there was a problem with NCPRR's politics of identity it was more related to the group's tendency to overextend itself without having the resources needed to fully meet its agenda than to having a narrow vision that hardened existing boundaries between Puerto Ricans and other groups. As Andreas Wimmer suggests, identity boundaries based on ethnicity are only partially self-determined. Institutional incentives also play a role as well as a given group's position in existing hierarchies of economic, political, and symbolic power.[34] He also shows that, if anything, what both produces and hardens identity boundaries is "inequality (and associated forms of closure) [...] because the privileged will add markers of cultural distinction to differentiate themselves from subordinate actors and to make boundary crossing more difficult."[35] Both propositions apply to the Puerto Rican case, and in both instances Puerto Ricans refused to be stifled by these external inducements to becoming isolated.

Ironically, the biggest fights NCPRR had were with other Puerto Rican organizations and their representatives rather than with blacks, Asians, or other outgroups. The controversy over the Coors agreement recalled in Chapter 6 is a good illustration of this point. NCPRR's most significant obstacle was not that it was parochial but that it had a weak position in the existing hierarchy of power, that it was marked as not just inferior but as an antagonist by those who had power, and that it wanted to be "at all activities of the Puerto Rican community."[36]

Ultimately, if on the question of moral learning the main challenge of the relationship between liberalism and identity politics is finding a way to remain faithful to the group while preserving enough critical distance to allow for the repudiation of constraining or disagreeable aspects of community life—as Michael Walzer suggests in *Interpretation and Social Criticism*—one could argue that it is in the ability to surmount that challenge that one can find an element of compatibility between the two.[37] In their rivalries, divisions, disagreements, and conflictive perspectives on issues, Puerto Ricans engaged in identity politics found ways of making that happen, thus crossing the aporetic bridge between liberalism and identity politics.

The practice of citizenship by Puerto Ricans promoted integration and community by affirming rather than suppressing meaningful differences of treatment and status directly attributable to differences in ascriptive traits. The point of emphasizing these differences was to pursue liberal integration, that is, to obtain acceptance as legitimate citizens of members of a racial and ethnic minority group incorporated as colonial subjects.

Organizations had different agendas, but their common denominator was identity—a civic club was not just civic but civic from Humacao or Arecibo; chauffeurs organized as *Puerto Rican* chauffeurs and Bronx organizations were united by issues as well as by leaders whose priority was serving Puerto Ricans who were affected by those issues, be it child care, housing, or education. The Grand Council of Hispanic Societies organized to serve Hispanics first, but it did so also to promote patriotism, tolerance, and equality, not to establish impermeable barriers between itself and other groups.

The work of NCPRR also illustrates this point: most of their language campaigns were carried out in coalitions that included Haitians, blacks, Italians, and Asians. The work was done by groups as diverse as LUPA, the Center for Puerto Rican Studies, and it included unexpected partners such as Ramitas de Borinquen. Although at the group level the common denominator in their efforts was Puerto Rican identity, in their relationship with the NPRC, for example, class and ideology tempered their solidarity in ways that challenge the common assumption that identity politics is not only exclusionary but cemented in the principle that blood is thicker than water.

All in all, at the end of 1989, the institutional capacity of the Puerto Rican community was significant. In each year between 1970 and 1988 for which there are records, the citywide number of Puerto Rican organizations was never below 200. In 1972, there were 469 groups accounted for by the Office of the Commonwealth of Puerto Rico; the second highest number was 428 in 1976. The greatest number of groups operated in Manhattan, followed by the Bronx, Brooklyn, Queens, and Staten Island.[38] While the available numbers are not definitive, they are suggestive of a highly organized and engaged community, a community striving for full-membership as cultural citizens.

As for collective action, between 1960 and 1990, Puerto Ricans participated in two major civil disturbances, collaborated with blacks in one school boycott, and staged hundreds of demand-protest actions in the city and beyond. These activities were varied in nature, but they all had a common denominator—redress of grievances structured by either attacks targeted against Puerto Ricans or by conditions affecting them that were deemed unacceptable.

In 1989, more than anything else, the appointment of New York-born, Puerto Rican educator, Joseph Fernández, as chancellor of the city's public schools under an eighteen-month contract, put the words "Puerto Rican" on everybody's lips in the city. Fernández was hailed as an administrator, but his real charm was his background. He succeeded Richard Green, who had passed away in May, suddenly, from a severe asthma attack. With a background that seemed lifted from a Horatio Alger's story, Fernández was hailed as a role model for the minority student population. His administrative prowess qualified him for the job, but in a city where blacks and Latinos were 80 percent of the city's public schools, the job was secured by his identity.

When the Federación de Organizaciones de Brooklyn met at the Las Vegas Restaurant in 1966, it was clear that the focus of the group's activities should be issues Puerto Ricans confronted in Brooklyn. A separate group had not appreciated Mayor Lindsay's exhortation to Puerto Ricans to be Americans first, New Yorkers second, and Puerto Ricans last. Yet, even among those that welcomed the remark, the sense was that the priority for civic and political action should be "their children born here," that is, in Brooklyn, Manhattan, or the Bronx, not in Puerto Rico. Identity politics was grounded in a sense of self, shaped by context and issues as well as by heritage.

Similarly, whether it was getting involved in educational issues, War on Poverty initiatives, fighting police brutality, or developing groups such as the Grand Council of Hispanic Societies, the lens through which participation and integration were refracted was that of Puerto Rican identity. The establishment of Hostos Community College and the fight to save it from dissolution reflected a concern with access to higher education but not access in the abstract, occurring instead in a setting structured around Puerto Rican history and identity. Self-sufficiency remained elusive since resources were prominently provided by the city, the state legislature, or federal programs, but identity was central.

Whether the petitioners were Lincoln Hospital or the Sociedad Maricaeña, resources were leveraged to address Puerto Rican issues and problems. In fact, if there was one key limitation to Puerto Rican identity politics, it was not that it contravened basic liberal principles and values but that it pursued goals way beyond its resource capacity or that, as the fight of CAFA against *Fort Apache* illustrates, its chosen targets had more resources and were engaged in actions that did not provoke a generalized moral outrage. As Mayor Koch himself put it, *Fort Apache* may have been offensive to Puerto Ricans, but it was a good movie.

The preceding recollection supports the thesis that community-based collective action among Puerto Ricans in New York City blended liberalism and identity politics in ways that seem impossible through abstract considerations alone. In theory, individualism and community clash, but in the Puerto Rican experience, individuals created community through the affirmation of a collective identity that served both the group and its members. When students at Bronx Community College took over the college, they acted as a group because they had been treated as a group: "We have been treated rudely," they protested, "and now we are treating them in kind."[39] The liberal objection to group rights, that they provide blanket benefits that serve both the deserving and the undeserving, fails to recognize the possibility that the so-called undeserving might appear capable as individuals but are nevertheless vulnerable in virtue of membership in a group over which they have no control. At Bronx Community College, all Puerto Rican students had been mistreated—the good, the bad, and the mediocre.

Be that as it may, there is still the question whether identity politics has consequences that can only be avoided by the pursuit of a pure form of liberalism. When Ramón Colón wrote to Mayor Lindsay that "A million Puerto Ricans living in New York must fight for and honor their children born here,"[40] what was the appropriate prescription for action that followed? Did it follow that parents had to make sure that their children learn English and limit their use of Spanish in their own homes? Or should they organize, as they did, to work on the issues that affected them in Brooklyn through an organization whose logo—an image of El Morro—sent the symbolic message that their Puerto Rican culture should not be a private matter?

IDENTITY POLITICS RECONSIDERED

This leads me back to the set of questions that in Michael Kenny's view ought to be answered in order to ascertain the impact of identity politics and to assess whether it is really incompatible with liberalism. Once again, what follows is not a comprehensive critique but a pragmatic assembly of concise propositions based on the preceding empirical recollection. They are offered not as generalizations but as hypotheses for practice.

Is the pluralism of identity politics a pluralism of diversity or a pluralism of difference—is conflict in identity politics about interests or about principles? The distinction between diversity and difference in this question implies that one might be preferable to the other. In fact, it is a distinction without a difference, no pun intended, because one condition presupposes the other. Diversity implies difference and vice versa. Further, if the distinction between interests and principles is meant to suggest that conflict based on interests is amenable to compromise, whereas conflict based on principles is not, it is then important to establish the basis of conflict in identity politics along those lines.

The fact of the matter is, however, that conflict resolution depends not just on its basis but also on a variety of structural as well as contingent factors. Therefore, establishing whether conflict in identity politics is based on interests or principles is only a starting point; once that question is answered, one must determine whether any given conflict has precedents, study its institutional basis, elaborate the resources that might be needed to resolve it, and find out whether those resources are scarce, plentiful or even available, among other factors.

What the record suggests in the case of Puerto Ricans is that conflict was not predominantly about proposing alternative normative frameworks but rather about bridging the gap between existing normative ideals and socio-economic and political practice. To Mayor Lindsay, the normative ideal was the subordination of Puerto Rican to American identity. But to the Puerto Ricans that met with him in February 1966, this idea was not only offensive but unnecessary: they already knew they were Americans and being Puerto Rican did not make them forget they had an allegiance to New York and the United States. By emphasizing their Puerto Rican identity, all they wanted was for New York, represented by the mayor, not to forget that as citizens they had rights and that to fight for those rights they needed to come together and be treated as Puerto Ricans. That much was understood by the group that decided to use El Morro as their logo, as well as by those who organized based on their town of origin: this was not an exercise in nostalgia but a mechanism to secure participation, not to transform the system root and branch but to secure rights as a class of individuals in order to enjoy them as individuals who happened to belong to a class.

The record also suggests that the institutional order included mechanisms that could be used to contain and/or resolve conflict within reasonable parameters and that when conflict became disruptive or violent there were always elements within the political system and within the community willing and able to manage it. When teachers went on strike in 1968, the conflict was brought to an end through the intervention of Mayor Lindsay using the institutional tools available to him. But he was not alone: Puerto Rican elected officials, community organizations, and community leaders also jumped into the fray to help bring the conflict to closure.

When people like Ralph Poynter called for the burning of "whitey" textbooks from the pages of *The Guardian* and *Workers World*, the criticism was overwhelming. When a student barged into the classroom of a Jewish teacher asking how many were Christians, there was alarm but no violence. When whites called blacks watermelon-eating pigs or when Jews in the Bronx were beaten by Puerto Ricans, identity politics was at its ugliest even if it all boiled down, mostly, to name-calling and very little if any violence. Incidents like this did not proliferate and were brought under control not just by governmental and school leaders, but by the very individuals who were in the thick of conflict and did not approve. In fact, the most troubling aspect of expressions of this kind was that the impartiality of the authorities with the power to enforce the law could not be taken for granted.

Is the liberal idea of citizenship, that is, as individuals equal under the law, replaced in identity politics by the idea of singular group personality, of groups unequal under the law and therefore each requiring their own law? This question implies that identity politics rejects the possibility of commonality, that the boundaries between groups are permanently fixed and impenetrable. Puerto Ricans in New York City never saw themselves as such, not even in the context of anti-colonial sentiments and activities. Groups such as the National Association for the Advancement of the Hispanic American People of African Origin, Inc., and leaders like Julio Sabater, a.k.a Oggun Nike, were aberrations. In fact, in the majority of times when identity politics was at its worst, for example, when calls to complete the work initiated by

Hitler, to "kill whitey," and to build walls to separate school children were issued, or when books were banned because they allegedly did not fit the dominant identity discourse, Puerto Ricans were not the proponents or protagonists.

Resistance to bilingual education was a form of nefarious identity politics and in this case it was so because it represented the attempt by a majority ethnic group to impose its language over the language of an ethnic minority looking to integrate in two languages—the majority language and its own. When it came to language, Puerto Ricans did demand a law of their own; yet the country had had a Bilingual Education Act since 1968, four years before ASPIRA won the consent decree establishing bilingual education in New York, and the demand for bilingual education had been sanctioned and expanded by the U.S Supreme Court in *Lau vs. Nichols* (1974) on behalf of Chinese students in California. In this case, bilingual education was special for Puerto Ricans, but it was also a collective good enjoyed by all individuals who needed it in order to have access to a "meaningful education," a universal right.

What identity politics gave Puerto Ricans was not a singular personality irreducible to a common law but rather ethnic awareness and power awareness, that is, a sense of self in the context of place and a sense of how political actors were favored by the polity, respectively.[41] Ethnic awareness and power awareness gave them a vantage point to assess the degree to which they received equal or unequal treatment under the law; it never gave them a reason to reject this principle nor to promote public policies favoring segregation. And if they claimed to have a personality as Puerto Ricans, it was as a point of cultural and historical pride, as well as an attempt to make the point that Puertorricanness was used against them in the allocation of resources and benefits and that it was often the reason behind the violation of their citizen rights.

Put in perspective, if there was a problem with this it was that, in some cases—for example, the creation of the Puerto Rican Legal Institute—initiatives to seek redress were ephemeral, and their impact was limited or inconsequential. No group illustrated this point better than the NCPRR, with its extremely overextended agendas, a phenomenon that, when one takes a hard look at it, it is difficult to avoid the conclusion that Puerto Ricans were beset by so many problems that they were bound to fall into a state of overreach, and end up trying to do everything about everything. Thus, the problem was not so much that identity politics was divisive, that it drove wedges that made it impossible to bridge the gap between liberal and group rights, but that using a collective identity as the basis for the pursuit of liberal rights required commensurate resources to the same extent as in struggles where liberal means and ends were in synch.

As noted in Chapter 7, by April 1989, eight years after its founding, the attendance goal of NCPRR for its annual convention was a mere 250 people. This is all the group thought it could show for itself and the goal stands to reason as a function of limited growth. With only sixteen chapters nationally, organized under a loose federal structure, many of which were simply inactive, the organization could hardly set for itself a more ambitious goal. Actually, given the group's history, it could have, but it was precisely that history that told the organization, as it were, that it had been there and done that, with disappointing results, especially in New York.

Is it true that under identity politics each group has an "irreducible individuality and that each must struggle to achieve its self-realization, whatever the social and political costs?"[42] Nothing is worth pursuing "whatever the social and political costs." I repeat: nothing; the question is loaded. Yet, raising it helps articulate the notion that the costs of identity politics will vary depending on the context and circumstances in which they occur.

Puerto Ricans had a distinctive socio-cultural individuality that fit comfortably—at least in *their* view—within the parameters of a broader American identity. "We don't need to be reminded we are Americans first," is how some responded to Mayor Lindsay's hierarchy of identity at the 1966 meeting. It is reasonable to conclude that based on that understanding of identity, the social and political costs of identity politics would be minimal provided that demands were made according to the understanding that a Puerto Rican and an American identity were two sides of the same coin.

Even though the Puerto Rican Parade is not the focus of attention here, the literature shows, and the practical experience of the Parade confirms, that it was never an exercise in virulent, separatist nationalism.[43] During the 1967 riots in El Barrio, some Puerto Ricans exhorted the rioters to stop and go home...in Spanish! As much as inter-group relations were at times conflictive, ethnic pride was foremost an affirmation of self that was predicated on solidarity and cooperation rather than on the repression of different or even competing groups.

What was more consistently the case was action and efforts that were in synch with "the central norms of liberal politics—democratic inclusion, non-discrimination and equality of respect above all."[44] Puerto Rican identity politics at the community level and the instances of collective action in which Puerto Ricans were protagonists were for the most part constitutional, responsible, and effective in the sense specified by Richard Hofstadter. In other words, Puerto Ricans were bound by the rules of the existing constitutional consensus and legal framework, they formulated policies that were feasible, and they were capable of fashioning alliances and/or winning positions of power that provided opportunities to satisfy their policy preferences.[45]

Puerto Rican community institutions provided services, advocated for socio-economic benefits, asserted Puerto Rican culture, campaigned for bilingual education, and against racial segregation and police brutality. Collective action was in some cases disruptive but never destructive in a political sense, that is, rallies, marches, protests, boycotts, and civil disturbances did not undermine the viability of the political system. Disruptive collective action, in fact, belies in the most powerful way the notion that political viability requires exclusion; in fact, it is the other way around: to the extent that exclusion leads to disruptive action, it threatens political viability, liberal or otherwise.

Collective action was often spontaneous and triggered by neglect, e.g., students protesting the 1967 teacher strike, charging that their teachers did not care about them (See Chapter 3). The demands that followed action were affirmative rather than destructive, e.g., students occupying the registrar's office at Brooklyn College to demand courses on black history and the hiring of more black and Puerto Rican faculty, counselors, and staff (See Chapter 3), and the fights to improve services at Lincoln Hospital (See Chapter 4) and to save Hostos Community College (See Chapter 5).

Expressions of disrespect were another trigger, e.g., the implication in 1986 by Mayor Koch that Puerto Ricans and Latinos didn't count and that they only made it to positions of responsibility on the basis of ethnic identity rather than competence (See Chapter 7). Racist expressions and police brutality also provoked Puerto Rican action, e.g., the remarks by the Prime Minister of Japan that blacks, Puerto Ricans and Mexicans lowered the level of intelligence in the U.S. (See Chapter 7) and the shootings of James Powell in 1964 (See Chapter 2) and of Reinaldo Rodríguez in 1967 (See Chapter 3), respectively. Concerns about Puerto Rico were also part of the repertoire of causes for collective action, e.g., protests demanding the withdrawal of the U.S. Navy from the Puerto Rican offshore islands of Culebra (See Chapter 4) and Vieques (See Chapter 6).

The political system did not lose its stability and least of all collapse as a result of such actions. Instead, the scope of political participation was broadened and the pool of participants was enlarged. Collective action also helped articulate various claims. For example, the 1964 riot was used to demand a civilian review board, to exact promises to recruit more minorities for the police force, and to work towards better communication with citizens, which actually meant blacks and Puerto Ricans (See Chapter 2). In 1967, the leaders of the group El Grito del Barrio used the teacher's strike to call attention to the disparities in access to War on Poverty funds experienced by Puerto Rican organizations (See Chapter 3). These claims and demands were sometimes satisfied, sometimes not, but the point was never to question liberal democratic governance but to make it work for all.

This was not always understood by Puerto Ricans who saw no value in certain expressions of identity politics. For example, during the CAFA campaign against *Fort Apache*, Herman Badillo and Michael C. D. Macdonald published an Op Ed piece in the *New York Times* targeting Mayor Koch. Who cared about *Fort Apache* and negative representations of Puerto Ricans?, they asked, rhetorically. More important was the fact that the services provided by the city were in crisis, crime was up, the subway system was collapsing, housing blight was spreading, and racial polarization was intensifying. This was no movie! This was for real, and what Puerto Ricans needed was not a boycott of some racist film but "a mayor willing to fight the bankers on restructured debt and the realtors on higher assessments." Mayor Koch, not Paul Newman, was the person that needed to be challenged in 1981.[46]

This is not how CAFA saw it; the campaign against the movie provided a platform for subsequent organization that targeted Mayor Koch and his policies. In fact, it could actually be argued that had there been no CAFA campaign the point of contrast around which Badillo and MacDonald made their argument would not have been there, perhaps making their piece, if they had bothered to write it in the first place without the CAFA foil to provide a dramatic contrast, less gripping and therefore less effective.

In contrast to the position taken by Badillo and MacDonald, Richie Pérez emphasized that, "CAFA was the spearhead of a mass community movement. It was a broad coalition, uniting different sectors of our community and different perspectives. This was its main strength."[47] In this view, *Fort Apache* was more than just a movie. It was a galvanizing trigger that helped mobilized the community against distorted representations of its collective identity. The campaign against the film unified black and Puerto Rican groups and enabled cooperation between Puerto Ricans, Gays, Native Americans, and the Chinese community.[48] And this unity was not pursued for its own sake but to advance a political agenda against racism, for education, and democratic rights. This was identity politics at its best.

It is possible for identity politics to produce "rival visions of public life and social authority" that are incompatible with each other and it is possible to lose a sense of "shared moral and political purpose" in such a context.[49] Yet identity politics does not have a monopoly on these kinds of consequences. Regardless, this case study does not provide sufficient evidence to substantiate those possible outcomes. In their pursuit of claims based on identity, Puerto Ricans did clash with blacks, e.g., when Major Owens and African Americans were charged by Puerto Ricans for taking part in a conspiracy to destroy Puerto Rican groups, in which anti-poverty resources were disproportionately channelled towards black organizations (See Chapter 4).

But even in these cases, blacks were as much the target as were the policies that produced a context for rivalry, such as deciding that instead of allocating money to provide services to individuals, funds should be used to help organizations offer technical services to groups. In these types of conflicts, Puerto Ricans often could count on the support of notable political elites such as Arthur Goldberg, who saw his support as important in his quest for the governorship in 1970, as well as from Governor Rockefeller, who did so to take the wind out of Goldberg's sails (See Chapter 4). These were "social authorities" and protagonists in conflict, fighting for resources and political support but not to change the moral compass of the state nor its political principles and values.

In any event, even if competing aspirations were principled and resolved by compromise, resorting to compromise would be a problem only if these aspirations could be separated clearly and without a doubt as right or wrong, as good or evil, as extremes. Compromise would be problematic if, as Kukathas suggests, at one end of a liberal society there was a commitment to a common enterprise, and at the other end the only commitment was to the pursuit of separate ends, with nothing in between.[50]

This scenario is extreme and rarely if ever a generalized feature of any given society. In the absence of that kind of polarization, there is no reason to reject accommodation on the basis of identity as illiberal and no reason to reject the possibility that identity politics, when it entails compromise, is still compatible with liberalism and its commitment to a specific set of values.

CODA

In sum, in their quest for self-sufficiency, Puerto Rican community institutions embedded themselves in the fabric of the liberal democratic order. Identity politics was the thread that kept them in place. Antonia Pantoja had been half right: self-sufficiency was good as a normative goal but it had no chance of ever becoming real or sustainable over the long-run. Even today, organizations that eschew government funding because it threatens their autonomy still must raise money from others and are beholden to their policy preferences.

On the other hand, ethnic pride, which is only a measure of the quality of ethnic identity, was a constant and also provided the basis for community organization and mobilization more or less consistently over time. Along with the various instances of collective action that took place between 1960 and 1990, community institutions engaged in action that was driven by the ideal of a democratic community grounded in the principles of unity within diversity and equal treatment under the law.

Identity was the engine that propelled Puerto Ricans to pursue integration and liberal democratic justice. As Mario Figueroa, from the Comité del Estado 51 [Committee for State 51] put it in 1980, while marching in the Puerto Rican Parade, identity politics was a way of showing Americans that Puerto Ricans were "American citizens and Puerto Ricans at the same time."[51] For them, however, the synthesis of these two ingredients was embodied in the category of "Puerto Rican." That synthesis encapsulated a vision for advancement based on a framework of inclusive difference.

In *The Puerto Rican Journey,* C. Wright Mills and his collaborators noted that:

> The willful feeling that the individual can command the future to serve his own ends may be historically characteristic of industrial Protestant culture, but it is not a signal feature of the Latin American. [...] [S]ome few [Puerto Ricans] have begun planfully to strive but most retain the heritage of their island background.[52]

Puerto Ricans refuted this canard about Latin American culture in practice. Further, those Puerto Ricans who were willing and ready to strive, to serve their own ends willfully, did so, not in spite of their desire to retain their Puerto Rican identity, but as a result of using it to move forward.

One significant irony of the use of identity politics by Puerto Ricans to advance group interests can be found in an unintended consequence of the War on Poverty. War on Poverty programs helped develop a substantial group of Puerto Rican and Latino *individuals* as professionals working in governmental programs. These individuals, in many cases more so than the community at large, often were the major and immediate beneficiaries of programs intended to serve group needs.[53] In the process, these professionals fought to protect their autonomy, to secure their individual rights, and to express their singular place in the liberal socio-political system as Puerto Ricans, as Latinos, and as U.S. citizens.

In 2016, 150 Puerto Ricans gathered in Camden, New Jersey, to formulate a program of advocacy for Puerto Ricans in Puerto Rico and the United States. They highlighted the need for reforms on electoral representation, educational access, employment, health care, and the colonial condition of Puerto Rico, among other issues. The meeting established the National Puerto Rican Agenda and its Board of Directors included local, state, and congressional elected officials. José "Che" Velázquez, a high-ranking official in the New York branch of the Puerto Rican Socialist Party in the 1970s, wrote the story of the Camden event, and from its content, it could have had the title "Puerto Ricans in the U.S. Fight for Living Democracy," which would have been similar to the title of the article written by Art Shields for *The Daily Worker* in 1938, cited in the introduction: "Puerto Ricans in Harlem Fight for Living Democracy."

The new group included in its Steering Committee former revolutionaries, but its agenda did not give a hint of transformational aspirations, not even in regards to the question of colonialism. In this "new" iteration of identity politics, the old call for "¡Independencia Ya, Socialismo Ahora Mismo!" [Independence Now, Socialism Right Now!] that was proffered by pro-independence organizations during the 1970s, was now a call for "decolonization or ending the territorial status of Puerto Rico," a formulation that left the door open for statehood. Some participants in the Camden event described themselves as activists without acknowledging their socialist background.[54] In a way, their orientation could be interpreted as a small-scale incidence of *corsi e ricorsi,* loosely understood, marked by an agenda rooted both in the affirmation of identity claims and liberal values.

NOTES

Introduction

[1] See José E. Cruz, *Puerto Rican Identity, Political Development, and Democracy in New York, 1960-1990* (Lanham, MD: Lexington Books/Rowman & Littlefield, 2017).

[2] I first offered this definition of ethnic identity in José E. Cruz, *Identity and Power: Puerto Rican Politics and the Challenge of Ethnicity* (Philadelphia: Temple University Press, 1998), p. 11; For a similar definition based on a case study of West Indians in New York City see Philip Kasinitz, *Caribbean New York* (Ithaca: Cornell University Press, 1992), pp. 4-5.

[3] See Nicholas Rescher, *Aporetics, Rational Deliberation in the Face of Inconsistency* (Pittsburgh: University of Pittsburgh Press, 2009), p. 5.

[4] Phillip Cole, *Philosophies of Exclusion: Liberal Political Theory and Immigration* (Edinburgh: Edinburgh University Press, 2000), p. 2.

[5] Melissa S. Williams, *Voice, Trust, and Memory, Marginalized Groups and the Failings of Liberal Representation* (Princeton, NJ: Princeton University Press, 1998), pp. 15-16; 8.

[6] Thomas W. Pogge, "Group Rights and Ethnicity," in Ian Shapiro and Will Kymlicka, eds., *Ethnicity and Group Rights* (New York: New York University Press, 1997), p. 188.

[7] Chandran Kukathas, *The Liberal Archipelago* (Oxford: Oxford University Press, 2003), pp. 4-9.

[8] Ibid., pp. 262-263.

[9] Ibid., p. 268.

[10] Steven Kautz, *Liberalism and Community* (Ithaca, NY: Cornell University Press, 1995), pp. 23, 28.

[11] See Carol Horton, *Race and the Making of American Liberalism* (New York: Oxford University Press, 2005).

[12] See Will Kymlicka, *Multicultural Citizenship* (New York: Oxford University Press, 1995) and *Liberalism, Community, and Culture* (Oxford: Clarendon Press, 1989), pp. 135-161; Iris Marion Young, *La justicia y la política de la diferencia* (Madrid: Ediciones Cátedra, 2000), pp. 12, 266; and David Ingram, *Group Rights, Reconciling Equality and Difference* (Lawrence, KS: University Press of Kansas, 2000).

[13] Kenneth R. Hoover, *A Politics of Identity, Liberation and the Natural Community* (Urbana, IL: University of Illinois Press, 1975). p. 2

[14] Ibid., p. 156.

[15] Santosh C. Saha, "Introduction," in Santosh C. Saha, ed., *The Politics of Ethnicity and National Identity* (New York: Peter Lang, 2007), p. 1.

[16] Paul J. Magnarella, "The Black Panther Party's Confrontation with Ethnicity, Race and Class," in Santosh C. Saha, ed., *The Politics of Ethnicity and National Identity* (New York: Peter Lang, 2007), pp. 56-62.

[17] Angelo Falcón, "Puerto Ricans and the Politics of Racial Identity," in Herbert W. Harris, et al., eds., *Racial and Ethnic Identity: Psychological Development and Creative Expression* (New York: Routledge, 1995), pp. 193-194; 200-203; 193-207.

[18] Ibid. p. 205.

[19] Aristotle, *The Politics* (New York: Penguin Books, 1982), p. 169.

20 Ibid., p. 179.
21 See Tamar Carroll, *Mobilizing New York: AIDS, Antipoverty, and Feminist Activism* (Chapell Hill, NC: University of North Carolina Press, 2015).
22 A. L. Epstein, *Ethos and Identity* (London: Tavistock Publications, 1978), p. 101.
23 James Baldwin, "Princes and Powers," in *Nobody Knows My Name* (New York: Dell Publishing, 1961), p. 26.
24 Xavier F. Totti and Félix V. Matos Rodríguez, "Activism and Change Among Puerto Ricans in New York, 1960s and 1970s" *CENTRO Journal* 21: 2 (Fall 2009), p. 4.
25 Antonia Pantoja, "Puerto Ricans in New York: A Historical and Community Development Perspective," *Centro* 2:5 (Primavera 1989), p. 24.
26 Ibid.
27 Ibid., p. 31.
28 Carlos Vargas-Ramos, "Puerto Rican Political and Civic Engagement in the United States," In Edwin Meléndez and Carlos Vargas-Ramos, eds., *Puerto Ricans at the Dawn of the New Millennium* (New York: Centro de Estudios Puertorriqueños, 2014), p. 262.
29 Ernest Gellner, "Introduction," in Ernest Gellner and César Cansino, *Liberalism in Modern Times* (Budapest: Central European University Press, 1996), p. 4.
30 Art Shields, "Puerto Ricans in Harlem Fight for Living Democracy," *The Daily Worker*, September 28, 1938, p. 4.
31 Judith F. Herbstein claims that the Forum was created in 1954, and she cites a 1973 agency newsletter. See Rituals and Politics of the Puerto Rican "Community" in New York City, Ph.D. Dissertation, City University of New York, 1978, p. 130. The newsletter account in all likelihood confused and conflated the creation of the Forum with the establishment of the Hispanic Young Adults Association (HYAA). A Puerto Rican Association for Community Affairs brochure says HYAA started in 1953. In her interview on May 24, 1988 with Amílcar Tirado and Carlos Sanabria, Josephine Nieves says that HYAA started in 1954. According to Nieves, the funding for ASPIRA was provided by the New York Foundation in 1957 in the amount of $70,000. This contradicts Toni Pantoja's account in her memoir. According to Pantoja, funding to establish ASPIRA from the New York, Field, Hofheimer, Rockefeller Brothers, and Taconic Foundations was obtained in 1961. See Antonia Pantoja, *Memoir of a Visionary: Antonia Pantoja* (Houston, TX: Arte Público Press, 2002), p. 99. In a 2002 interview with Lillian Jiménez, Maria Canino mentions Charles Silverman, from Consolidated Cigar, as a major donor. The interviews of Josephine Nieves and Maria Canino are at the Archives of the Puerto Rican Diaspora, Centro de Estudios Puertorriqueños, Hunter College, CUNY, hereinafter referred to as Centro Archives, and at the Latino Educational Media Center, Bronx, NY, respectively.
32 Michael Kenny, The Politics of Identity (Malden, MA: Polity, 2004), p. 3.
33 Renato Rosaldo, "Cultural Citizenship and Educational Democracy," *Cultural Anthropology* 9 (August 1994): 402-11.
34 Rina Benmayor, "Gender, College, and Cultural Citizenship: A Case Study of Mexican-Heritage Students in Higher Education," in Kia Lilly Caldwell, et al., eds., *Gendered Citizenships* (New York: Palgrave Macmillan, 2009), pp. 138-139.
35 María Teresa Babín, "Lengua y Ciudadanía," *La Voz de Puerto Rico en U.S.A.*, April 1956, p.

3. Archival collection/newspapers, reel 6. Centro Archives.
[36] Kenny, op. cit, p. 4.
[37] Ibid., p. 10.
[38] Ibid.
[39] Ibid., p. 17.
[40] Ibid., p. 19.
[41] Ibid.
[42] The three following references from the literature on Puerto Rican radical politics illustrate the points made above, respectively. Johanna L. del C. Fernández, Radicals in the late 1960s: A history of the Young Lords Party in New York City, 1969-1974, Ph.D. dissertation, Columbia University, 2004; Rose Muzio, *Radical Imagination, Radical Humanity: Puerto Rican Political Activism in New York* (Albany: SUNY Press, 2017); José E. Cruz, "Pushing Left to Get to the Center: Puerto Rican Radicalism in Hartford, Connecticut," in Andrés Torres and José E. Vélazquez, eds., *The Puerto Rican Movement, Voices from the Diaspora* (Philadelphia: Temple University Press, 1998).
[43] Even though I've applied this method in previous publications, it will probably become better known through the book *1947* by Elisabeth Åsbrink. Her book was reviewed in the "Briefly Noted" section of *The New Yorker* issue of March 12, 2018, p. 77. Åsbrink described the book as a "splintered whole" and the reviewer described it as a "careful juxtaposition of disparate events."
[44] Alasdair MacIntyre, "The Indispensability of Political Theory," in David Miller and Larry Siedentop, eds., *The Nature of Political Theory* (Oxford: Clarendon Press, 1983), p. 32.
[45] A note on style: The capitalization of headlines in *El Diario-La Prensa* is different at different times. The format of the title of the journal of the Center for Puerto Rican studies also varies over time. In all citations I followed the style of the source. In the text, regarding accents, I followed the rule for all Spanish words and names rather than usage by individuals and sources. Except where indicated, all citations from Spanish sources translated from Spanish to English are mine.

Chapter 1

[1] Edwin Meléndez, ed., Puerto Rico Post-Maria (New York: Center for Puerto Rican Studies, 2018), p. 4.
[2] Danielle Paquette, "Why a White Town Paid for a Class Called 'Hispanics 101'," *The Washington Post*, March 7, 2018. Thanks to Greg Nowell for bringing this article to my attention.
[3] Edgardo Meléndez, *Sponsored Migration, The State and Puerto Rican Postwar Migration to the United States* (Columbus, OH: Ohio State University Press, 2017).
[4] For documentation on Hawaii, Connecticut, and New Jersey as destinations see respectively, Blase Camacho Souza, "Trabajo y Tristeza—"Work and Sorrow": The Puerto Ricans of Hawaii 1900-1902," *The Hawaiian Journal of History* 18 (1984), pp. 156-173; Edna Acosta-Belén, et al., "Adiós Borinquen Querida:" *The Puerto Rican Diaspora, Its History and Contributions* (Albany, NY: CELAC, 2000), pp. 19-20; Cruz, *Identity and Power*, pp. 47-48;

Meléndez, *Sponsored Migration*, pp. 198-204.

5 "Boricuas Se Diseminan en Todo N. York," *El Diario de Nueva York*, November 2, 1962, p. 2.

6 Douglas D. Richards, "Censo Revela Electores Boricuas en N.Y. son 300,000," *El Mundo*, September 4, 1963, p. 1.

7 Thanks to Carlos E. Santiago for his research on this section when we collaborated on the paper "The Changing Socioeconomic and Political Fortunes of Puerto Ricans in New York City: 1960-1990," for the 2000 symposium honoring Antonia Pantoja held at the Center for Puerto Rican Studies.

8 Paul W. McCraken, "Economic Policy and the Lessons of Experience," in Melvin R. Laird, ed., *Republican Papers* (New York: Praeger, 1968), p. 378.

9 Fred Ferretti, *The Year the Big Apple Went Bust* (New York: G.P. Putnam's Sons, 1976), p. 28.

10 For a discussion of the political dimensions of New York City's financial crisis, see Martin Shefter, *Political Crisis, Fiscal Crisis: The Collapse and Revival of New York City* (New York: Columbia University Press, 1992); Ester Fuchs, *Mayors and Money: Fiscal Policy in New York and Chicago* (Chicago: University of Chicago Press, 1992).

11 Ferretti, op. cit., p. 129.

12 In a *New York Times* article published on December 28, 2006, Sam Roberts tried to rehabilitate Ford by noting that he never said those words. But this is beside the point. Ford thought that the government of New York City was irresponsible and undeserving of federal help. See http://www.nytimes.com/2006/12/28/nyregion/28veto.html?_r=0 <Accessed July 21, 2014>

13 Ferretti, op. cit., pp. 181-182.

14 Ibid., p. 366.

15 Data from U.S. Department of Labor, U.S. Department of Commerce, Manpower Report of the President, 1964; New York City Council Against Poverty, December 1965. Edward Mercado Papers, Series VII Subject Files, Box 10, Folder 29. Centro Archives.

16 Carlos E. Santiago, "The Migratory Impact of Minimum Wage Legislation: Puerto Rico, 1970-1987," *International Migration Review*, 27: 4 (Winter 1992).

17 Ibid., p. 791.

18 Francisco Rivera-Batiz and Carlos E. Santiago, *Puerto Ricans in the United States: A Changing Reality* (Washington, D.C.: National Puerto Rican Coalition, 1994), pp. 114-115.

19 Vargas-Ramos, op. cit.

20 David Zarefsky, *President Johnson's War on Poverty, Rhetoric and History* (Tuscaloosa, AL: University of Alabama Press, 1986), p. 21. This section is based on Zarefsky's account.

21 Ibid., p. 34.

22 Ibid., pp. 38-39.

23 Mason B. Williams, *City of Ambition, FDR, La Guardia, and the Making of Modern New York* (New York: W. W. Norton & Company, 2013), p. 109.

24 See Desmond S. King and Rogers M. Smith, "Racial Orders in American Political Development," *The American Political Science Review* 99: 1 (February 2005): 75-92.

25 Michael Lapp, Managing Migration: The Migration Division of Puerto Rico and Puerto Ricans in New York City, 1948-1968, Ph.D. Dissertation, Johns Hopkins University, 1990, p. 307.

26 Judith Herbstein, Rituals and Politics of the Puerto Rican "Community" in New York City, Ph.D. Dissertation, City University of New York, 1978, p. 130.
27 "The Puerto Rican Forum," Editorial, *El Diario-La Prensa*, November 10, 1964, p. 17.
28 Lapp, op. cit., pp. 300-303.
29 Interview of Josephine Nieves by Amílcar Tirado and Carlos Sanabria, May 24, 1988.
30 Flyer for National Puerto Rican March for Justice, Diana Caballero Papers, Series V, National Congress for Puerto Rican Rights, Box 17, Folder 4. Centro Archives.
31 Press Release, "National Movement for Puerto Rican Empowerment to March on Washington-Oct. 4," September 26, 1986. Diana Caballero Papers, Series V, National Congress for Puerto Rican Rights, Box 15, Folder 1. Centro Archives.
32 Summary of Work Done by the Women's T.F. of the Last Two Years, 1984-1986. Lourdes Torres Papers, Series V, Committee Against Fort Apache, Box 8, Folder 3. Centro Archives.
33 Puerto Rican Worker, Report of the Labor Task Force of the New York Chapter of the Congress for Puerto Rican Rights, c. 1986. Lourdes Torres Papers, Series IV, National Congress for Puerto Rican Rights, Box 4, Folder 15. Centro Archives.
34 Isabel Malavet, "Let's Vote to Elect a Mayor for the People," *En Nueva York*, Newsletter of the N.Y.C. chapter of the National Congress for Puerto Rican Rights, January 1989, Diana Caballero Papers, Series V, National Congress for Puerto Rican Rights, Box 16, Folder 12. Centro Archives.
35 Letter of Eddie Baca to Dear Alice, February 20, 1989. Diana Caballero Papers, Series VII, Subject Files, Box 28, Folder 2. Centro Archives.
36 Nathan Glazer and Daniel Patrick Moynihan, *Beyond the Melting Pot: The Negroes, Puerto Ricans, Jews, Italians, and Irish of New York City*, 2nd Edition (Cambridge, MA: MIT Press, 1970), xxiii-xxiv.

Chapter 2

1 See Herman Badillo, *One Nation, One Standard, An Ex-Liberal on How Hispanics Can Succeed Just Like Other Immigrant Groups* (New York: Sentinel, 2006), pp. 1-8.
2 Phil Santora, "A Stepchild Torn by Two Loyalties," *Daily News*, December 15, 1964, p. 1.
3 "Puerto Rican Groups Here in Vote Registration Drive," *The Worker*, October 6, 1963, p. 1.
4 Angel M. Arroyo, "Gotitas de mi Tintero," *El Imparcial*, September 18, 1963, p. 18.
5 Douglas D. Richards, "Censo Revela Electores Boricuas en N.Y. son 300,000," *El Mundo*, September 4, 1963, p. 1.
6 Commonwealth of Puerto Rico, Department of Labor, Migration Division, *Monthly Activities Report of the Migration Division, July 1964*, pp. 6, 13. Migration Division Collection, Monthly Reports, Box 3. Centro Archives.
7 "Mobilization of the Legion of Voters," Editorial, *El Diario La Prensa*, November 9, 1964, p. 15.
8 Luisa A. Quintero, "Marginalia," *El Diario-La Prensa*, June 30, 1964, p. 16.
9 Peter Kihss, "City's Puerto Rican Voters Appear Heavily Pro-Johnson, but G.O.P. Believes It Can Cut the Margin," *New York Times*, September 15, 1964, p. 22.
10 "The Puerto Rican Forum," Editorial, *El Diario-La Prensa*, November 10, 1964, p. 17.

[11] Luisa A. Quintero, "Boricua es el Más Sufrido En su Pobreza," *El Diario-La Prensa*, November 8, 1964, p. 2.

[12] Screvane was council president from 1962 to 1965. Erazo claims that when Screvane decided to run in the primary for the mayoral candidacy against Abe Beame in 1965, he came to "call in the chit." Erazo did not support Screvane, which allegedly made the latter very angry at Erazo. Interview of Joseph Erazo by Lillian Jiménez, March 20, 2002. Latino Educational Media Center, Bronx, NY.

[13] Outline of the Puerto Rican Community Development Project, n.d., Frank Torres Papers, Series VI Organizations, Box 21, Folder 3. Centro Archives.

[14] Video interview of Manuel "Manny" Díaz, Jr., used for production of documentary *Politics con Sabor*, Terramax Entertainment, LLC, 2004. Centro Archives. All interviews from this source hereafter referred to as "Terramax."

[15] Erazo interview, 2002.

[16] Díaz, Jr., Terramax, 2004.

[17] Estado Libre Asociado de Puerto Rico, Departamento del Trabajo, División de Migración, *Informe Anual, Año Fiscal 1964-65*, pp. 103-104, 106. Migration Division Collection, Annual Reports, Box 2. Centro Archives.

[18] Esli Ramón González, "Piquetearán City College Por Discrimen Contra Hispanos," *El Diario de Nueva York*, November 1, 1962, p. 3; Esli Ramón González, "Siguen Preparando Piquetes Hispanos Al City College," *El Diario de Nueva York*, November 2, 1962, p. 2.

[19] "City College," Editorial, *El Diario de Nueva York*, November 19, 1962, p. 14; "El Diario y La Prensa Donan $500 Para la Compra Libros en Español Para City College," *El Diario de Nueva York*, November 20, 1962, p. 2.

[20] "Organizaciones del Bronx Apoyan Depto. Hispano En El City College," *El Diario de Nueva York*, November 16, 1962, p.15.

[21] "Piquete Contra City College es Aplazado," *El Diario de Nueva York*, November 15, 1962, p. 2.

[22] Esli Ramón González, "Sale a Relucir Nombre del Rector Benítez En la Controversia Del City College de N.Y.," *El Diario de Nueva York*, November 14, 1962, p. 2.

[23] Esli Ramón González, "City College Vela Por El Maestro, No Por Su Origen," *El Diario de Nueva York*, November 13, 1962, p. 3.

[24] Esli Ramón González, "Explica City College Cese Maestros Hispanos," *El Diario de Nueva York*, November 9, 1962, p. 3.

[25] Esli Ramón González, "Niega Discrimen en City College," *El Diario de Nueva York*, November 8, 1962, p. 5.

[26] "Wagner Pedirá Informe del Caso City Hall," *El Diario de Nueva York*, November 4, 1962, p. 3.

[27] "Anuncia el Lic. John Carro Que la Organización ASPIRA Inaugurará Centro de Estudios Puertorriqueños el Día 19," *El Diario de Nueva York*, November 16, 1962, p. 2.

[28] Leonard Buder, "Boycott Cripples City Schools," *The New York Times*, February 4, 1964, p. 1. Buder may have cited Rustin incorrectly.

[29] Jerald E. Podair, *The Strike that Changed New York, Blacks, Whites, and the Ocean Hill-Brownville Crisis* (New Haven: Yale University Press, 2002), p. 31.

[30] "School Board Members Picketed in Snowfall," *The Worker*, January 12, 1965, p. 2.

31 "Rev. Galamison Arrested," January 24, 1965; "B'klyn School Pickets Hit Overcrowding," January 26, 1965; "School Boycott Gains Momentum," January 31, 1965. Jesús Colón Papers, Newspaper Clippings, Box 2, Folder 5, Centro Archives.

32 "More Schools Boycotted." February 9, 1965. Jesús Colón Papers, Newspaper Clippings, Box 2, Folder 5, Centro Archives.

33 "20 Schools Now in Boycott." February 14, 1965. Ibid.

34 "More Schools Boycotted."

35 John I. Ortiz, Jr. "Platicas en el Batey Neoyorquino," *El Diario de Nueva York*, November 3, 1961, p. 18.

36 "Always a Problem: Low Rent Housing," *El Diario-La Prensa*, November 8, 1963, p. 21.

37 Memo from Andrew P. Kerr to John V. Lindsay, et al., October 15, 1971. John V. Lindsay Papers, Subject Files 1966-1973, Box 16 Folder 190. Municipal Archives, New York City, hereafter referred to as NYC Archives.

38 "Blockbusting: A Low Tactic," *El Diario-La Prensa*, November 11, 1963, p. 15.

39 "Mayores Quejas a Nuestra Unidad Móvil: Sobre Alquileres," *El Diario-La Prensa*, November 7, 1963, p. 10.

40 "Declaran Huelga Varios Inquilinos de Harlem," *El Diario-La Prensa*, November 6, 1963, p. 12.

41 Esli Ramón González, "Continúa Huelga De 110 Familias en Pago de Alquileres," *El Diario-La Prensa*, November 7, 1963, p. 5.

42 "Acusan a 2 de Haber Pegado Fuego a Casas en 'El Barrio,'" *El Diario-La Prensa*, November 7, 1963, p. 4.

43 "Discutirán Problemas Afectan a los Hispanos," *El Diario-La Prensa*, November 11, 1963, p. 10.

44 Fred Gilman, "Harlem Tenant Pickets Jolt a Smug City Hall," *The Worker*, January 26, 1965. Jesús Colón Papers, Newspaper Clippings, Box 2, Folder 5, Centro Archives.

45 Woody Klein, *Lindsay's Promise, The Dream That Failed* (London: The Macmillan Company, 1970), pp. 81-83.

46 Doug Archer, "Angry Tenants Stage Housing Office Sit-in" March 9, 1965. Jesús Colón Papers, Newspaper Clippings, Box 2, Folder 5, Centro Archives.

47 "Remember," Editorial, *El Diario-La Prensa*, November 6, 1966, p. 25.

48 Mike A. Correa, "Inician Juicio a Policías Acusados Golpear Boricua," *El Diario-La Prensa*, November 4, 1965, p. 5.

49 "Remember." In this editorial his name is spelled "Trifulo." Trífilo is used in "Recopilan Datos Rodearon Muerte de Trífilo Rubero," *El Diario-La Prensa*, November 3, 1966, p. 2.

50 Mario González, "Constituyen Comité Boricua Contra Brutalidad Policíaca," *El Diario-La Prensa*, November 15, 1966, p. 4.

51 Fred Gilman, "Public Refuses to Take Cops' Alibi on Killing," *The Worker*, February 25, 1964. Jesús Colón Papers, Newspaper Clippings, Box 2, Folder 2. Centro Archives.

52 Mike Davidow, "6,000 Cross Brooklyn Bridge in Unity Anti-Bias March," *The Worker*, March 3, 1964. Ibid.

53 Doug Archer, "Seven Arrested During Sitdown Protesting Police Brutality," March 10, 1964. Ibid.

54 Mike Davidow, "City Hall March Sunday Will Protest Slaying," *The Worker*, March 1, 1964; Fred Gilman, "City Sued for $1,000,000 for Cop's Slaying of Youth," *The Worker*, March 3,

1964, p. 8; Fred Gilman, "Committee Fights Police Brutality," *The Worker*, March 8, 1964. Ibid.
55 Fred Gilman, "Harlem Rally Denounces 'Frisk' and 'No Knock' Laws," *The Worker*, March 10, 1964, p. 8.
56 Local 1199 of the Retail Drug Employees Union was formed by blacks and Puerto Ricans pushing for a more responsive union. See Johanna L. del C. Fernández, op. cit., p. 57.
57 Mike Davidow, "City Hall March Sunday Will Protest Slaying," *The Worker*, March 1, 1964. Jesús Colón Papers, Newspaper Clippings, Box 2, Folder 2. Centro Archives.
58 Fred Gilman, "Harlem Rally Denounces 'Frisk' and 'No Knock' Laws," *The Worker*, March 10, 1964, p. 8.
59 "Remember."
60 Luisa A. Quintero, "Badillo y Heuvel Preparan Plan en Pro de Boricuas," *El Diario-La Prensa*, December 8, 1971, p. 4.
61 Selwyn Raab, "Pickets to Protest Prisoner Hangings," *New York World Telegram and Sun*, March 31, 1965; "Boricuas Piquetearán los Sábados Cuarteles Policía," *El Tiempo*, April 9, 1965. Jesús Colón Papers, Newspaper Clippings, Box 2, Folder 6, Centro Archives.
62 Memo from Gilberto Gerena Valentín to National Association for Puerto Rican Civil Rights members, no date. Jesús Colón Papers, Correspondence, Box 4, Folder 1, Centro Archives.
63 "Police Establish Puerto Rican Aids," *The New York Times*, March 29, 1965, p. 35.
64 "City Hall Readying Another Police Whitewash." April 13, 1965. Jesús Colón Papers, Newspaper Clippings, Box 2, Folder 5, Centro Archives.
65 Peter Kihss, "Police Assailed by Puerto Ricans," *The New York Times*, April 7, 1965, p. 45.
66 "Puerto Ricans Picket Police," *New York Times*, April 11, 1965, p. 80.
67 Thomas Buckley, "Councilmen Seek Panel on Police," *The New York Times*, May 16, 1965, p. 1.
68 "Police Board Plan Stirring Protests," *The New York Times*, May 18, 1965, p. 24; "Mr. Murphy Resigns," *The New York Times*, May 19, 1965, p. 46.
69 Richard Witkin, "Lindsay Proposes Adding Civilians to Police Board," *The New York Times*, May 21, 1965, p. 1.
70 Homer Bigart, "5,000 Policemen Picket City Hall," *The New York Times*, June 30, 1965, p. 1.
71 "Council to Consider Review Board Issue," *The New York Times*, July 15, 1965, p. 26.
72 "Puerto Rican Community Hails 'Police Friend' Plan," *The New York Times*, June 1, 1965, p. 29.
73 Homer Bigart, "Policeman Kills Brooklyn Negro," *The New York Times*, July 16, 1965, p. 1; Homer Bigart, "Protest is Renewed," *The New York Times*, July 17, 1965, p. 1.
74 Theodore Jones, "Police-Review Rules Revised; Right to Question is Extended," *The New York Times*, July 18, 1965, p. 1.
75 Spanish Press Digest, Mayor's Press Office, August 15-27, 1971. John V. Lindsay Papers, Subject Files 1966-1973, Box 104 Folder 1966. NYC Archives.
76 Fred C. Shapiro and James W. Sullivan, *Race Riots, New York 1964* (New York: Thomas Y. Crowell Company, 1964), pp. 1-2; 43.
77 Ibid., p. 94.
78 Ibid., p. 127.
79 Ibid., pp. 5-6.
80 Ibid., pp. 8-9.

81 Ibid., p. 82.
82 Ibid., pp. 63-64.
83 Ibid., p. 88.
84 Ibid., p. 172.
85 Ibid., p. 65.
86 Ibid., p. 86.
87 Ibid., p. 158.
88 Ibid., pp. 88-89; 206.

Chapter 3

1 "Primera Reunión Pro Federación Organizaciones de Brooklyn." Jesús Colón Papers, New York Organizations, Box 1, Folder 5. Centro Archives.
2 Charles G. Bennett, "Lindsay Rejects Ethnic Job Rule," *New York Times*, February 3, 1966, p. 27.
3 Paul Hoffman, "Mayor Criticized by Puerto Ricans," *New York Times*, February 5, 1966, p. 20; Western Union Telegram from Ramon Colon to John V. Lindsay, March 11, 1966. John V. Lindsay Papers, Subject Files 1966-1973, Box 94, Folder 1714, NYC Archives.
4 Jean-Jacques Rousseau, *The Social Contract and Discourses* (London: J.M. Dent Ltd, 1973), p. 204.
5 Commonwealth of Puerto Rico, Department of Labor, Migration Division, *Monthly Activities Report of the Migration Division, August 1966; September 1966*, pp. 6, 7, respectively. Migration Division Collection, Monthly Reports, Box 4, Centro Archives.
6 Commonwealth of Puerto Rico, Department of Labor, Migration Division, *Monthly Activities Report of the Migration Division, September 1967*, p. 2. Migration Division Collection, Monthly Reports, Box 4. Centro Archives.
7 Estado Libre Asociado de Puerto Rico, Departamento del Trabajo, División de Migración, *Informe Anual, Año Fiscal 1968-69*, pp. 119-123. Migration Division Collection, Annual Reports, Box 3. Centro Archives.
8 "Favorece Boricuas en EU Voten en Plebiscito," *El Diario-La Prensa*, December 30, 1966, p. 5; "Comité Pro Voto de Boricuas en NY," *El Diario-La Prensa*, December 18, 1966, p. 2.
9 "93 de Cada 100 Boricuas en E.U. Quieren Votar en Plebiscito P.R.," *El Diario-La Prensa*, December 21, 1966, p. 3. An earlier story puts the proportion at 91 percent. See "91% Quiere Votar en Plebiscito de P. Rico," *El Diario-La Prensa*, December 16, 1966, p. 5.
10 "A RSV: No Ignore Sentimientos de Boricuas: Ramos," *El Diario-La Prensa*, December 15, 1966, p. 5.
11 José Lumen Román, "El Plebiscito de Puerto Rico," *El Imparcial*, January 30, 1967, P. 12.
12 Salvador Guzmán, "Dice Boricuas Exterior Tienen Derecho a Votar," *El Imparcial*, March 3, 1967. Jesús Colón Papers, Newspaper Clippings, Box 2, Folder 8. Centro Archives.
13 "Hacen Llamamiento a los que Desean la Estadidad Para PR," *El Diario-La Prensa*, March 27, 1967, p. 10.
14 The airport is now named after Governor Luis Muñoz Marín.
15 "No Los Escucharon," photo, *El Diario-La Prensa*, April 24, 1967, p. 21; "Considerarán Hoy Peregrinación de Boricuas a San Juan Desde N.Y.," *El Diario-La Prensa*, April, 24, 1967, p. 6.

16 "Puerto Rican Rally Assails Plebiscite," *New York Times,* July 17, 1967, p. 9; Henry Giniger, "Puerto Rico Vote Strongly Favors Commonwealth," *New York Times,* July 24, 1967, p. 1; Carmen E. Gautier, "The Flaw in Puerto Rico's Plebiscite," Letter to the Editor, *New York Times,* September 20, 1972, p. 46.

17 Hereafter this council is referred to as Council Against Poverty or CAP.

18 Letter of Rev. Ruben Dario Colon to John V. Lindsay, May 11, 1966; Letter of John V. Lindsay to Rev. Ruben Dario Colon, June 1, 1966. John V. Lindsay Papers, Subject Files 1966-1973, Box 94, Folder 1714. NYC Archives.

19 Memo to Arnold Fraiman From Undisclosed Source, May 1, 1967. John V. Lindsay Papers, Subject Files 1966-1973, Box 30, Folder 544. NYC Archives.

20 Quarterly Report, April/June 1966, The City of New York, Commission on Human Rights. John V. Lindsay Papers, Subject Files 1966-1973, Box 30, Folder 544. NYC Archives.

21 Luisa A. Quintero, "Marginalia—Gran Jurado," *El Diario-La Prensa,* October 6, 1966, p. 22.

22 Esli Ramón González, "Que se Vaya Marks, Piden Los Boricuas," *El Diario-La Prensa,* December 22, 1966, p. 4.

23 Esli Ramón González, "Acuerdan Hacer Nuevos Piquetes Contra Marks," *El Diario-La Prensa,* January 8, 1967, p. 2.

24 Ibid., p. 128.

25 Luisa A. Quintero, "Marginalia-Corporación Comunal," *El Diario-La Prensa,* December 19, 1966, p. 18.

26 New York City People's Board of Education, Press Release, February 28, 1967. John V. Lindsay Papers, Subject Files 1966-1973, Box 22, Folder 390. NYC Archives.

27 Ibid.

28 Remarks by Mayor John V. Lindsay Before the Conference: "Puerto Ricans Confront the Problems of Urban Society: A Design for Change," April 15, 1967. John V. Lindsay Papers, Subject Files 1966-1973, Box 94, Folder 1714. NYC Archives. In the conference program the title is "Puerto Ricans Confront Problems of the Complex Urban Society: A Design for Change," Edward Mercado Papers, Series VII Subject Files, Box 14, Folder 18. Centro Archives.

29 Commonwealth of Puerto Rico, Department of Labor, Migration Division, *Monthly Activities Report of the Migration Division, April 1967,* p. 7. Migration Division Collection, Monthly Reports, Box 4. Centro Archives.

30 "Recomendaciones para la conferencia puertorriqueña (Abril 15-16, 1967)." Jesús Colón Papers, Series VI, Box 1, Folder 9. Centro Archives.

31 Program of "Puerto Ricans Confront Problems of the Complex Urban Society: A Design for Change," Edward Mercado Papers, Series VII Subject Files, Box 14, Folder 18. Centro Archives.

32 Letter of G. Gerena-Valentin to John V. Lindsay, August 8, 1967, with accompanying recommendations. John V. Lindsay Papers, Subject Files 1966-1973, Box 94, Folder 1714. NYC Archives.

33 Letter of John V. Lindsay to Antonia Pantoja, September 26, 1967. Ibid.

34 Memo of Jason R. Nathan to John V. Lindsay, August 4, 1967; Memo of Walter Washington to Jason R. Nathan, August 4, 1967; Memo of Samuel Ganz to John V. Lindsay, n.d. (c. August 1967); Memo of Timothy W. Costello to John V. Lindsay, August 4, 1967; Report to the Mayor

of Follow Up Activities in the Department of Social Services to the Puerto Rican Community Conference, August 4, 1967; Memorandum to Mayor Lindsay from August Heckscher, August 4, 1967; Memo of Deputy Commissioner in Charge of Community Relations to Police Commissioner, August 4, 1967. John V. Lindsay Papers, Subject Files 1966-1973, Box 94, Folder 1712. NYC Archives.

[35] "Sociedades de Servicio Civil," photo by M. Santini, *El Diario-La Prensa*, September 17, 1967, p. 4.

[36] The Grand Council Newsletters, n.d.; The Grand Council of Hispanic Societies in Civil Service, Inc., n.d. Edward Mercado Papers, Series VI Organizations Box 9, Folder 10. Centro Archives.

[37] Grand Council of Hispanic Societies in Public Service, Inc., Executive Board 1987-1988. Frank Torres Papers, Series VI Organizations, Box 17, Folder 18. Centro Archives.

[38] "Formarán Frente Unido de Defensa Puertorriqueños," *El Diario-La Prensa*, February 21, 1969, p. 4.

[39] "Se Trabaja en Ultimar Detalles de La Conferencia Puertorriqueña N.Y.," *El Diario-La Prensa*, April 18, 1969, p. 2.

[40] "Badillo Hace Llamado a Conferencia Boricua," *El Tiempo*, March 5, 1969, p. 15.

[41] Luisa A. Quintero, "Impiden Hablar a Delegado JVL en Conferencia Boricua," *El Diario-La Prensa*, April 21, 1969, p. 2.

[42] Mike A. Correa, "Alumnos Piquetean Contra Maestros," *El Diario-La Prensa*, September 14, 1967, p. 2; reference to Vietnam summer and summer of urban riots in Lauren Stokes, "Marjorie Murphy Discusses the Lasting Effects of a Brooklyn Teachers' Strike," *The Daily Gazette*, February 13, 2007 at http://daily.swarthmore.edu/2007/2/13/marjorie-murphy-discusses-the-lasting-effects-of-a-brooklyn-teachers-strike/<accessed July 27, 2010>

[43] Esli Ramón González, "Hispana Acusa de Negligencia a la Unión de Maestros," *El Diario-La Prensa*, September 15, 1967, p. 4.

[44] Luisa A. Quintero, "Solicitan más Fondos Para Actividades en 'El Barrio,'" *El Diario-La Prensa*, September 17, 1967, p. 4.

[45] "B'klyn College Hearings Open on 35 Expulsions," May 28, 1968. Jesús Colón Papers, Newspaper Clippings, Box 3, Folder 1. Centro Archives.

[46] "Item #1," No Date. John V. Lindsay Papers, Subject Files 1966-1973, Box 22, Folder 391. NYC Archives.

[47] Jerald E. Podair, *The Strike that Changed New York, Blacks, Whites, and the Ocean Hill-Brownville Crisis* (New Haven: Yale University Press, 2002), p. 67.

[48] Anthony De Jesús and Madeline Pérez, "From Community Control to Consent Decree: Puerto Ricans Organizing for Education and Language Rights in 1960s and '70s New York City," *CENTRO Journal* XXI: 2 (Fall 2009), pp. 13-16.

[49] Luis Fuentes, "The Struggle for Local Political Control," in Clara E. Rodríguez and Virginia Sánchez-Korrol, eds., *Historical Perspectives on Puerto Rican Survival in the United States*, (Princeton: Markus Wiener Publishers, 1996), p. 134.

[50] Diana Caballero, "School Board Elections: Parents Against the Odds," *CENTRO Journal* 2:5 (1989), p. 85.

[51] Luisa A. Quintero, "Boricuas Deben Tomar Participación Activa Para Forjar Los Destinos de Esta Ciudad," *El Diario-La Prensa*, September 29, 1968. Jesús Colón Papers, Newspaper

Clippings, Box 3, Folder 1. Centro Archives. Vazquez left the Board in May of 1969 and was honored for his service by Mayor Lindsay at Gracie Mansion. Letter of John V. Lindsay to Hector I. Vazquez, May 14, 1969. John V. Lindsay Papers, Subject Files 1966-1973, Box 114, Folder 2159. NYC Archives.

52 Boricuas Atacan Maestros Por Huelga en Escuelas, n.d. John V. Lindsay Papers, Subject Files 1966-1973, Box 102, Folder 1883. NYC Archives.

53 "Congreso Municipalidades no Está de Acuerdo con Huelga de Maestros," *El Diario-La Prensa*, September 1, 1967, p. 4.

54 Item #55. John V. Lindsay Papers, Subject Files 1966-1973, Box 22, Folder 393. NYC Archives.

55 "Escuelas Este de Harlem Apoyan Junta de Ocean-Hill," *El Diario-La Prensa*, October 9, 1968. Jesús Colón Papers, Newspaper Clippings, Box 3, Folder 1. Centro Archives.

56 Item #57. John V. Lindsay Papers, Subject Files 1966-1973, Box 22, Folder 393. NYC Archives.

57 Memorandum Re Data Submitted by the New York City Commission on Human Rights. No Date. John V. Lindsay Papers, Subject Files 1966-1973, Box 22, Folder 393. NYC Archives.

58 Letter of Donald Morey to Bernard Botein, November 27, 1968; Letter of Robert Grobstein to Frank Hogan, November 27, 1968; Statement by Mrs. Florence Nizin. No Date; Letter of Mrs. Fred Bauer. No Date; Statement by Burt London. No Date; Statement by Joshua Scherer, November 20, 1968. John V. Lindsay Papers, Subject Files 1966-1973, Box 22, Folder 393. NYC Archives.

59 "Piden se Espere Descentralización De las Escuelas," *El Diario-La Prensa*, November 1, 1968, p. 10.

60 Jay Maeder, "Absolute Control Ocean Hill-Brownsville, November-December 1968," *Daily News*, June 3, 2001, p. 41.

61 Lindsay Anuncia Arreglo de Huelga; Maestros Abuchean Informe Shanker, November 18, 1968. John V. Lindsay Papers, Subject Files 1966-1973, Box 102, Folder 1883. NYC Archives.

62 Maeder, "Absolute Control..."

63 See Conrad M. Dyer, Protest and the Politics of Open Admissions: The Impact of the Black and Puerto Rican Students' Community (of City College), Ph.D. Dissertation, City University of New York, 1990, pp. 53-54; 63; 80-81; 75-76.

64 Luisa Quintero, "Marginalia," *El Diario-La Prensa*, January 7, 1969.

65 Lillian Jiménez, "Puerto Ricans and Educational Civil Rights: A History of the 1969 City College Takeover (An Interview with Five Participants)," *CENTRO Journal* 21:2 (Fall 2009).

66 Ibid., p. 173.

67 "Piquete de Protesta Contra Centro Guerra Pobreza del bajo Manhattan," *El Diario-La Prensa*, March 5, 1967, p. 11.

68 "Piquetean Agencia Desarrollo Comunal," photo by Santini, *El Diario-La Prensa*, September 1, 1967, p. 1.

69 "Viviendas en el Bronx," photo by M. Santini, *El Diario-La Prensa*, September 22, 1967, p. 4.

70 "Piden Investigación Sobre Uso Fondos Contra Pobreza," *El Diario-La Prensa*, September 22, 1967, p. 4. In 1977, a founder of MEND, Anibal Solivan Román, Jr., vied for Frank Rossetti's position as Democratic leader for the East Harlem district with support from Angelo and William del Toro. William had just returned to his position as Executive Director of MEND

with back pay, after serving nine months in prison for conspiracy and perjury convictions related to his performance at MEND. See Frank Lynn, "Poverty Group Leader's Petitions For Rossetti's Post Are Invalidated," *The New York Times,* July 28, 1977, p. 23.

71 "Puerto Rican Poor Organize March," May 28, 1968. Jesús Colón Papers, Newspaper Clippings, Box 3, Folder 2. Centro Archives.

72 Commonwealth of Puerto Rico, Department of Labor, Migration Division, *Monthly Activities Report of the Migration Division, April 1968,* p. 8. Migration Division Collection, Monthly Reports, Box 5. Centro Archives.

73 Interview of Gilberto Gerena Valentín by Carlos Rodríguez Fraticelli and Amilcar Tirado, June 6, 1988. Centro Archives.

74 Interview of Herman Badillo by José E. Cruz, August 10, 2006.

75 Memo of Deputy Commissioner in Charge of Community Relations to Police Commissioner, August 4, 1967. John V. Lindsay Papers, Subject Files 1966-1973, Box 94, Folder 1712. NYC Archives.

76 Mike A. Correa, "Líderes Buscan Paz en 'El Barrio,'" *El Diario-La Prensa,* July 25, 1967, p. 3; "Comunidad Boricua y Alcalde Discuten Sobre el Problema," *El Diario-La Prensa,* July 25, 1967, p. 3.

77 "Esto no es un Motín," Front page photograph, *El Diario-La Prensa,* July 25, 1967. Jesús Colón Papers, Newspaper Clippings, Box 2, Folder 9. Centro Archives.

78 "Vuelvan a sus Casas," photograph, *El Diario-La Prensa,* July 25, 1967, p. 2.

79 More E. Side Violence: 4 Arrested, 3 Cops Hurt, July 25, 1968. John V. Lindsay Papers, Subject Files 1966-1973, Box 97, Folder 1787. NYC Archives.

80 Fernández, op. cit., p. 62; "Admiten Policías Mataron Dos en Motines de 'El Barrio,'" *El Diario-La Prensa,* September 27, 1967, p. 3.

81 Memo of Deputy Commissioner in Charge of Community Relations to Police Commissioner, August 4, 1967. John V. Lindsay Papers, Subject Files 1966-1973, Box 94, Folder 1712. NYC Archives.

82 "The Puerto Ricans: Behind the Flare-Up," *New York Times,* July 30, 1967. p. 133.

83 John V. Lindsay, *The City,* (New York: W.W. Norton & Company, 1970), p. 96.

84 Letter of Edward Mercado to John V. Lindsay, August 14, 1967. John V. Lindsay Papers, Subject Files 1966-1973, Box 97, Folder 1788. NYC Archives.

85 Youths Go on Rampage in South Bronx, July 21, 1968. John V. Lindsay Papers, Subject Files 1966-1973, Box 97, Folder 1787. NYC Archives.

86 Commonwealth of Puerto Rico, Department of Labor, Migration Division, *Monthly Activities Report of the Migration Division, June 1968; July 1968,* pp. 15, 8 respectively. Migration Division Collection, Monthly Reports, Box 5. Centro Archives.

87 Lindsay, *The City,* pp. 97-101.

Chapter 4

1 Antonio Gil de la Madrid, "Boricuas se Apoderan Bronx College," *El Diario-La Prensa,* February 18, 1970, p. 3.

2 Alfredo Izaguirre Horta, "Asociación de Mujeres Puertorriqueñas, Inc., Juramenta Directiva Mañana en la Noche," *El Diario-La Prensa, Suplemento Diario,* May 12, 1972, p. 1.

3 Esli Ramón González, "Acción Hispana Lucha Por Toda La Comunidad," *El Diario-La Prensa,*

November 9, 1970, p. 15.

[4] Estado Libre Asociado de Puerto Rico, Departamento del Trabajo, División de Migración, *Informe Anual, Año Fiscal 1971-72*. Migration Division Collection, Annual Reports, Box 2. Centro Archives.

[5] Commonwealth of Puerto Rico, Department of Labor, Migration Division, *Monthly Activities Report of the Migration Division, August 1971*, p. 13. Migration Division Collection, Monthly Reports, Box 6. Centro Archives.

[6] Interview of Manuel A. Casiano, Jr. by Peter Block. Migration Division Collection, Radio Broadcasts Transcripts, Box 1467, Folder 100. Centro Archives.

[7] Will Lissner, "Coalition Sought By Puerto Ricans," *New York Times*, September 30, 1971, p. 43.

[8] Commonwealth of Puerto Rico, Department of Labor, Migration Division, *Monthly Activities Report of the Migration Division, October 1971; December 1971*, pp. 15, 14 respectively. Migration Division Collection, Monthly Reports, Box 6. Centro Archives.

[9] César A. Marín, "Badillo y Abrams Serán Oradores En Mitin Boricua," *El Diario-La Prensa*, November 3, 1971, p. 5; Luisa A. Quintero, "Marginalia - Conferencia Puertorriqueña," *El Diario-La Prensa*, November 3, 1971, p. 22.

[10] Alfredo Izaguirre Horta, "Dedicarán Conferencia Boricua Bronx Educador Cándido de León," *El Diario-La Prensa*, November 4, 1971, p. 8.

[11] César A. Marín, "Boricuas Toman Vitales Acuerdos En Conferencia," *El Diario-La Prensa*, December 6, 1971, p. 4; Eurípides Ríos, "Expulsan al Padre Gigante de la Conferencia Puertorriqueña Bronx," *El Diario-La Prensa*, December 6, 1971, p. 4; "Padre Gigante Conspira Contra Mí, Dice Vélez," *El Diario-La Prensa*, December 6, 1971, p. 4.

[12] Form letter of John V. Lindsay and Eleanor Holmes, February 16, 1972. John V. Lindsay Papers, Subject Files 1966-1973, Box 53, Folder 953. NYC Archives.

[13] The Emergence of Ethnic Group Identity, Conference Program, March 7, 1972. John V. Lindsay Papers, Subject Files 1966-1973, Box 53, Folder 953. NYC Archives.

[14] Opening Remarks of Eleanor Holmes Norton at Conference on the Emergence of Ethnic Group Identity, March 7, 1972, p. 7. John V. Lindsay Papers, Subject Files 1966-1973, Box 53, Folder 953. NYC Archives.

[15] Form letter sent by Eleanor Holmes Norton, July 3, 1972. Ibid.

[16] News Release, Commission on Human Rights, March 12, 1973. John V. Lindsay Papers, Subject Files 1966-1973, Box 53, Folder 955. NYC Archives.

[17] For a complete listing see John V. Lindsay Papers, Subject Files 1966-1973, Box 53, Folder 956. NYC Archives.

[18] Pedro J. Linares, "Comité Vistas Públicas Boricuas Presenta Hoy a los Panelistas," *El Diario-La Prensa*, May 5, 1972, p. 4.

[19] "Habrá Mitin Mañana Para Arreglos Previos a Vistas Sobre Discrimen," *El Diario-La Prensa*, May 4, 1972, p. 4.

[20] "Puerto Rican People's Hearing," *El Diario-La Prensa*, May 14, 1972, p. 21.

[21] "Inician Audiencias Públicas Sobre Discrimen a Boricuas," *El Diario-La Prensa*, May 15, 1972, p. 3.

[22] "Candidato del Bronx Alega Discriminación," *El Diario-La Prensa*, May 15, 1972, p. 16.

[23] Pedro J. Linares, "Acusan Discrimen Comisión Estatal Derechos Humanos," *El Diario-La*

Prensa, May 18, 1972, p. 4.

24 Pedro J. Linares, "Denuncia Que Policías N.Y. Prejuician a Puertorriqueños," *El Diario-La Prensa*, May 21, 1972, p. 3.

25 Luisa A. Quintero, "Marginalia," *El Diario-La Prensa*, September 22, 1970, p. 18.

26 Esli Ramón Gonzalez, "Censura se Hagan Ataques Contra Alcalde de Culebra," *El Diario-La Prensa*, September 6, 1970, p. 10.

27 "Goldberg Luchará Para Que Se Haga Justicia a Culebra," *El Diario-La Prensa*, September 18, 1970, p. 2.

28 "Nixon Firma Ley Pentágono Estudie Caso de Culebra," *El Diario-La Prensa*, October 27, 1970, p. 3.

29 Luisa A. Quintero, "Marginalia," *El Diario-La Prensa*, October 8, 1970, p. 22; "Permiten Armada Bombardee Culebra," *El Diario-La Prensa*, October 16, 1970, p. 3.

30 "Prácticas Tiro en Culebra Deben Cesar, Dice Dodd," *El Diario-La Prensa*, September 22, 1970, p. 2.

31 Regia Asamblea de Puertoriquenos de Brownsville, No Date. Jesús Colón Papers, New York Organizations, Box 1, Folder 7. Centro Archives

32 "Reducirán Prácticas de Tiro en Culebra," *El Diario-La Prensa*, September 25, 1970, p. 3; "Senado Limita Operaciones Marina EE.UU. En Culebra," *El Diario-La Prensa*, October 1st, 1970, p. 2; "Derrotan Proposición Sobre Maniobras de Tiro en Culebra," *El Diario-La Prensa*, October 9, 1970, p. 3.

33 Cesar Marin, "Culebrenses Harán Marcha a Washington el 21 de Noviembre," *El Diario-La Prensa*, October 23, 1970, p. 12; César A. Marín, "Declaran Día Unidad Boricua Para la Marcha a Washington," *El Diario-La Prensa*, November 15, 1970, p. 4; Domingo Roche, Jr., "Suspenden la Marcha Culebra a Washington," *El Diario-La Prensa*, November 22, 1970, p. 3.

34 Gilberto Gerena Valentín, *Gilberto Gerena Valentín: My Life as a Community Activist, Labor Organizer, and Progressive Politician in New York City*, Carlos Rodríguez-Fraticelli, ed., (New York: Center For Puerto Rican Studies, 2013), p. 230.

35 Dana Adams Schmidt, "Navy to Yield Culebra Targets; 13-Year Island Struggle at End," *New York Times*, April 2, 1971, p. 64.

36 "Culebra Over Goliath," *New York Times*, May 28, 1973, p. 14.

37 Finn-Olaf Jones, "Einstein on the Beach: The Ph.D.'s of Culebra," *New York Times*, November 4, 2005, p. F8.

38 Statement of Joseph Monserrat on Parents Rights at Public Meeting, April 21, 1971; Statement Opposing the Action of Community School Board 25," Queens Division, American Jewish Congress, April 29, 1971; Memorandum from Sidney P. Nadel to Hon. Murry Bergtraum, May 25, 1971; "Book Ban is Eased by Queens Board," *New York Times*, June 3, 1971. Joseph Monserrat Papers, Series VI, Subject Files, Box 13, Folder 15. Centro Archives.

39 Pedro J. Linares, "Grupo Estudiantes Ocupa Oficinas Presidente del Manhattan College," *El Diario-La Prensa*, May 3, 1972, p. 16.

40 Gerena Valentín, op. cit., pp. 241-242.

41 "Protestan por Empleo de Maestro No Puertorriqueño en Hunter College," *El Diario-La Prensa*, May 9, 1972, p. 12.

42 César A. Marín, "Quero Chiesa Mantenido Rehén Por Estudiantes," *El Diario-La Prensa*, May 11, 1972, p. 4.
43 Luisa A. Quintero, "Piden Cese Discriminación a Boricuas en Univ. Columbia," *El Diario-La Prensa*, May 11, 1972, p. 8.
44 "Court Order Forbids Lincoln Hospital Take-Over," *New York Times*, February 2, 1970, p. 16.
45 John Sibley, "Lincoln Hospital Occupied for Two Hours in Protest," *New York Times*, February 3, 1970, p. 28.
46 "City Hall Appoints Puerto Rican Head of Lincoln Hospital," *New York Times*, March 6, 1970, p. 43.
47 Alfonso A. Narvaez, "Young Lords Seize Lincoln Hospital Building," *New York Times*, July 15, 1970, p. 34.
48 Alfonso A. Narvaez, "Lincoln Hospital Hears Demands," *New York Times*, July 16, 1970, p. 24.
49 Alfonso A. Narvaez, "Doctors at Lincoln Hospital Threaten to Resign," *New York Times*, July 29, 1970, p. 28.
50 Alfonso A. Narvaez, "Lincoln Doctors to Aid Militants," *New York Times*, July 30, 1970, p. 24.
51 Francis X. Clines, "City Gets Injunction in Lincoln Hospital Dispute," *New York Times*, August 27, 1970, p. 38; "Crisis at Lincoln Hospital," Editorial, *New York Times*, August 27, 1970, p. 34.
52 John Sibley, "Dr. Smith Is Back In Lincoln Post," *New York Times*, September 2, 1970, p. 75; Irving Spiegel, "Lincoln Doctors Asked to Return," *New York Times*, September 1, 1970, p. 26.
53 John Sibley, "Pediatrics Chief Out at Lincoln Hospital; Puerto Rican Named," *New York Times*, November 17, 1970, p. 1.
54 John Sibley, "Rights Commission Investigating Removal of Pediatrics Chief at Lincoln Hospital," *New York Times*, November 19, 1970, p. 51.
55 "Mayor Will Study Physician's Ouster at Lincoln Hospital," *New York Times*, November 21, 1970, p. 27.
56 John Sibley, "Einhorn 'Reinstated' at Lincoln, Indicates He May Not Go Back," *New York Times*, November 24, 1970, p. 32.
57 Michael T. Kaufman, "Lincoln Hospital: Case History of Dissension That Split Staff," *New York Times*, December 21, 1970, p. 1; Harry Schwartz, "Lincoln Hospital: Behind the Conflict Over the Pediatric Post," *New York Times*, November 29, 1970, p. 198.
58 Michael T. Kaufman, "Lincoln Hospital: Case History of Dissension That Split Staff," *New York Times*, December 21, 1970, p. 1.
59 SCA Resolution on Lincoln Hospital Controversy, May 24, 1971. John V. Lindsay Papers, Subject Files 1966-1973, Box 54, Folder 966. NYC Archives.
60 New York City Commission on Human Rights Report on the Einhorn Matter at Lincoln Hospital, July 1971, pp. 16, 20, 21, 24. John V. Lindsay Papers, Subject Files 1966-1973, Box 54, Folder 963. NYC Archives.
61 Letter of Jerome M. Becker to Herman Brown, July 19, 1971. Ibid.
62 Letter of Eugene S. Callender and Manuel Diaz, Jr. to Joseph Monserrat, March 9, 1971; Committee to Defend the Queens House of Detention 8, Narrative Account, n.d.; *New York Times* October 6, 1970 and *Village Voice* December 17, 1970 clippings. Joseph Monserrat Papers, Series V, Organizations, Box 11, Folder 4. Centro Archives.

63 César A. Marín, "Vaticinan Proyecto Boricua Será Cerrado en Diciembre," *El Diario-La Prensa*, September 6, 1970, p. 4.

64 Luisa A. Quintero, "Declaran Sin Lugar una Acusación Contra Empleados Puertorriqueños," *El Diario-La Prensa*, September 11, 1970, p. 4.

65 "Líderes Boricuas en Manifestación Protesta," *El Diario-La Prensa*, September 9, 1970, p. 2; Alfredo Izaguirre Horta, "Comunidad Protesta Por Reducción Fondos Pobreza," *El Diario-La Prensa*, September 9, 1970, p. 4; Alfredo Izaguirre Horta, "Boricuas Convocan a Mobilización Frente al C.D.A.," *El Diario-La Prensa*, September 10, 1970, p. 3; "Afirman Hay Discrimen Contra Puertorriqueños," *El Diario-La Prensa*, September 10, 1970, p. 12.

66 "Ultimátum a JVL Para Que Medie en Rebaja a Pobreza," *El Diario-La Prensa*, September 10, 1970, p. 4. In a subsequent news article, the organization is dubbed the "Frente Internacional Puertorriqueño" [International Puerto Rican Front]. See "Frente Puertorriqueño Informa De sus Gestiones con Lindsay," *El Diario-La Prensa*, September 15, 1970, p. 4.

67 Editorial, "Justified Protest," *El Diario-La Prensa*, September 10, 1970, p. 21.

68 Editorial, "A Conspiration [sic] Against Puerto Ricans," *El Diario-La Prensa*, September 11, 1970, p. 21.

69 Domingo Roche, Jr. "Más de Mil Protestan Rebaja de $$ Pobreza," *El Diario-La Prensa*, September 11, 1970, p. 3.

70 "Piden Investigación de Caso en Que Varios Boricuas Fueron 'Apaleados'," *El Diario-La Prensa*, September 20, 1970, p. 8.

71 "Goldberg Contra Rebaja de $$ a la Pobreza," *El Diario-La Prensa*, September 11, 1970, p. 4.

72 "Rockefeller Interviene en Caso De Fondos Para La Pobreza," *El Diario-La Prensa*, September 17, 1970, p. 4.

73 Alfredo Izaguirre Horta, "Prometen Ayuda de Rocky A Guerra Contra la Pobreza," *El Diario-La Prensa*, September 27, 1970, p. 8

74 "Vote Today!," Editorial, *El Diario-La Prensa*, September 15, 1970, p. 19.

75 Alfredo Izaguirre Horta, "Vélez Renuncia a Multiservice," *El Diario-La Prensa*, October 22, 1970, p. 3; Alfredo Izaguirre Horta, "Ciudad Provocó Mi Renuncia, Afirma Vélez," *El Diario-La Prensa*, October 29, 1970, p. 3.

76 Letter of David J. Billings, III to John V. Lindsay, October 29, 1970. John V. Lindsay Papers, Subject Files 1966-1973, Box 4, Folder 55. NYC Archives.

77 Pedro J. Linares, "Se Encadena Frente a Oficina Para Demostrar Que Hay 'Discriminación,'" *El Diario-La Prensa*, December 8, 1971, p. 4.

78 Luisa A. Quintero, "Marginalia," *El Diario-La Prensa*, May 4, 1972, p. 22.

79 "Boricua Inscríbete Hoy Sábado Para Poder Votar," *El Diario-La Prensa*, May 7, 1972, p. 8.

80 "JVL Proclama Semana Cultura Puertorriqueña," *El Diario-La Prensa*, May 28, 1972, p. 4.

Chapter 5

1 Letter of Andres Quiles to Herman Badillo, February 27, 1973; Letter of Jim Senyszyn to Herman Badillo, February 27, 1973; Borrador, Dictado por Don Luis Muñoz Marín, May 24, 1973. Congressman Herman Badillo Papers, Box G3. Boricua College Northside Library.

2 Invitation of the Committee Pro-Badillo for Mayor of New York to Cocktail reception in Honor of Herman Badillo on May 10 1973. Ibid.
3 Exchange of letters between Frank Bonilla, Víctor G. Alicea, and Thomas K. Glennon, Jr., from July 23, 1973 to December 18, 1973. United Bronx Parents Collection, Series II, Box 1, Subject File 3. Centro Archives.
4 Circular letter of Frank Bonilla, April 23, 1974; "Statement by Puerto Rican Educators," c. 1974. United Bronx Parents Collection, Series II, Box 1, Subject File 3. Centro Archives.
5 In 2008, PRLDEF changed its name to Latino Justice PRLDEF.
6 Isaura Santiago Santiago, *Aspira v. Board of Education of the City of New York*: A History and Policy Analysis, Ph.D. Dissertation, Fordham University, 1978, pp. 212-214.
7 Herbert Teitelbaum, "Bilingual Education Here," *New York Times,* May 26, 1975, p. 15.
8 Andres Roura, " Junta Educación Comienza Implementación de Educación Bilingüe," *El Diario-La Prensa*, November 5, 1975, p. 19.
9 David Vidal, "Bilingual Education Stirs Debate in New York City," *New York Times,* June 21, 1976, p. 35.
10 Ibid.
11 Kenneth B. Clark and Jorge Batista, "Hispanic and Unequal," *New York Times,* December 7, 1977, p. 43.
12 Michael Cortés, *Bilingual Education Issues Being Considered by the Ninety-Fifth Congress* (Washington, D.C.: National Council of La Raza, 1978); *Forum of National Hispanic organizations, Hispanic Dialogue Subcommittee, Bilingual Education Conference, Summary of Bilingual Education Conference Proceedings,* 1978. PRLDEF Collection, Legislative Comments, Box 1, Folder 2. Centro Archives; Statement of the Puerto Rican Legal Defense and Education Fund, Inc. regarding Reorganization Plan No. 1 of 1978 on Equal Employment Opportunity Enforcement, March 1978. PRLDEF Collection, Legislative Comments, Box 1, Folder 3. Centro Archives.
13 Murray Schumach, "Hispanic Queens Political Club Opens," *New York Times,* May 31, 1974, p. 37.
14 Migration Division, Commonwealth of Puerto Rico, Short Films, Herman Badillo and Robert García, Appeal for Voter Registration, c. 1978-1979. Migration Division Collection. Centro Archives.
15 Departamento del Trabajo, División de Migración, Estado Libre Asociado de Puerto Rico, *Informe Mensual, Abril 1979; Mayo 1979,* pp. 12, 11 respectively. Migration Division Collection, Monthly Reports, Box 8. Centro Archives.
16 Commonwealth of Puerto Rico, Department of Labor, Migration Division, *Monthly Activities Report of the Migration Division, August 1973,* p. 20. Migration Division Collection, Monthly Reports, Box 7. Centro Archives; Peter Kihss, "Migrant Division Held Ineffective," *New York Times*, September 23, 1973, p. 56.
17 Directories of Puerto Rican Organizations in the United States, Migration Division, Department of Labor, Commonwealth of Puerto Rico. Migration Division Collection, Community Organizations Directories, Box 1. Centro Archives.
18 Letter of Moises Ledesma to John V. Lindsay, August 26, 1972; Letter of Marvin Schick to Moises Ledesma, August 30, 1972. John V. Lindsay Papers, Subject Files 1966-1973, Box 53, Folder 953. NYC Archives.
19 Domingo Roche, Jr., "Niegan Oficina de Puerto Rico Trate de Controlar Desfile de NY," *El*

Diario-La Prensa, November 15, 1970, p. 4.

20 Estado Libre Asociado de Puerto Rico, Departamento del Trabajo, División de Migración, *Informe Anual, Año Fiscal 1974-75*, p. 35. Migration Division Collection, Annual Reports, Box 3. Centro Archives.

21 Estado Libre Asociado de Puerto Rico, Departamento del Trabajo, División de Migración, *Informe Anual, Año Fiscal 1964-65-Año Fiscal 1973-74*. Migration Division Collection, Annual Reports, Box 2 and 3. Centro Archives.

22 "Invitation to El Hipocampo." Ruth M. Reynolds Collection, Series VIII, Box 3, Folder 7. Centro Archives.

23 Ethnic Composition of Community School Boards Elected on May 3, 1983 and on May 1, 1973. Lourdes Torres Papers, Series VIII, Subject Files, Box 12, Folder 7. Centro Archives.

24 "Revisan Decisión Contra Negros y Puertorriqueños," *El Diario-La Prensa*, November 7, 1972, p. 2; "City Elections Cheat Hispanics, U. S. Says," *Daily News*, October 23, 1973.

25 *Torres v. Sachs*, 381 F. Supp. 309 (1974). http://www.leagle.com/decision/1974690381FSu pp309_1644/TORRES%20v.%20SACHS <Accessed September 11, 2016>

26 Juan E. Hernández Cruz, "El Instituto Legal de Puerto Rico Capítulo de Nueva York," December 1973. Juan Hernández Cruz Papers. Centro Archives.

27 Committee for Puerto Rican Decolonization, "Puerto Rico at the United Nations," No Date. Ruth M. Reynolds Collection, Series VIII, Box 3, Folder 6. Centro Archives.

28 Letter of Evelina Antonetti to Lucille Rose, April 10, 1975. United Bronx Parents, Administrative Records, Box 1, Folder 14. Centro Archives.

29 Circular Letter of Teresa Morales to Community Organizations, April 15, 1975. United Bronx Parents, Administrative Records, Box 1, Folder 14. Centro Archives.

30 Assorted documents. Lourdes Torres Papers, Series VII, Organizations, Box 9, Folder 16. Centro Archives.

31 Interview of Lourdes Torres by José E. Cruz, July 12, 2006.

32 "Conferencia Católica del Area del Bajo Manhattan," *El Diario-La Prensa*, November 4, 1982, p. 18.

33 Except where noted, this and the following three paragraphs are based on the Minutes of Meeting of December 11-12, 1977, of the National Puerto Rican Coalition. Records of United Bronx Parents, Series II, Box 1, Subject File 12. Centro Archives.

34 Luisa A. Quintero, "Líderes Crean Coalición Nacional Puertorriqueña," *El Diario-La Prensa*, December 28, 1977, p. 1.

35 Nieves interview, 1988.

36 Luis Fernández, "Funcionarios Niegan Cometieran Fraude En El Proyecto Puertorriqueño de Nueva York," *El Diario-La Prensa*, November 2, 1977, p. 4.

37 Peter Kihss, "Sit-In Group Demands Ouster of Directors of Puerto Rican Project," *New York Times*, March 7, 1978, p. 39; John Kifner, "Puerto Rican Poverty Agency Accused of Wasting 'Millions'," *New York Times*, March 25, 1978, p. 23; John Kifner, "Bronx Poverty Corporation Loses City Funds in Fraud Investigation," *New York Times*, April 26, 1978, section 2, p. 3; Charles Kaiser, "Ex-Officials of Puerto Rican Poverty Agency Indicted," *New York Times*, June 28, 1978, section 2, p. 3; "Funds Are Cut Off for Work Project," *New York Times*, July 21, 1978, section 2, p. 2.

[38] Letter of Angelo Del Toro to Edward Koch, June 21, 1979. Edward Koch Papers, Box 242, Folder 6. NYC Archives.
[39] Letter of Yolanda Sanchez to Evelina Antonetty, July 14, 1978. Records of United Bronx Parents, Series II, Box 1, Subject File 17. Centro Archives.
[40] Resolution, Puerto Rican Community Development Project, October 31, 1978; Letter of Haskell G. Ward to Luis A. Cardona, November 21, 1978. United Bronx Parents Collection, Series II, Box 1, Subject File 14. Centro Archives.
[41] Nieves interview, 1988.
[42] Mailgram from Haskell G. Ward to Evelina Antonetty, November 3, 1978. United Bronx Parents, Administrative Records, Box 5, Folder 4. Centro Archives.
[43] Edward I. Koch, *Mayor, An Autobiography* (New York: Warner Books, 1984), pp. 139-141.
[44] Plan for the Establishment of a City-wide Puerto Rican Community-based Organization to Provide Training and Technical Assistance to the City's Puerto Rican Community, No Date; Letter of Roger P. Alvarez to Evelina Antonetti [sic], July 13, 1979. United Bronx Parents, Administrative Records, Box 5, Folder 4. Centro Archives.
[45] Letter of Angelo Del Toro to Edward Koch, June 21, 1979. Edward Koch Papers, Box 242, Folder 6. NYC Archives.
[46] Fact Sheet on Achievements of Harvey Scribner, n.d. Joseph Monserrat Papers, Series IV, Board of Education of the City of New York, Box 10, Folder 3. Centro Archives.
[47] Iver Peterson, "Tight Supervision Is Set In Election," *New York Times*, May 12, 1974, p. 27.
[48] Iver Peterson, "U.F.T. Leads In District 1 Election," *New York Times*, May 18, 1974, p. 35; Paul L. Montgomery, "'U.F.T. Slate Wins In District 1 Vote," *New York Times*, May 19, 1974, p. 34.
[49] Robert Hanley, "New Board Votes to Oust Member," *New York Times*, June 14, 1974, p. 17.
[50] Iver Peterson, "Local School Board to Try To Suspend Fuentes Again, *New York Times*, August 6, 1974, p. 37.
[51] Leonard Buder, "Both Sides Claim School Victory," *New York Times*, May 8, 1975, p. 86; Leonard Buder, "Slate Opposed to U.F.T. Wins In District 16 School Election," *New York Times*, May 10, 1975, p. 27; Judith Cummings, "Big U.F.T. Victory Indicated in Vote," *New York Times*, May 12, 1975, p. 1; Leonard Buder, "U.F.T. To Control Fuentes District," *New York Times*, May 11, 1975, p. 1.
[52] Leonard Buder, "3,000 in Brooklyn Protest Feared Student Transfer," *The New York Times*, March 19, 1975, p. 51.
[53] Commonwealth of Puerto Rico, Department of Labor, Migration Division, *Monthly Activities Report of the Migration Division, May 1973*, p. 31. Migration Division Collection, Monthly Reports, Box 7. Centro Archives.
[54] Spanish Press Digest, Mayor's Press Office, June 23, 1971. John V. Lindsay Papers, Subject Files 1966-1973, Box 104, Folder 1966. NYC Archives.
[55] Jaime Rivera, "Abierta parcialidad contra un boricua," *El Diario-La Prensa*, June 17, 1980. P. 2.
[56] "The City," *New York Times*, February 23, 1979, p. B3.
[57] Lee Dembart, "Koch, Criticized by Many Blacks, Seeks to Repair Ties With Them," *New York Times*, February 27, 1979, p. A1.
[58] Black and Latino Coalition Against Police Brutality, The Case of Luis Baez, n.d. Lourdes Torres Papers, Series VIII, Subject Files, Box 13, Folder 24. Centro Archives.

[59] "Despiden a Galarcé De Director Hospital Lincoln," *El Diario-La Prensa*, November 3, 1976, p. 2; César A. Marín "Elementos Boricuas Ocupan el Hospital," *El Diario-La Prensa*, November 3, 1976, p. 2; Mike A. Correa, "Están Jugando con la Salud de Enfermos: Dr. Izquierdo," *El Diario-La Prensa*, November 3, 1976, p. 4; Luisa A. Quintero, "Badillo Pide Dr. Holloman Proteja Pacientes Lincoln," *El Diario-La Prensa*, November 3, 1976, p. 4.

[60] Carlos Rodríguez-Fraticelli, "Hostos Community College and the Puerto Rican Struggle for Equity in Education," *Centro* 2:2 (Invierno 1987-88).

[61] A fuller account of the campaign to save Hostos is provided by Gerald Meyer in "Save Hostos: Politics and Community Mobilization to Save a College in the Bronx, 1973-1978," *CENTRO Journal* XV:I (Spring 2003). A personal perspective on this campaign can be found in Ramón J. Jiménez, "Hostos Community College: Battle of the Seventies," *CENTRO Journal* XV:I (Spring 2003). My account is based on Meyer's article.

[62] Meyer, op. cit., p. 89.

Chapter 6

[1] Departamento del Trabajo, División de Migración, Estado Libre Asociado de Puerto Rico, Informe Mensual, Enero 1980, p. 11. Migration Division Collection, Monthly Reports, Box 8. Centro Archives.

[2] Migration Division, Department of Labor and Human Resources, Government of Puerto Rico, Press Release, February 14, 1980. Migration Division Collection, Press Releases, Box 1490, Folder 18. Centro Archives.

[3] Program for Primera Convencion Nacional Puertorriquena, Lourdes Torres Papers, Series IV, National Congress for Puerto Rican Rights, Box 3, Folder 1. Centro Archives.

[4] Keynote Speech by Juan Gonzalez, Documents of the First National Convention, April 25-26, 1981, pp. 2-3, 7-9. Lourdes Torres Papers, Series IV, National Congress for Puerto Rican Rights, Box 3, Folder 1. Centro Archives.

[5] Letter of Juan Gonzalez to Manny Diaz, November 11, 1981. Lourdes Torres Papers, Series IV, National Congress for Puerto Rican Rights, Box 4, Folder 1. Centro Archives.

[6] Agenda of National Congress for Puerto Rican Rights by Topic. Diana Caballero Papers, Series V, National Congress for Puerto Rican Rights, Box 12, Folder 7. Centro Archives.

[7] Torres interview, 2006.

[8] Summary of Work Done by the Women's T.F. of the Last Two Years, 1984-1986. Lourdes Torres Papers, Series V, Committee Against Fort Apache, Box 8, Folder 3. Centro Archives.

[9] A Proposal to Continue the Basic Program of the National Congress for Puerto Rican Rights," c. August 1984, p. 5. Lourdes Torres Papers, Series IV, National Congress for Puerto Rican Rights, Box 7, Folder 3. Centro Archives.

[10] Letters of Yourlagnes Bonano and Richie Pérez to Puertorriquena/os, n.d. Lourdes Torres Papers, Series IV, National Congress for Puerto Rican Rights, Box 4, Folder 1. Centro Archives.

[11] Report on Transition Period of New Leadership, Coordinating Committee, NCPRR/NYC Chapter, November 1986-January 1987. c. September 1986. Diana Caballero Papers, Series V, National Congress for Puerto Rican Rights, Box 17, Folder 4. Centro Archives.

[12] Internal Memo, National Congress for Puerto Rican Rights, n.d. Diana Caballero Papers,

Series V, National Congress for Puerto Rican Rights, Box 17, Folder 2. Centro Archives. The Latin Union for Political Action was the same as Latinos United for Political Action or LUPA.

[13] Letter of Juan Gonzalez to Enrique Irizarry, November 14, 1981. Diana Caballero Papers, Series V, National Congress for Puerto Rican Rights, Box 12, Folder 9. Centro Archives.

[14] Letter of Juan Gonzalez to Isidoro Rodriguez, July 28, 1981. Lourdes Torres Papers, Series IV, National Congress for Puerto Rican Rights, Box 4, Folder 1. Centro Archives. Rodriguez was not listed as a Board member in the official program of the December conference; Letter of Juan Gonzalez to Luis Nunez, November 4, 1981. Lourdes Torres Papers, Series IV, National Congress for Puerto Rican Rights, Box 4, Folder 1. Centro Archives.

[15] Fact Sheet, n.d. Lourdes Torres Papers, Series IV, National Congress for Puerto Rican Rights, Box 4, Folder 4. Centro Archives.

[16] Letter of Juan Gonzalez to Dear, January 18, 1982. Lourdes Torres Papers, Series IV, National Congress for Puerto Rican Rights, Box 4, Folder 1. Centro Archives. Emphases in the original.

[17] First National Conference of the National Puerto Rican Coalition, December 3-5, 1981, Official Program. Lourdes Torres Papers, Series IV, National Congress for Puerto Rican Rights, Box 4, Folder 8. Centro Archives.

[18] Memo from Juan Gonzalez to NCPRR Board Members, December 8, 1981. Lourdes Torres Papers, Series IV, National Congress for Puerto Rican Rights, Box 5, Folder 4. Centro Archives.

[19] Juan Gonzalez, Summary Analysis of NCPRR Work, March 18, 1982. Lourdes Torres Papers, Series IV, National Congress for Puerto Rican Rights, Box 5, Folder 1. Centro Archives.

[20] Summary of Executive Committee and Major NCPRR Work Since Last National Board Meeting of November 14, 1981. Lourdes Torres Papers, Series IV, National Congress for Puerto Rican Rights, Box 5, Folder 1. Centro Archives.

[21] Minutes, National Executive Committee, National Congress for Puerto Rican Rights, April 30, 1982. Lourdes Torres Papers, Series IV, National Congress for Puerto Rican Rights, Box 5, Folder 8. Centro Archives.

[22] Diana Caballero, "Testimony in Opposition to S. 2002," April 26, 1982. Lourdes Torres Papers, Series VIII, Bilingual Education, Box 11, Folder 13. Centro Archives.

[23] Letter of Richie Pérez to Friends, April 16, 1982. Diana Caballero Papers, Series V, National Congress for Puerto Rican Rights, Box 17, Folder 2. Centro Archives.

[24] The New York Congress for Puerto Rican Rights and the Electoral Question. n.d. Lourdes Torres Papers, Series IV, National Congress for Puerto Rican Rights, Box 4, Folder 1. Centro Archives.

[25] Memo from Judy Bonano, et al. to New York City Coordinating Committee, September 15, 1982. Lourdes Torres Papers, Series IV, National Congress for Puerto Rican Rights, Box 5, Folder 5. Centro Archives.

[26] Draft Minutes, National Board Meeting, National Congress for Puerto Rican Rights, October 16, 1982. Lourdes Torres Papers, Series IV, National Congress for Puerto Rican Rights, Box 5, Folder 1. Centro Archives.

[27] Letter of Richie Pérez to Friends, April 16, 1982; Letter of Isabel Malavet to Dear Friends, July 16, 1982; Letter of the Women's Task Force, National Congress for Puerto Rican Rights to Dear Friends, September 8, 1982; Letter from Judy Bonano, et al. to Hermanas y Hermanos, September 13, 1982. Lourdes Torres Papers, Series IV, National Congress for Puerto Rican

Rights, Box 4, Folder 1. Centro Archives.

[28] Assorted documents. Lourdes Torres Papers, Series IV, National Congress for Puerto Rican Rights, Box 6, Folder 12. Centro Archives.

[29] "Puerto Rican Community Rejects Lew Lehrman," October 29, 1982. Diana Caballero Papers, Series V, National Congress for Puerto Rican Rights, Box 15, Folder 1. Centro Archives.

[30] D.G., "The Role of Puerto Rican Communists in the National Movement," February 1, 1980. Lourdes Torres Papers, Series VIII, Subject Files, Box 14, Folder 7. Centro Archives.

[31] Ibid.

[32] Diana Caballero Pérez, National Bilingual Education Task Force, Summary of work and workplan for 1983, January 22-23, 1983. Lourdes Torres Papers, Series IV, National Congress for Puerto Rican Rights, Box 5, Folder 1. Centro Archives.

[33] Diana Caballero Pérez, National Bilingual Education Task Force, Summary of work and workplan for 1983, January 22-23, 1983. Ibid.

[34] Zoilo Torres, "The New York City Mayoral Elections: A Call to Action," n.d. Lourdes Torres Papers, Series IV, National Congress for Puerto Rican Rights, Box 4, Folder 4. Centro Archives.

[35] New York City Chapter: Evaluation and Analysis of Past Year's Work, March 1983-March 1984, n.d., Diana Caballero Papers, Series V, National Congress for Puerto Rican Rights, Box 17, Folder 2. Centro Archives.

[36] Documentation of the Concerns and recommendations at the April 15th, NYC Chapter Retreat, n.d. Diana Caballero Papers, Series V, National Congress for Puerto Rican Rights, Box 15, Folder 5. Centro Archives.

[37] National Congress for Puerto Rican Rights, Organizational Development, Analysis Report, June 4, 1983. Lourdes Torres Papers, Series IV, National Congress for Puerto Rican Rights, Box 3, Folder 2. Centro Archives.

[38] National Congress for Puerto Rican Rights, National Board Minutes, March 30, 1985. Lourdes Torres Papers, Series IV, National Congress for Puerto Rican Rights, Box 5 Folder 1. Centro Archives.

[39] Letter of Frank Solís to Louis Núñez, February 6, 1985; Memorandum of Annabelle Jaramillo to Louis Núñez, January 31, 1985. Diana Caballero Papers, Series VII, Subject Files, Box 29, Folder 4. Centro Archives.

[40] Letter of Louis Núnez to Angelo Falcón, January 3, 1985; Letter of Angelo Falcón to Louis Núñez, January 11, 1985. Ibid.

[41] Institute for Puerto Rican Policy, Attachment, Excerpt from National Agreement Between Adolph Coors Company and a Coalition of Hispanic Organizations, n.d. Ibid.

[42] Juan González, "Latino Groups 'Sold Out for a Glass of Beer,'" *Daily News*, February 1, 1985. Ibid.

[43] Letter of Frank Solís to Louis Núñez, February 6, 1985. Ibid.

[44] Memorandum of Annabelle Jaramillo to Louis Núñez, January 31, 1985. Ibid.

[45] Letter of Louis Núñez to Angelo Falcón, January 3, 1985; Memorandum of Annabelle Jaramillo to Louis Núñez, January 31, 1985; Gonzalez, "Latino Groups 'Sold Out....'" Ibid.

[46] Letter of Angelo Falcón to Annabelle Jaramillo, February 19, 1985; Memorandum of Annabelle Jaramillo to Louis Núñez, January 31, 1985; Letter of Frank Solís to Louis Núñez, February 6,

1985. Ibid.

47 National Congress for Puerto Rican Rights, October 20, 1982. Luis O. Reyes Papers, Series VII, Organizations, Box 29, Folder 8. Centro Archives.

48 National Congress for Puerto Rican Rights, October 20, 1982. Ibid.

49 "Bilingual Education Under Fire...Again," El Pitirre (Winter 1982-83), p. 1. Luis O. Reyes Papers, Series IV, Aspira of New York, Box 8, Folder 2. Centro Archives.

50 "New York Coalition to Defend Bilingual Education to Protest Dismantling of Bilingual Programs by Chancellor Macchiarola," Luis O. Reyes Papers, Series VII, Organizations, Box 29, Folder 13. Centro Archives.

51 Press Advisory, Puerto Rican legal Defense and Education Fund, November 17, 1982 and December 15, 1982. Diana Caballero Papers, Series VI, Organizations, Box 24, Folder 12. Centro Archives.

52 Letter of Diana Caballero to Dear Friends of Bilingual Education, May 26, 1983. Lourdes Torres Papers, Series VII, Organizations, Box 10, Folder 20. Centro Archives.

53 Letter of Diana Caballero and Luis O. Reyes to Dear Friends of Bilingual Education, May 26, 1983; Flyer of the New York Coalition for Bilingual Education. Diana Caballero Papers, Series VI, Organizations, Box 23, Folder 17. Centro Archives.

54 See Robert E. Rossier, "Bilingual Education, Training for the Ghetto," *Policy Review* (Summer 1983): 36-45.

55 *Variety*, March 12, 1980, p. 28.

56 Eli Teiber, "Uprising at Fort Apache: Angered Residents Demand Newman Film be Stopped," *New York Post*, March 22, 1980, p. 3.

57 Ibid.

58 Press release, Office of Congressman Bob García, May 19, 1980. Records of United Bronx Parents, Series II, Box 1, Subject File 7. Centro Archives.

59 Press release, Office of the Roman Catholic Vicariate of the South Bronx, April 19, 1980. Ibid.

60 Records of United Bronx Parents, Series II, Box 1, Subject File 7. Centro Archives.

61 "Latin Cops Storm Fort Apache," *Daily News* April 30, 1980, p. 38.

62 Letter of Jaime Inclán to Committee Against Fort Apache, May 1st, 1980. Records of United Bronx Parents, Series II, Box 1, Subject File 7. Centro Archives.

63 Lillian Jiménez, "Fort Apache: Legacy of Shame Continued," *The Independent*, May 1980, p. 11.

64 Chronological History of the Committee Against Fort Apache, c. 1980. Records of United Bronx Parents, Series II, Box 1, Subject File 7. Centro Archives.

65 "Contra Fuerte Apache," *El Diario-La Prensa*, May 20, 1980, p. 2.

66 Records of United Bronx Parents, Series II, Box 1, Subject File 7. Centro Archives.

67 "Judíos protestan por la cinta Fort Apache," *El Diario-La Prensa*, June 6, 1980, p. 6.

68 Vincent Canby, "Screen: 'Fort Apache, the Bronx,' With Paul Newman," *New York Times*, February 6, 1981, p. C6.

69 Selwyn Raab, "Film Image Provokes Outcry in South Bronx," *New York Times*, February 6, 1981, p. C6.

70 Letter of William H. Gray, III to Norman Levy, January 29, 1981. Diana Caballero Papers, Series VII, Subject Files, Box 34, Folder 2. Centro Archives.

71 "El Concejo Municipal de N.Y.: Condena para 'Fuerte Apache,'" *El Diario-La Prensa*, Febru-

ary 10, 1981, p. 1.

72 Nat Hentoff, "New York City Council Cavalry Rides on 'Fort Apache,'" *Village Voice*, February 25-March 3, 1981, p. 8.

73 "Day of Unity & Pride," leaflet, no date. Diana Caballero Papers, Series V, National Congress for Puerto Rican Rights, Box 12, Folder 6. Centro Archives.

74 Assorted documents, Lourdes Torres Papers, Series VIII, Subject Files, Box 14, Folder 12. Centro Archives.

75 Letter of Rev. Neil A. Connolly to Jose Cintron, November 21, 1980. Lourdes Torres Papers, Series VIII, Subject Files, Box 14, Folder 13. Centro Archives.

76 Lincoln Hospital Sterilization Audit, January 1 to June 30, 1980. Ibid.

77 Memo of Joseph N. Cintron to Esta Armstrong, November 25, 1980. Ibid.

78 Ronald Sullivan, "2 City Hospitals to Do Abortions Despite Archdiocese," *New York Times*, May 16, 1979, p. B1.

79 Josue Rivas, "Sacerdotes y Otros Líderes Comunitarios Piden Cancelación de Médico del Lincoln," *Noticias del Mundo*, January 29, 1982, p. 9.

80 Assorted documents, Lourdes Torres Papers, Series VIII, Subject Files, Box 14, Folder 12. Centro Archives.

81 Letters of Bronx Coalition Against Sterilization Abuse to Members and Friends, February 1982 and March 1, 1982. Lourdes Torres Papers, Series VIII, Subject Files, Box 14, Folder 13. Centro Archives.

82 Letter of Linda Curtis to Dear Friends, April 22, 1982. Ibid.

83 Flyer of Coalicion Contra Esterilizaciones Abusivas, c. May 1982. Ibid.

84 Chikako Takeshita, *The Global Biopolitics of the IUD* (Cambridge, MA: MIT Press, 2012), p. 80.

85 María E. Pérez y González, *Puerto Ricans in the United States* (Westport, CT: Greewood Press, 2000), p. 89.

86 Assorted documents, flyers, and newsclippings. Lourdes Torres Papers, Series IV, National Congress for Puerto Rican Rights, Box 4, Folder 19. Centro Archives.

87 Minutes, National Congress for Puerto Rican Rights, Executive Committee, September 25, 1983, p. 3. Lourdes Torres Papers, Series IV, National Congress for Puerto Rican Rights, Box 5, Folder 8. Centro Archives.

88 "Marcha a Washington Sabado 17 de Mayo, 1980 ¡Un Compromiso No Falte!" advertisement in *El Diario-La Prensa*, May 14, 1980, p. 15; Fernando Moreno, "Boricuas van a Washington a protestar por lo de Vieques," *El Diario-La Prensa*, May 14, 1980, p. 5.

89 Elisabeth Pérez Luna, "Manifestación extraordinaria efectuarán a Vieques," *El Diario-La Prensa*, May 22, 1980, p. 4.

90 Larry Rohter, "Hispanics in State in Worst Poverty," *New York Times*, August 26, 1985, p. 1.

91 Larry Rohter, "El Barrio Residents Worry and Wait," *New York Times*, October 10, 1985, p. B16.

92 William G. Blair, "City to Give Hispanic Groups $1 Million to Aid Job Training," *New York Times*, December 5, 1985, p. B8.

Chapter 7

1 Letter of Ed Koch to Guillermo Linares, Diana Caballero, Dr. Luis Reyes, Coalition for Latino

Representation on the Board of Education, February 28, 1986. Diana Caballero Papers, Series V, National Congress for Puerto Rican Rights, Box 12, Folder 9. Centro Archives.

[2] Luis A. Miranda, "The Mayor is a *Paisano*," *New York Newsday*, August 14, 1987, p. 76.

[3] Institute for Puerto Rican Policy, "Testimony Before Manhattan Public Hearings of Mayor Koch's Commission on Hispanic Concerns," March 1986. Lourdes Torres Papers, Series VII, Organizations, Box 10, Folder 6. Centro Archives.

[4] Ibid.

[5] Evido de la Cruz, "Comisión de Asuntos Hispanos se reúne con Koch," *El Diario-La Prensa*, December 5, 1986, p. 2.

[6] Evido de la Cruz, "Koch se niega a nombrar hispano a la junta de educación," *El Diario-La Prensa*, December 11, 1986, p. 7; José Lumen Román, "Nueva York debe ayudar a sus pobres," *El Diario-La Prensa*, December 12, 1986, p. 14.

[7] Evido de la Cruz, "Comisión pide mayor representación hispana en el gobierno municipal," *El Diario-La Prensa*, December 10, 1986, p. 3.

[8] Evido de la Cruz, "Koch se niega a nombrar hispano a la junta de educación," *El Diario-La Prensa*, December 11, 1986, p. 7.

[9] "When Koch says no," Editorial, *El Diario-La Prensa*, December 12, 1986, p. 14.

[10] Press Release, "Naksone's Racial Purity Theory Supported by Leading Reaganites," September 30, 1986. Diana Caballero Papers, Series V, National Congress for Puerto Rican Rights, Box 15, Folder 1. Centro Archives.

[11] Carlos Alberto Montaner, "El señor Nakasone se hace el harakiri," *El Diario-La Prensa*, December 12, 1986, p. 15.

[12] Memo to National Board from Executive Committee, March 21, 1987. Lourdes Torres Papers, Series IV, National Congress for Puerto Rican Rights, Box 5, Folder 4. Centro Archives.

[13] Fifth National Puerto Rican Convention, New York City Mobilization, Outreach Tasks, April 20, 1989. Lourdes Torres Papers, Series IV, National Congress for Puerto Rican Rights, Box 3, Folder 6, Centro Archives.

[14] Letter of Julio Sabater to Frank Torres, June 14, 1989. Frank Torres Papers, Series VI, Organizations, Box 19, Folder 2. Centro Archives.

[15] Letter of Angelo Falcón to Edward I. Koch, January 14, 1986. Diana Caballero Papers, Series V, National Congress for Puerto Rican Rights, Box 21, Folder 1. Centro Archives.

[16] Letter of Angelo González to Edward I. Koch, January 15, 1986. Ibid.

[17] Letter of Edward I Koch to Angelo Falcón, January 17, 1986. Ibid.

[18] Coalition for Latino Representation on the Board of Education, Statement to Mayor Edward I. Koch, February 26, 1986. Ibid.

[19] Koch, *Mayor*, p. 33.

[20] Letter of Nydia M. Velázquez to Edward I. Koch, August 29, 1986; Letter of Stanley Brezenoff to Nydia M. Velázquez, October 7, 1986. Diana Caballero Papers, Series V, National Congress for Puerto Rican Rights, Box 21, Folder 1. Centro Archives.

[21] Letter of Ana I. Amaez and Joseph Pacheco to Dear Colleague, October 2, 1987. Diana Caballero Papers, Series VI, Organizations, Box 24, Folder 1. Centro Archives.

[22] "Puerto Rican/Latino Organizations Call for Clarity on Recent Promises," Joint Statement

to the Press, September 14, 1987. Luis O. Reyes Papers, Box 8, Folder 3. Centro Archives.

[23] Carlos García, "Exigen a Wagner Nombre Hispano En la Junta de Educación de N.Y.; Frank Sobrino, "Wagner Afirma que debería haber un hispano en Junta de Educación." Ibid.

[24] Frank Sobrino, "Adquiere mayor gravedad la falta de representatción latina en Educación," *El Diario-La Prensa*, October 25, 1987. Ibid.

[25] Evido de la Cruz, "Latinos califican de inaceptable la selección del nuevo canciller;" "Coalición tendrá cita con Wagner,"September 15, 1987; Frank Sobrino, "Educadores hispanos celebran reunión con Wagner," September 20, 1987. Ibid.

[26] Letter of Elizabeth Colón et al. to Robert Wagner, Jr., September 22, 1987. Ibid.

[27] New York City Board of Education Press Release, September 30, 1987. Ibid.

[28] Frank Sobrino, "Denuncian falta de liderazgo de algunos políticos hispanos," *El Diario-La Prensa*, November 2, 1987, p. 3.

[29] Frank Sobrino, " Serrano: Ya escribí mi carta a Ed Koch sobre representación latina en Junta de Educación," *El Diario-La Prensa*, November 4, 1987, p. 2.

[30] Sobrino, "Denuncian..."

[31] "Otro líder comunitario se alista a huelga de hambre," *El Diario-La Prensa*, November 4, 1987, p. 2.

[32] Rafael Anglada, "Un homenaje a Evelina Antonetty," *El Diario-La Prensa*, December 5, 1986, p. 14.

[33] Emily Sachar, "38 Contenders for Chancellor's Job," *New York Newsday*, November 1, 1987; Jane Perlez, "Board Might Name Temporary Chief," *New York Times*, November 1, 1987. Luis O. Reyes Papers, Box 8, Folder 3. Centro Archives.

[34] "Emergency Coalition for Latino Representation on the Board of Education, Address in Honor of Evelina Lopez Antonetty, November 19, 1987, given by Luis Garden Acosta." Ibid.

[35] Evelyn Hernandez, "Hispanics: Koch Remark 'Crass,'" *New York Newsday*, November 19,1987. Ibid.

[36] Frank Sobrino and Rossana Rosado, "Mil Manifestantes latinos exigen representación" *El Diario-La Prensa* November 20, 1987. Ibid.

[37] Jane Perlez, "Hispanic Woman to Fill School Board Vacancy," *New York Times*, December 8, 1987, p. B5.

[38] Ibid.

[39] Diana Caballero, "A Latino Rights Course for Pols," *New York Newsday*, December 14, 1987. Luis O Reyes Papers, Box 8, Folder 3. Centro Archives; Julio Laboy, "Hispanic Demands Met by Kock with New appointment to City's Board of Education," *Hispanic*, April 1988, p. 17.

[40] Jane Perlez, "Koch Seeks Bigger School Board To Allow for a Hispanic Member," *The New York Times*, November 24, 1987, p. B3.

[41] News from Assemblyman Roger Green, December 30, 1987. Diana Caballero Papers, Series VII, Subject Files, Box 38, Folder 4. Centro Archives.

[42] Joaquin Torres Feliciano, "Los Ayudantes Hispanos de Koch." Diana Caballero Papers, Series VII, Subject Files, Box 35, Folder 3. Centro Archives; Suzanne Daley, "Hispanic Dropout Rate Is Highest In Study of New York City Schools," *New York Times,* June 21, 1988, p. A1.

[43] Neil A. Lewis, "Early Education of Green: Ethnic Wars of New York," *New York Times,* September 5, 1988, p. 23.

44 Robert Lindsey, "Debates Growing On Use Of English," *New York Times,* July 26, 1986, p. A1.
45 Luis Fernandez, "Caucus lanza proyecto para hacer a Nueva York un estado multilingüe," *El Diario-La Prensa,* November 11, 1986, p. 5.
46 Luis Fernández, "Más dinero para enseñar ingles," *El Diario-La Prensa,* November 11, 1986, p. 2.
47 Evido de la Cruz, "Quinones: peligro que hay que detener," *El Diario-La Prensa,* November 7, 1986, p. 3.
48 Luis Fernandez, "Tratan de Imponer US English en NY y NJ," *El Diario-La Prensa,* November 7, 1986, p. 3.
49 Luis Fernández, "Minorías crean comité para combatir el US English," *El Diario-La Prensa,* November 13, 1986, p. 6.
50 "Beyond U.S. English," Editorial, *El Diario-La Prensa,* November 7, 1986, p. 12.
51 Miguel Pérez, "In any language, a small but growing effort," *Daily News,* February 19, 1987, p. 37.
52 Frank Sobrino, "Derrotan proyecto de 'US English' en Nueva York," *El Diario-La Prensa,* May 13, 1987, p. 3.
53 Flyer announcing NCPRR Northeast Regional Strategy Conference on the English Only Movement. Diana Caballero Papers, Series VII, Subject Files, Box 32, Folder 6. Centro Archives; Jeffrey Schmalz, "Hispanic Influx Spurs 3 Ballots on Language," *New York Times,* October 26, 1988, p. A1.
54 Letter of the Committee for a Multilingual New York, November 1, 1988. Luis O. Reyes Papers, Box 29, Folder 14. Centro Archives.
55 Ibid.; Flyer for Demonstrate Against English-only Rules at the Workplace, Diana Caballero Papers, Series V, National Congress for Puerto Rican Rights, Box 21, Folder 6. Centro Archives.
56 Eric Schmitt, "English-Only Bill Ignites Debate and Fear in L.I.," *New York Times,* February 14, 1989, p. B3.
57 Letter of Committee for a Multilingual New York to Dear Alice, May 26, 1987. Diana Caballero Papers, Series V, National Congress for Puerto Rican Rights, Box 21, Folder 7. Centro Archives.
58 Letter of Committee for a Multilingual New York to Dear Friends/Members, February 3, 1989; Letter of Committee for a Multilingual New York to Dear Friend/Member, January 20, 1989. Ibid.
59 Flyer announcing NCPRR Northeast Regional Strategy Conference on the English Only Movement. Diana Caballero Papers, Series VII, Subject Files, Box 32, Folder 6. Centro Archives.
60 Invitation to CSS Institute For Community Empowerment, "The English Only Attack." Ibid.
61 Flyer for Hostos Stop English Only, English Only vs. Language Freedom program. Ibid.
62 Press Release, APRED Condemns Attack on Bilingual Education, July 25, 1989. Diana Caballero Papers, Series VI, Organizations, Box 19, Folder 9. Centro Archives.
63 "Police Brutality Must be Investigated," *El Diario-La Prensa,* January 2, 1987, p. 12; Enrique Soria, "Denuncian que Policía Golpeó Brutalmente a Tres Mujeres," *El Diario-La Prensa,* January 1, 1987, p. 3.
64 Press Statement of the Puerto Rican Legal Defense and Education Fund, Inc. on the Brutal Attack of Two Women by Transit Police Officers, February 2, 1987. Lourdes Torres Papers, Series VIII, Subject Files, Box 13, Folder 25. Centro Archives.

[65] Ron Davis, "Giving the Slip to Protesters," *New York Newsday*, April 13, 1988; Flyer for Acto de Presencia Frente a la Alcaldia, Jueves 21 de Abril de 1988. Diana Caballero Papers, Series V, National Congress for Puerto Rican Rights, Box 17, Folder 1. Centro Archives; José Luis Morín, "A Community Under Siege: Racial Violence and Police Brutality Against Latinos," *Centro* 2:5 (Primavera 1989), p. 97.

[66] Richie Pérez, National Congress for Puerto Rican Rights, New York City Chapter, n.d. Diana Caballero Papers, Series V, National Congress for Puerto Rican Rights, Box 17, Folder 1. Centro Archives.

[67] National Congress for Puerto Rican Rights, President's Report, March 1988. Diana Caballero Papers, Series V, National Congress for Puerto Rican Rights, Box 15, Folder 4. Centro Archives.

[68] "Se Enfrentan Policías y Manifestantes," *El Diario-La Prensa*, April 13, 1988, Diana Caballero Papers, Series V, National Congress for Puerto Rican Rights, Box 17, Folder 1. Centro Archives.

[69] "¡Que Pasa!," *Unidad Borinqueña* 7:1 (May 1988). Diana Caballero Papers, Series V, National Congress for Puerto Rican Rights, Box 16, Folder 15. Centro Archives.

[70] Richard Pérez, "Racism isn't black and white," *New York Newsday*, August 2, 1988, p. 52.

[71] Flyer of Demostración Colectiva, Coalición Latina Para Justicia Racial, Diana Caballero Papers, Series V, National Congress for Puerto Rican Rights, Box 21, Folder 2. Centro Archives.

[72] Evido de la Cruz, "Sugieren Policía contrate a más minorías," *El Diario-La Prensa*, November 11, 1986, p. 3.

[73] "Take a Stand Against Apartheid," *En Nueva York*, Newsletter of the NYC Chapter - National Congress for Puerto Rican Rights. c. 1986. Diana Caballero Papers, Series V, National Congress for Puerto Rican Rights, Box 15, Folder 1. Centro Archives.

[74] "Anti-Machine Candidates or Business as Usual?," n.d. Lourdes Torres Papers, Series VIII, Subject Files, Box 14, Folder 4. Centro Archives.

[75] Educadores del Pueblo Flyer, c. 1986. Lourdes Torres Papers, Series VII, Organizations, Box 10, Folder 3. Centro Archives.

[76] "Coalition for Racial Justice Postpones March," n.d.; "LUPA Affirms New York City has Declared Open Season on Puerto Ricans," August 1, 1986. Lourdes Torres Papers, Series VIII, Subject Files, Box 12, Folder 6. Centro Archives.

[77] News from District 65, August 6, 1986. Ibid.

[78] El Grito de Williamsburg, September 24, 1986. Lourdes Torres Papers, Series VII, Organizations, Box 9, Folder 7. Centro Archives.

[79] "Dos hispanos casi pierden la vida en Howard Beach," *El Diario-La Prensa*, December 23, 1986, p. 3.

[80] Enrique Soria and Manuel Avendaño, "Identifican a segundo agresor de hispanos," *El Diario-La Prensa*, December 26, 1986, p. 3.

[81] Evido de la Cruz, "Marcha contra el racismo en Howard Beach," *El Diario-La Prensa*, December 25, 1986, p. 3.

[82] Enrique Soria, "Hieren a hispano porque hablaba español," *El Diario-La Prensa*, Sunday Supplement, December 28, 1986, p. 1.

[83] Enrique Soria, "Koch pide comisión nacional contra el racismo," *El Diario-La Prensa*, December 29, 1986, p. 3.

[84] "¿Cuantos otros incidents raciales?" Editorial, *El Diario-La Prensa*, December 22, 1986, p. 14.

85 Soria, "Hieren a hispano..."
86 "Marcha contra el racismo en Howard Beach," *El Diario-La Prensa*, Sunday Supplement, December 28, 1986, p. 3.
87 Evido de la Cruz, "Las tensiones raciales no son nada nuevo en Howard Beach," *El Diario-La Prensa*, Sunday Supplement, December 28, 1986, p. 3.
88 Enrique Soria, "Koch pide comisión nacional contra el racismo," *El Diario-La Prensa*, December 29, 1986, p. 3.
89 Rossana Rosado, "Tolerando al racismo," *El Diario-La Prensa*, December 29, 1986, p. 11.
90 Manuel Santana, "Reclaman Fiscal Especial Investigue Ataque Racial Contra Dos Hispanos," *Noticias del Mundo*, January 14, 1987, p. 2; Lydia Chavez, "Ethnic Groups Cite an Attack on 2 in Queens," *New York Times*, January 14, 1987, p. B4; Elaine Rivera, "Hispanics Seek Probe," *New York Newsday*, January 14, 1987, p. 23; Manuel Avendaño, "Cuomo nombra fiscal especial en caso de Howard Beach," *El Diario-La Prensa*, January 14, 1987, p. 3.
91 Puerto Rican Organization for Growth, Research, Education and Self-Sufficiency, "Racism on the Rise in New York City," *Progress Report*, vol. 6, no. 1, January 1987, p. 1. Diana Caballero Papers, Series VI, Organizations, Box 24, Folder 13. Centro Archives.
92 Ibid.
93 Ibid.

Chapter 8

1 Gerena Valentín, op. cit., pp. 108-117.
2 Nick Lugo, Terramax, 2004.
3 *The New York Red Book*, 1941.
4 Díaz, Jr., Terramax, June 10, 2004.
5 "Las Inscripciones," *El Diario de Nueva York*, November 2, 1960, p. 15.
6 César Andreu Iglesias, ed., *Memoirs of Bernardo Vega* (New York: Monthly Review Press, 1984), p. 121.
7 Ibid., pp. 129-130.
8 Ibid., p. 131.
9 See Virginia E. Sánchez Korrol, *From Colonia to Community* (Berkeley: University of California Press, 1994), pp. 147-150.
10 Lawrence R. Chenault, *The Puerto Rican Migrant in New York City* (New York: Russell & Russell, 1938), p. 128.
11 Ibid., pp. 153-155.
12 Art Shields, "Puerto Ricans Find a Friend in Harlem—The Workers Alliance," *The Daily Worker*, September 30, 1938, p. 4.
13 David Badillo, From South of the Border: Latino Experiences in Urban America, Ph.D. Dissertation, City University of New York, 1988, p. 84.
14 Edgardo Meléndez, "Vito Marcantonio, Puerto Rican Migration, and the 1949 Mayoral Election in New York City," *CENTRO Journal* XXII: 2 (Fall 2010), pp. 200-201.
15 "El Diario y WWRL Darán Amplia Información Sobre Elecciones," *El Diario de Nueva York*, November 7, 1960, p. 5.

16 Ismael Fernández, "Campaña Política Por Cartas De Boricuas De N.Y. Para Los De P.R.," *El Diario de Nueva York*, November 3, 1960, p. 4.

17 "Procurador General Combate Táctica De Intimidar a Ciertos Electores," *El Diario de Nueva York*, November 2, 1960, p. 3.

18 José J. Torres Cintrón, "Líderes Boricuas Plantean a Wagner Tácticas Dilatorias En Inscripciones," *El Diario de Nueva York*, November 3, 1960, p. 2.

19 "Los Liberales," editorial, *El Diario de Nueva York*, November 14, 1960, p. 14.

20 Lugo, Terramax, 2004.

21 Gonzalo Jusino, "Nueva York Hispano," *El Diario de Nueva York*, November 4, 1960, p. 15.

22 "¡Hispanos!," political advertisement, *El Diario de Nueva York*, November 4, 1960, p. 12.

23 "¡Hispanos!," political advertisement, *El Diario de Nueva York*, November 2, 1960, p. 6.

24 The two political advertisements cited above include the following caption: "This ad was paid by the Spanish-Speaking Citizens Committee for Nixon, Lodge, and Puerto Rican candidates."

25 "Kennedy and the Spanish People," *El Diario de Nueva York*, November 4, 1962, p. 16.

26 Ramón Grosfoguel, *Colonial Subjects, Puerto Ricans in a Global Perspective* (Berkeley: University of California Press, 2003), p. 140.

27 Ibid., pp. 140-141.

28 Michael Lapp, "Managing Migration: The Migration Division of Puerto Rico and Puerto Ricans in New York City, 1948-1968," Ph.D. Dissertation, Johns Hopkins University, 1990, pp. 295, 296.

29 Interview of John Carro by Carlos Sanabria, June 3, 1988. Centro Archives.

30 Ibid.

31 Erazo interview, 2002.

32 Carro interview, 1988.

33 Commonwealth of Puerto Rico, Department of Labor, Migration Division, *Monthly Activities Report of the Migration Division, August 1969; September 1969, October 1969, November 1969*, pp. 7, 7, 7, 9 respectively. Migration Division Collection, Monthly Reports, Box 5, Centro Archives.

34 Andreas Wimmer, *Ethnic Boundary Making* (New York: Oxford University Press, 2013), p. 208.

35 Ibid., p. 210.

36 Documentation of the Concerns and recommendations at the April 15, NYC Chapter Retreat, op. cit.

37 Michael Walzer, *Interpretation and Social Criticism* (Cambridge: Harvard University Press, 1987), pp. 21-22.

38 Directories of Puerto Rican Organizations in the United States, Migration Division, Department of Labor, Commonwealth of Puerto Rico. Migration Division Collection, Community Organizations Directories, Box 1. Centro Archives.

39 Gil de la Madrid, "Boricuas se Apoderan Bronx College...,"

40 Hoffman, "Mayor Criticized by Puerto Ricans...."

41 See Cruz, *Identity and Power*, pp. 10-12.

42 Kenny, op. cit., p. 10.

43 See Herbstein, op. cit.; Rosa Estades, "Symbolic Unity: The Puerto Rican Day Parade," in Clara E. Rodríguez and Virginia Sánchez-Korrol, eds., *Historical Perspectives on Puerto Rican*

Survival in the United States, (Princeton: Markus Wiener Publishers, 1996). The main problem of the Parade over the years has been corruption rather than Balkanization.

44 Kenny, op. cit., p. 10.

45 Richard Hofstadter, *The Idea of a Party System* (Berkeley: University of California Press, 1969), pp. 4-5.

46 Herman Badillo and Michael C. D. Macdonald, "Koch Says: Etc., Etc.; But, Let's Look," *New York Times,* February 16, 1981, p. A19.

47 Richard Pérez, "Fort Apache: Did We Win or Lose?," *Don Peyo,* newspaper of the Puerto Rican Educators Association. c. 1982. Diana Caballero Papers, Series V, National Congress for Puerto Rican Rights, Box 12, Folder 6. Centro Archives.

48 "CAFA: An Evaluation," *PAW PRINTS,* Newsletter of People Against White Supremacy, March/April, c. 1981. Diana Caballero Papers, Series V, National Congress for Puerto Rican Rights, Box 12, Folder 6. Centro Archives.

49 Hofstadter, op. cit., pp. 17, 19.

50 Kukathas, op. cit., p. 268.

51 "Comité del Estado 51 al Desfile," *El Diario-La Prensa,* June 8, 1980, p. 4.

52 C. Wright Mills, Clarence O. Senior, and Rose K. Goldsen, *The Puerto Rican Journey: New York's Newest Migrants* (New York: Russell and Russell, 1967), p. 212. The book was originally published in 1950.

53 Daniel Patrick Moynihan, *Maximum Feasible Misunderstanding, Community Action in the War on Poverty* (New York: The Free Press, 1970), pp. 129-130.

54 José E. Velázquez Luyanda, "The National Puerto Rican Agenda (NPRA) Reaches New Heights," *The NiLP Report,* July 27, 2016. Author's collection.

BIBLIOGRAPHY

Books

Acosta-Belén, Edna, et al. *"Adiós Borinquen Querida:" The Puerto Rican Diaspora, Its History and Contributions.* Albany, NY: CELAC, 2000.

Andreu Iglesias, César, ed., Juan Flores, trans. *Memoirs of Bernardo Vega: A Contribution to the History of the Puerto Rican Community in New York,* New York: Monthly Review Press, 1984.

Aristotle. *The Politics.* New York: Penguin Books, 1982.

Badillo, Herman. *One Nation, One Standard, An Ex-Liberal on How Hispanics Can Succeed Just Like Other Immigrant Groups.* New York: Sentinel, 2006.

Carroll, Tamar. *Mobilizing New York: AIDS, Antipoverty, and Feminist Activism.* Chapell Hill, NC: University of North Carolina Press, 2015.

Chenault, Lawrence R. *The Puerto Rican Migrant in New York City.* New York: Russell & Russell, 1938 (Reissued 1970).

Cole, Phillip. *Philosophies of Exclusion: Liberal Political Theory and Immigration.* Edinburgh: Edinburgh University Press, 2000.

Cruz, José E. *Identity and Power: Puerto Rican Politics and the Challenge of Ethnicity.* Philadelphia: Temple University Press, 1998.

Dávila, Arlene. *Barrio Dreams, Puerto Ricans, Latinos, and the Neoliberal City.* Berkeley: University of California Press, 2004.

Epstein, A.L. *Ethos and Identity.* London: Tavistock Publications, 1978.

Ferretti, Fred. *The Year the Big Apple Went Bust.* New York: G.P. Putnam's Sons, 1976.

Fuchs, Ester. *Mayors and Money: Fiscal Policy in New York and Chicago.* Chicago: University of Chicago Press, 1992.

Gerena Valentín, Gilberto. *Gilberto Gerena Valentín: My Life as a Community Activist, Labor Organizer, and Progressive Politician in New York City.* Edited by Carlos Rodríguez-Fraticelli. New York: Center for Puerto Rican Studies, 2013.

Glazer, Nathan and Daniel Patrick Moynihan. *Beyond the Melting Pot; The Negroes, Puerto Ricans, Jews, Italians, and Irish of New York City.* Cambridge: M.I.T. Press, 1970.

Grosfoguel, Ramón. *Colonial Subjects, Puerto Ricans in a Global Perspective.* Berkeley: University of California Press, 2003.

Hofstadter, Richard. *The Idea of a Party System.* Berkeley: University of California Press, 1969.

Hoover, Kenneth R. *A Politics of Identity, Liberation and the Natural Community.* Urbana, IL: University of Illinois Press, 1975.

Ingram, David. *Group Rights, Reconciling Equality and Difference.* Lawrence, KS: University Press of Kansas, 2000.

Kasinitz, Philip. *Caribbean New York.* Ithaca: Cornell University Press, 1992.

Klein, Woody. *Lindsay's Promise, The Dream That Failed.* London: The Macmillan Company, 1970.

Kukathas, Chandran. *The Liberal Archipelago.* Oxford: Oxford University Press, 2003.

Kymlicka, Will. *Multicultural Citizenship.* New York: Oxford University Press, 1995.

Koch, Edward I. *Mayor, An Autobiography*. New York: Warner Books, 1984.
Lindsay, John V. *The City*. New York: W.W. Norton & Company, 1970.
Marion Young, Iris. *La justicia y la política de la diferencia*. Madrid: Ediciones Cátedra, 2000.
Meléndez, Edgardo. *Sponsored Migration, The State and Puerto Rican Postwar Migration to the United States*. Columbus, OH: Ohio State University Press, 2017.
Mills, C. Wright, Clarence O. Senior and Rose K. Goldsen. *The Puerto Rican Journey: New York's Newest Migrants*. New York: Russell and Russell, 1967.
Moynihan, Daniel Patrick. *Maximum Feasible Misunderstanding, Community Action in the War on Poverty*. New York: The Free Press, 1970.
Pantoja, Antonia. *Memoir of a Visionary: Antonia Pantoja*. Houston, TX: Arte Público Press, 2002.
Pérez y González, María E. *Puerto Ricans in the United States*. Westport, CT: Greewood Press, 2000.
Podair, Jerald E. *The Strike that Changed New York, Blacks, Whites, and the Ocean Hill-Brownville Crisis*. New Haven: Yale University Press, 2002.
Rivera-Batiz, Francisco L. and Carlos E. Santiago. *Puerto Ricans in the United States: A Changing Reality*. Washington, D.C.: National Puerto Rican Coalition, 1994.
Rousseau, Jean-Jacques. *The Social Contract* and *Discourses*. London: J.M. Dent Ltd, 1973.
Sánchez-Korrol, Virginia. *From Colonia to Community: The History of Puerto Ricans in New York City*. Berkeley, CA: The University of California Press, 1994.
Shapiro, Fred C. and James W. Sullivan. *Race Riots, New York 1964*. New York: Thomas Y. Crowell Company, 1964.
Shefter, Martin. *Political Crisis, Fiscal Crisis: The Collapse and Revival of New York City*. New York: Columbia University Press, 1992.
Schlesinger, Arthur M., Jr. *The Disuniting of America: Reflections on a Multicultural Society*. New York: W.W. Norton, 1998.
Sotomayor, Sonia. *My Beloved World*. (New York: Vintage Books, 2014).
Takeshita, Chikako. *The Global Biopolitics of the IUD*. Cambridge, MA: MIT Press, 2012.
Walzer, Michael. *Interpretation and Social Criticism*. Cambridge: Harvard University Press, 1987.
Williams, Mason B. *City of Ambition, FDR, La Guardia, and the Making of Modern New York*. New York: W. W. Norton & Company, 2013.
Williams, Melissa S. *Voice, Trust, and Memory, Marginalized Groups and the Failings of Liberal Representation*. Princeton, NJ: Princeton University Press, 1998.
Wimmer, Andreas. *Ethnic Boundary Making*. New York: Oxford University Press, 2013.
Zarefsky, David. *President Johnson's War on Poverty, Rhetoric and History*. Tuscaloosa, AL: University of Alabama Press, 1986.

Book Chapters
Baldwin, James. "Princes and Powers." In *Nobody Knows My Name*, James Baldwin, pp. 24-54. New York: Dell Publishing, 1961.
Benmayor, Rina. "Gender, College, and Cultural Citizenship: A Case Study of Mexican-Heritage Students in Higher Education." In *Gendered Citizenships*, Kia Lilly Caldwell, et al., eds., pp. 137-156. (New York: Palgrave Macmillan, 2009).
Cruz, José E. "Pushing Left to Get to the Center: Puerto Rican Radicalism in Hartford,

Connecticut." In *The Puerto Rican Movement, Voices from the Diaspora*, Andrés Torres and José E. Vélazquez, eds., pp. 69–87. Philadelphia: Temple University Press, 1998.

Estades, Rosa. "Symbolic Unity: The Puerto Rican Day Parade." In *Historical Perspectives on Puerto Rican Survival in the United States*, Clara E. Rodríguez and Virginia Sánchez-Korrol, eds., pp. 99-106. Princeton: Markus Wiener Publishers, 1996.

Falcón, Angelo. "Puerto Ricans and the Politics of Racial Identity." In *Racial and Ethnic Identity: Psychological Development and Creative Expression*. Herbert W. Harris, et al., eds., pp. 193-207. New York: Routledge, 1995.

Gellner, Ernest. "Introduction." In *Liberalism in Modern Times*, Ernest Gellner and César Cansino, eds., pp. 1-4. Budapest: Central European University Press, 1996.

Magnarella, Paul J. "The Black Panther Party's Confrontation with Ethnicity, Race and Class." In *The Politics of Ethnicity and National Identity*, Santosh C. Saha, ed., pp. 53-68. New York: Peter Lang, 2007.

MacIntyre, Alasdair. "The Indispensability of Political Theory." In *The Nature of Political Theory*, David Miller and Larry Siedentop, eds., pp. 17-33. Oxford: Clarendon Press, 1983.

McCraken, Paul W. "Economic Policy and the Lessons of Experience." In *Republican Papers*, Melvin R. Laird, ed., pp. 372-390. New York: Praeger, 1968.

Pogge, Thomas W. "Group Rights and Ethnicity." In *Ethnicity and Group Rights*, Ian Shapiro and Will Kymlicka, eds., pp. 187-221. New York: New York University Press, 1997.

Saha, Santosh C. "Introduction." In *The Politics of Ethnicity and National Identity*, Sattosh C. Saha, ed., pp. pp. 1-6. New York: Peter Lang, 2007.

Vargas-Ramos, Carlos. "Puerto Rican Political and Civic Engagement in the United States." In *Puerto Ricans at the Dawn of the New Millennium*, Edwin Meléndez and Carlos Vargas-Ramos, eds., pp. 260-283. New York: Centro de Estudios Puertorriqueños, 2014.

Journal and Periodical Articles

Caballero, Diana. "School Board Elections: Parents Against the Odds." *CENTRO Journal* 2:5 (1989), p. 85.

Camacho Souza, Blase. "Trabajo y Tristeza—"Work and Sorrow: The Puerto Ricans of Hawaii 1900-1902." *The Hawaiian Journal of History* 18 (1984): 156-173.

De Jesús, Anthony and Madeline Pérez. "From Community Control to Consent Decree: Puerto Ricans Organizing for Education and Language Rights in 1960s and '70s New York City." *CENTRO Journal* 21: 2 (Fall 2009): 7-31.

Jiménez, Ramón J. "Hostos Community College: Battle of the Seventies." *CENTRO Journal* XV:I (Spring 2003): 99-111.

King, Desmond S. and Rogers M. Smith. "Racial Orders in American Political Development." *The American Political Science Review* 99: 1 (February 2005): 75-92.

Meléndez, Edgardo. "Vito Marcantonio, Puerto Rican migration, and the 1949 mayoral election in New York City." *CENTRO Journal* 22:2 (2010): 198–233.

Meyer, Gerald J. "Save Hostos: Politics and Community Mobilization to Save a College in the Bronx, 1973-1978." *CENTRO Journal* 15:I (Spring 2003): 73-97.

Pantoja, Antonia. "Puerto Ricans in New York: A Historical and Community Development Perspective." *CENTRO Journal* 2:5 (Primavera 1989): 20-31.

Rossier, Robert E. "Bilingual Education, Training for the Ghetto." *Policy Review* (Summer 1983): 36-45.
Santiago, Carlos E. "The Migratory Impact of Minimum Wage Legislation: Puerto Rico, 1970-1987." *International Migration Review*, 27: 4 (Winter 1992): 772-795.
Santiago, Carlos E. and Erik Thorbecke. "A Multisectoral Framework for the Analysis of Labor Mobility and Development in LDCs: An Application to Postwar Puerto Rico." *Economic Development and Cultural Change*, 37:1 (October 1988): 127-148.
Totti, Xavier F. and Félix V. Matos Rodríguez. "Activism and Change Among Puerto Ricans in New York, 1960s and 1970s" *CENTRO Journal* 21: 2 (Fall 2009): 4-5.

Doctoral Dissertations

Badillo, David. From South of the Border: Latino Experiences in Urban America. City University of New York, 1988.
Dyer, Conrad M. Protest and the Politics of Open Admissions: The Impact of the Black and Puerto Rican Students' Community (of City College). City University of New York, 1990.
Herbstein, Judith F. Rituals and Politics of the Puerto Rican "Community" in New York City. City University of New York, 1978.
Lapp, Michael. Managing Migration: The Migration Division of Puerto Rico and Puerto Ricans in New York City, 1948-1968. Johns Hopkins University, 1990.
Santiago Santiago, Isaura. *Aspira v. Board of Education of the City of New York*: A History and Policy Analysis. Fordham University, 1978.

Reports

Meléndez, Edwin, ed. *Puerto Rico Post-Maria*. New York: Center for Puerto Rican Studies, 2018.

Government Documents

United States Commission on Civil Rights. *Puerto Ricans in the Continental United States: An Uncertain Future*. Washington, D.C.: U.S. Commission on Civil Rights, 1976.

Archival and Private Collections

Author's collection
Herman Badillo Papers, Boricua College.
Diana Caballero Papers, Centro Archives.
Jesús Colón Papers, Centro Archives.
Commonwealth of Puerto Rico, Department of Labor, Migration Division Collection, Centro Archives.
Edward Koch Papers, New York City Municipal Archives.
John V. Lindsay Papers, New York City Municipal Archives.
Edward Mercado Papers, Centro Archives.
Joseph Monserrat Papers, Centro Archives.
Luis O. Reyes Papers, Centro Archives.
Ruth Reynolds Collection, Centro Archives.

Records of United Bronx Parents, Centro Archives.
Frank Torres Papers, Centro Archives.
Lourdes Torres Papers, Centro Archives.

Newspaper Collections & Clippings
El Diario de Nueva York
El Diario-La Prensa
El Imparcial
El Mundo
El Tiempo
La Voz de Puerto Rico en U.S.A.
New York Newsday
New York Times
Noticias del Mundo
The Guardian
The New York Telegram and Sun
The Worker

Interviews
Herman Badillo, August 10, 2006, by José E. Cruz.
María Canino, April 26, 2002, by Lillian Jiménez.
John Carro, June 3, 1988; June 7, 1988, by Carlos Sanabria,
Manuel "Manny" Díaz, video interview for documentary Politics con Sabor, June 10, 2004, Terramax Entertainment, LLC, Centro Archives.
Joseph Erazo, March 20, 2002, by Lillian Jiménez.
Gilberto Gerena Valentín, June 6, 1988, by Carlos Rodríguez-Fraticelli and Amílcar Tirado.
Nick Lugo, video interview for documentary Politics con Sabor, 2004, Terramax Entertainment, LLC. Centro Archives.
Josephine Nieves, May 24, 1988, by Amílcar Tirado and Carlos Sanabria.
Lourdes Torres, July 12, 2006, by José E. Cruz.

Other Sources
Nuyoricans: Puerto Ricans in New York. VHS. Glazen Creative Group in association with Thirteen/WNET New York. 2002.
Palante, Siempre Palante. Video Documentary. Produced and Directed by Iris Morales. Latino Education Network Service, 1996.
Politics con Sabor, A History of Puerto Ricans and Other Hispanics in New York State Politics. Terramax Entertainment, LLC & Centro/Hunter College/CUNY. 2006.
Puerto Ricans. Andrew Schlessinger, Executive Producer. Bala Cynwyd, PA: Schlessinger Video Productions, 1993.

INDEX

Abad, Luis Rodríguez, 92
Abrams, Robert, 38, 43, 86
Abreu, Mario, 69
Acción Hispana, 85
Advisory Committee for Hispanic Affairs, 138
affirmative action, 18, 88, 105, 124
African Americans, 18, 21, 22, 78, 87, 98, 117, 127, 141, 143, 168
Alianza Obrera, 155
Alianza Puertorriqueña, 155
Alicea, Víctor, 53
Alvarado, Rafael, 93
Alvarez, Luis, 110, 111
American Friends Service Committee, 134
American Labor Party, 25, 153
Andrade, Kathy, 124
Anglada, Mario, 103
Anglophone political theory, 26–27
Anker, Irving, 105
Anti-Apartheid Coordinating Council of New York, 149
Anti-Defamation League, 97
anti-poverty funds, 47, 68, 73, 79, 86, 87, 101, 112, 168
Anti-Poverty Operations Board, 52
anti-Semitism, 76, 96, 97
Antonetty, Evelina, 53, 74, 97, 103, 108–9, 112, 113, 119, 142
Aponte, Humberto, 97
Aprea, Joseph, 150–51
APRED. See Association of Puerto Rican Executive Directors (APRED)
Arce, Henry, 78
Arce, Oscar, 105
Aristotle, 21–22
Arm, Walter, 60
Arroyo, Anthony Stevens, 109–10, 123
Asociación Comunal de Dominicanos Progresistas, 129, 141
Asociación Nacionalista, 155
ASPIRA, 25, 44, 52, 55, 68, 87, 98, 103-05, 110, 122, 128, 129, 140-42, 144, 145, 150, 153, 160, 165, 173n31
Association of Hispanic Police Officers, 149
Association of Puerto Rican Executive Directors (APRED), 135, 141, 147
autonomy, 17, 25, 44, 47, 50, 72, 75, 118, 153, 169, 170
Aviles, Miguel Joey, 34
Azabache, 78

Babín, Maria Teresa, 27–28, 103
Baca, Eddie, 48
Badillo, Américo, 92
Badillo, Herman, 35, 50, 60, 70, 72, 78–79, 81, 86, 93, 97, 102, 105, 106, 112, 116, 117, 154, 155, 157, 158, 167, 168
Baez, Luis, 115–16
Baldwin, James, 23
Barretto, Ray, 107, 119, 130
Barrios-Paoli, Lillian 137
Batista, Jorge, 105

Beame, Abraham D., 37, 117, 177n12
Beattie, Richard, 140, 143
Bedford Stuyvesant Youth and Action, 52
Bellamy, Carol, 112
Benítez, Jaime, 54
Bennett, Charles, 90
Betancourt, Alfonso, 60
Betanzos, Amalia, 68, 88, 93, 101, 110, 143
Big MAC, 38
bilingual education, bilingualism, 47, 76, 84, 103–4, 114, 117, 125, 128, 145, 146, 147, 153, 165
Billings, David, Jr., 98
bill S-901, 145–46
Bithorn, María, 98
Black and Latino Coalition Against Police Brutality, 115, 120, 130
Black Panthers, 20, 28, 96
Black Student Union, 118
Black United Front, 130
Board of Education, 55, 58, 69, 74–76, 78, 91, 97, 103, 104, 114–15, 128–29, 137, 141–45
Board of Higher Education, 75, 79, 92, 117–18
Bonilla, Edwin Seda, 88
Bonilla, Frank, 47, 69, 103, 119, 159
Botein, Bernard, 77
Bowker, Albert, 142
Brezenoff, Stanley, 141
Bronx, conference at, 85–87, 86
Bronx Coalition Against Sterilization Abuse, 132, 133–34
Bronx Community College, 84, 162–63
Brooklyn College, 73–74
Brooklyn League of Afro-American Collegians, 73
Brotherhood of Arecibeños Campeche, 101
Brownsville Spanish Community Club, 57
Bustelo, Manuel, 110

Caballero, Diana, 75, 120, 123, 129, 141, 142, 143
Cabán, Luis, 123
Cabranes, Manuel, 159
CAFA. See Committee Against Fort Apache (CAFA)
Camacho v. Rogers, 51
Canby, Vincent, 131
Canino, María Josefa, 103, 173n31
CAP. See Council Against Poverty (CAP)
capitalism, 20, 34
Capó, Félix Rodríguez "Bobby," 106, 119
Cardona, Louis, 70
Cardona, Luis, 112
Carey, Hugh, 38, 118, 130
Carmichael, Stokely, 74
Carrión, Enio, 124
Carro, John, 51, 60, 88, 113, 154, 159
Carroll, Tamar, 22
Carter, Jimmy, 110
Carter, Robert, 129
Casiano, Manuel, Jr., 85
Catholicism, 109–10, 146
Cavanagh, Edward F., Jr., 61

CCFIS. See Citywide Committee for Integrated Schools (CCFIS)
CDA. See Community Development Agency (CDA)
Cedeño, Blanca, 52
Center for Puerto Rican Studies, CUNY, 102, 110, 122, 141, 161
Central Commercial High School, 72–73
Cerpa, Frances, 120
Chalk, O. Roy, 157
Chávez, Linda, 146
CHE. See Comunidad Hispana Para Educacion [Hispanic Community for Education] (CHE)
Chenault, Lawrence, 155–56
Chinese American Progressive Association, 146
Chinese for Affirmative Action, 105
Chinese Progressive Association of New York, 147
Chisholm, Shirley, 97
Chong, Celia, 145
Christian Leadership Conference, 134
Church of Nuestra Señora de la Medalla Milagrosa, 156
Cintrón, Bernardo, 62
Cintrón, Elma, 124
Cintrón, Joseph, 133
citizen, citizenship, 21, 164.
  See also cultural citizenship
City College, CUNY, 54–55, 78–79
Citywide Committee for Integrated Schools (CCFIS), 55–56
Citywide Intergroup Coalition, 87
Civic Community Center, 57
Clark, Kenneth B., 105
Cloward, Richard, 53
Club Betances, 155
Club Cívico Hijos de Vieques (Sons of Vieques Civic Club), 135–36
Club Latinoamericano, 155
CNPP. See Comité Nacional Pro Plebiscito (CNPP) [National Pro-Plebiscite Committee]
Coalition for Latino Representation on the Board of Education, 137, 141
Coalition for Racial Justice, 150, 151
Coalition for the Control of East Harlem Schools, 76
Coalition in Defense of Puerto Rican and Hispanic Rights, 130
Cohen, Henry, 52
Cole, Phillip, 18
collective action, 17, 23-26, 30-33, 35, 44, 46-48, 50, 116, 154-55, 157, 160-62, 166-67, 169
collective identity, 17, 22, 23, 30, 33, 44, 46, 47, 140, 162, 165, 168
collective interests, 27, 44
Colón, Darío, 53
Colón, Elizabeth, 141, 142, 147
Colón, Rafael Hernández, 145
Colón, Ramón, 64, 163
Colón, Rubén Darío, 67, 88, 89
Colón, Willie, 35
colonialism, 34, 35, 66, 107, 170
Comité Boricua Contra la Brutalidad Policíaca

[Puerto Rican Committee Against Police Brutality], 58
Comité Boricuas Ausentes Pro-Voto Plebiscitario, 66–67
Comité del Estado 51 [Committee for State 51], 169
Comité Nacional Pro Plebiscito (CNPP) [National Pro-Plebiscite Committee], 65–66
Comité Pro Defensa de Culebra de Brownsville [Brownsville Committee in Support of Culebra], 90
Comité Pro Voto de Boricuas en NY (CPVBNY) [Committee For the Puerto Rican Absentee Voter], 65, 66
Commission on Hispanic Concerns, 137–38
Commission on Human Rights, 67, 76, 87, 88, 148
Committee Against Fort Apache (CAFA), 130–31, 132, 162, 167–68
Committee for a Multilingual New York, 146
Committee for Prison Justice, 97
Committee of Six, 54
Committee on Police Community Relations (CPCR), 59
Committee Pro-Badillo for Mayor of New York, 102
Committee to Defend the Queens House of Detention Eight, 97
Committee to Save Our Studies, 92
Communist Party, 156
communitarian, 18, 20
community-based activities, 17, 23–26, 30–32, 33, 35, 44, 46–49, 154, 155
community control:
  of Lincoln Hospital, 92–97;
  of local schools, 74–78
Community Development Agency (CDA), 98, 112–13
Community Housing Council, 56
community politics, 17, 23, 24, 25–26, 48
Community Service Society, 147
Comunidad Hispana Para Educacion [Hispanic Community for Education] (CHE), 76
Concerned Parents of Brooklyn, 141
Congress for Racial Equality, 97
Congress of Puerto Rican Hometowns, 75, 153, 155
Conigliaro, Ana Alvarez, 75
Conjunto Libre, 120
Connolly, Neil, 130, 132, 133
Coors, 126–28, 160
Cordero, Rafael, 124
Corso, Dominick, 61
Cortijo, Rafael, 130
Cosme, Inocencia, 71
Cotto, Pablo, 59
Council Against Poverty (CAP), 67, 98, 100
Council of Puerto Rican, 87
CPCR. See Committee on Police Community Relations (CPCR)
CPVBNY. See Comité Pro Voto de Boricuas en NY (CPVBNY) [Committee For the Puerto Rican Absentee Voter]
Creitoff, Raquel, 106
Crespo, Marcos, 44
Cronkite, Walter, 146

Cruz, Gregorio, 58
Cruz, Pablo, 78
Cruzada Cívica del Voto [Civic Crusade for Voting], 106
Culebra, 89–91, 157, 167
cultural citizenship, 27–28, 31, 50, 103, 128
cultural pluralism, 104
Cuomo, Andrew, 43
Cuomo, Mario, 138, 146

Daily News, 38, 50, 97, 107, 120, 127, 146
Davidow, Mike, 59
de Borinquen, Ramitas, 122, 161
de Carter, Myrna Hernandez, 102
decentralization of public school system, 69, 74–78, 79
de Gautier, Felisa Rincón, 35
De Jesús, Anthony, 74
De León, Alberto, 54
de León, Cándido, 69, 101, 118
deLeon, Dennis, 138
del Toro, Angelo, 112, 113, 145
demand-protest, 23, 33, 47, 48–49, 54;
    1964 Harlem riot, 62–63;
    1967-1968 riots, 80–83;
    Culebra issue, 89–91;
    education, 54–56, 72–79, 91–92, 113–15, 128–30, 140–44;
    Fort Apache, 130-132
        housing, 56–58;
        language, 144–47;
        Lincoln Hospital, 92–97, 116, 132–34;
        March on Washington, 134–35;
        police brutality, 58–62, 115–16, 147–49; 167
        poverty, 79–80;
        prisoner riot, 97;
        race, 149–52;
    resource allocations, 98–101
        Save Hostos campaign, 116–18
    Vieques, 135-36
democracy of communities, 64–65
Democratic Party, 45, 156, 157, 158
democratization of community school boards, 153
De Sapio, Carmine, 157
Díaz, Distinto, 71
Díaz, Manuel "Manny," Jr., 52, 53, 69, 97, 102, 113, 154–55, 156
Díaz, Olga, 124
Díaz, William, 142
Dinkins, David, 143
diversity and difference, distinction between, 163
Dodd, Thomas, 90
Dominican Club, 118
Dontzin, Michael, 97
Down These Mean Streets, ban of, 91
Draper, Edgar, 91

East Harlem, 57, 154
East Harlem Planning Committee, 79
East Harlem Tenants Council (EHTC), 57, 76, 97, 122
economic crisis, 34, 35, 154

Economic Opportunity Act of 1964, 45
Educadores del Pueblo [People's Educators], 141, 149–50
education, demand-protests, 54–56, 72–79, 91–92, 102–5, 113–15, 128–30, 140–44
EHTC. See East Harlem Tenants Council (EHTC)
Einhorn, Arnold, 94, 95–96
El Barrio riot, 80–82
El Comite MINP, 120
El Diario de Nueva York, 54, 155, 157
El Diario-La Prensa, 56, 82, 90, 99, 101, 103, 112, 130, 138, 145, 146, 147, 151, 152, 155
electoral politics, 25, 35, 44, 50–51, 65–67, 105–6, 123, 139.
    See also voting
Elementary and Secondary Education Act, 105
El Grito de Lares, 107
El Grito del Barrio, 73, 79, 167
El Puente de Brooklyn, 141, 142
Emergency Financial Control Board, 38
Encenado, Peter, 133
English, Joseph T., 96
English Only movement, 103, 108, 130, 145–47, 153
Epstein, A. L., 23
Equal Employment Opportunity Commission, 52
Erazo, Joseph, 52, 53, 157, 159, 177, n12
Eric, Dámaso, 53
Espada, Frank, 53, 80, 85, 97, 110
Espaillat, Edwin, 124
Espinosa, Lin, 89, 90
ethnic identity, ethnicity, 17, 20–21, 24, 25, 33, 72, 79, 116
ethnic pride, 24, 26, 87, 166, 169
Evers, Medgar, 118
exclusion, 18, 21–22

Fair Labor Standards Act of 1976, 39
Falcón, Angelo, 20–21, 127–28, 140, 142
Federación Organizaciones de Brooklyn, 162
Federation of Puerto Rican University Socialist Students, 118
Federation of Teachers, 73
Feliciano, Juan, 90
Feliciano, Ramón, 90
Fernández, Dolores M., 144
Fernández, Joseph, 162
Fernández, Manuel, 70
Figueroa, Mario, 169
First Presbyterian Church of Jamaica, 97
Flores, Monserrate, 54, 92–93, 94–95, 99
Fonollosa, Luz María, 85
Ford, Gerald, 38
Forner, Tomás, 88
Fort Apache, The Bronx (film), 130–32, 162, 167–68
Foster, Elmer, 95
Fraiman, Arnold G., 95
Francione, Russell, 112
freedom of association, 18–19
Frente Nacional Puertorriqueño [Puerto Rican

National Front], 98
Fuentes, Luis, 74, 113, 114
Fulbright, William, 90

Galarcé, Julio César, 116
Gallagher, Buell, 54, 55
García, David, 130, 132, 134
García, Faustino Luis, 157
García, Robert, 75, 88, 105, 159
García Rivera, Oscar, 25, 154, 156, 157
Garden Acosta, Luis, 142, 143
Garvey, Marcus, 74
Gellner, Ernest, 25
Gerena Valentín, Gilberto, 53, 54, 58–59, 60, 61–62, 69, 71, 80, 88, 90–91, 101, 111, 119, 130, 134, 154
Gifford, Bernard, 104
Gigante, Louis, 86
Gilligan, Thomas, 62–63
Glazer, Nathan, 48
Glennon, Thomas K., Jr., 103
Golar, Simeon, 72
Gold, Eugene, 62
Goldberg, Arthur J., 89, 99, 168
Golden, Howard, 143
Goldin, Harrison, 111
Gómez, Jorge L., 157
González, Angelo, 140, 141, 144–45, 151
González, Emilio, 92
González, Jaime, 60
González, Juan, 120, 122–23, 127, 134
González, Rafael, 150–51, 152
González, Virginia, 85
Grand Council of Hispanic Societies, 71, 161
Graves End, Brooklyn, 151
Gray, William H., III, 132
Great Depression, 154
Green, Richard R., 144
Green, Roger, 143, 144
group-based representation, 18, 22
group identity, 19, 22, 30, 47, 153
group rights, 18–20, 22, 25, 30, 47, 163, 165
Gutierrez, Gilbert, 78
Guzmán, Pablo "Yoruba," 119

Halpin, Patrick G., 147
Hands Off Culebra Association, 90
Harlem Parents Committee (HPC), 55–56
Harlem Youth, Inc, 52
Health and Hospitals Corporation (HHC), 116
Health Revolutionary Unity Movement, 94
Hentoff, Nat, 132
Herbstein, Judith F., 173, n31
Hernández, Amelia, 85
Hernández, Luis, 51, 58
HHC. See Health and Hospitals Corporation (HHC)
Hispanic Day Parade, 87
Hispanic Democratic Club, 105
Hispanic Labor Committee of NYC of the Central Labor Council, 120
Hispanic Organization of Park Slope, 122
Hispanic Organizations of the Lower East Side, 87
Hispanics, 51, 85, 104, 137
Hispanic Society of City Police Officers, 131
Hispanic Young Adults Association (HYAA), 44, 173n31
Hispanic Youth Pastoral Council of the Northeastern United States, 109
historical collage, 29, 30–31, 158
Holmes Norton, Eleanor, 87
Holtzman, Elizabeth, 148
Hoover, Kenneth, 20
Horton, Carol, 19
Hostos Community College, 116–18, 147, 162
Howard Beach, 150–52
HPC. See Harlem Parents Committee (HPC)
human diversity, 19, 21
Human Rights Commission, 96
"100 Scholars," 78
Hunter College, 92
Hunts Point Community Corporation, 98, 111
Hunts Point Multi-Service Agency, 98
HYAA. See Hispanic Young Adults Association (HYAA)

identity politics, defined, 17
    aporetic relationship with liberalism, 18–22;
    blended with liberalism, 162-169
individualism, 25, 30
Ingram, David, 20
Institute for Puerto Rican Policy (IPRP), 137–38, 140
integration, 26
inter-ethnic alliances, 53
IPRP. See Institute for Puerto Rican Policy (IPRP)
Iris Marion Young, 19
Irizarry, Eunice, 54, 122
Irizarry, José Antonio, 91
Irrizary, Jesús, 98
Izquierdo, Rafael, 116

Jack, Hulan, 154
Jaramillo, Anabelle, 127
Javits, Jacob, 63
Jiménez, Lillian, 52, 173n31, 177n12
Johnson, Lyndon B., 37, 44–45
Jordan, Howard, 148, 150
Juan, Pedro San, 158
Jusino, Gonzalo, 158

Kain, Gylan, 130
Kaplowitz, Hyman, 56–57
Kautz, Steven, 19
Kennedy, John F., 158
Kenny, Michael, 26, 28, 29, 163
Kessler, Claire, 77
King, Martin Luther, Jr., 83
Klein, Woody, 57
Koch, Edward, 12, 112, 115, 119, 125, 131, 135, 136, 137, 138–39, 140–41, 143–44, 148, 149, 151–52, 160, 162, 167
Korrol, Virginia Sánchez, 155
Kukathas, Chandran, 18–19, 168

Kunstler, William, 88
Kymlicka, Will, 19

Laboriel, Juan, 124
Lacot, Antero, 93-95
Lafontaine, Hernán, 143
Laird, Melvin, 91
Landrau, Santa, 57
Lapp, Michael, 159
La Prensa, 54
Latin American Students Club, 118
Latino Coalition for Racial Justice, 148, 149
Latino Institute, 110
Latino organizations, 128
Latinos for a Free South Africa, 149
Latinos United for Political Action (LUPA), 122, 145, 150, 161, 193n12
Lau v. Nichols, 104, 165
Laviera, Tato, 35
La Voz Hispana, 156
League of United Latin American Citizens (LULAC), 105, 127
League of Women Voters, 51, 101
Legion of Voters in New York City, 51
Lehrman, Lew, 124
Lemus, Felícita, 85
Levy, Norman, 131-32
Liberalism, defined, 17
    aporetic relationship with identity politics, 18-22; blended with identity politics, 162-169
liberal democracy, 26, 28, 30, 47, 53, 102
Liberal Party, 157
Libre and Friends, 130
Liga Puertorriqueña, 155
Linares, Florencio, 88
Lincoln Hospital, 92-97, 116, 132-34, 162
Lindsay, John V., 37, 57, 61, 64, 69, 70, 71-72, 77, 78, 80, 82, 83-84, 86, 87, 88, 93, 95-96, 98, 100, 101, 162, 163, 164, 166
Local 1199, 146
Long Island, 123
López, José Ramos, 155, 157
López, Juan, 92
López, Ramonita, 85
López, Víctor, 124
Los Cuarenta, 122
Lower Manhattan Community Corporation, 79
low-income housing, 70, 130
Lugo, Nick, Jr., 101, 154
LULAC. See League of United Latin American Citizens (LULAC)
LUPA. See Latinos United for Political Action (LUPA)

Macchiarola, Frank, 128, 129
MacDonald, Michael C. D., 167, 168
MacIntyre, Alasdair, 32
Magnarela, Paul J., 20
Malaret, Marisol, 84
Malavé, Fred, 71

Malavet, Isabel, 48
Malcolm X, 28, 74
Maldonado, Victor, 60
Mangual, Victor, 82
Mangum, Robert J., 70
Manhattan Democratic Organization, 63
Marcantonio, Vito, 156
Marchi, John, 145
Marfisi, Iran, 70
marginality, 18
Marks, Charles, 68
Marrero, Víctor, 142
Martínez, Manuel, 115
Martínez, Miguel O., 140, 142
Martinez, Ralph, 59
Marx, Karl, 28
McClellan, Graydon E., 56
McGrath, George F., 97
Medina, Ramiro, 65-66
Meléndez, Edgardo, 34
Meléndez, Johnny, 111
Méndez, Olga, 68, 143, 145
Méndez, Tony, 154-55
Mendoza, Esther, 85
Mercado, Edward, 70, 83
Messinger, Ruth, 132
Mexican American Legal Defense and Education Fund (MALDEF), 105, 147
Mexican American Political Association, 105
Meyer, Gerald, 117, 118
MFY. See Mobilization for Youth (MFY)
migration, 34-35
Migration Division, 50-51, 158-59
Mills, C. Wright, 169
minority rights, 19
Miranda, Frank, 131
Miranda, Ismael, 107
Miranda, Luis, 137
Miranda-King, Lourdes, 103
Mobilization for Youth (MFY), 52
Molina, Pedro, 149-50
Mollen, Milton, 57
Monserrat, Joseph, 59, 80, 91, 97, 115, 145, 159
Montalvo, Elba, 141
Montaner, Carlos Alberto, 139
Montano, Armando, 100, 133
Morales, Domingo, 115
Morales, Iris, 78
Morales, José, 52
Morales, Julio, 76
Morales, Teresa, 109
moral learning, 160
Morey, Donald, 77
Morín, José Luis, 148
Mott Haven Planning Committee, 79
Moynihan, Patrick, 48
Municipal Assistance Corporation. See Big MAC
Murphy, Joseph, 147
Murphy, Michael J., 59, 61, 63

NAACP. See National Association for the Advancement of Colored People (NAACP)
Naborí, 109–10
NACOPRW. See National Conference of Puerto Rican Women (NACOPRW)
Nakasone, Yasuhiro, 139, 167
NAPRA. See National Association for Puerto Rican Affairs (NAPRA)
NAPRCR. See National Association for Puerto Rican Civil Rights (NAPRCR)
National Association for Puerto Rican Affairs (NAPRA), 60, 87
National Association for Puerto Rican Civil Rights (NAPRCR) (Also National Association for Civil Rights), 60, 61, 68, 119, 135, 154
National Association for the Advancement of Colored People (NAACP), 55, 59, 64, 120, 127, 134
National Association for the Advancement of the Hispanic American People of African Origin, Inc., 140, 164
National Bilingual Education Task Force, 123
National Conference of Puerto Rican Women (NACOPRW), 106, 110
National Congress for Puerto Rican Rights (NCPRR), 48, 119–20, 120–26, 128, 129, 132, 134–35, 137, 139, 141, 145, 147, 148, 149, 152, 153, 160, 161, 165–66
National Council of La Raza, 105
National Institute of Education (NIE), 102–3
National Italian Civil Rights League, 120
National Organization of Women, 134
National Puerto Rican Coalition (NPRC), 110, 111, 122, 124, 153
National Puerto Rican Conference, 110, 132
NCPRR. See National Congress for Puerto Rican Rights (NCPRR)
Neco, Luis, 89
New Alliance Party, 130
Newfield, Jack, 97
New Rican Village Club, 120, 130
Newton, Huey, 20
New York Coalition for Bilingual Education, 121, 129
New York Daily News, 103
New York Newsday, 143
New York State Association for Bilingual Education, 129
New York Times, 82, 95, 103, 143
New York Urban Coalition, 97
Nichols, Bill, 79
Nick Lugo, Sr., 157
NIE. See National Institute of Education (NIE)
Nieves, Josephine, 47, 52, 54, 70, 103, 111, 173n31
Nike, Oggun, 140
Nine, Louis, 100
Nixon, Richard, 90
NPRC. See National Puerto Rican Coalition (NPRC)
Núñez, Louis, 53, 75, 110, 111, 126
NY Puerto Rican/Hispanic Voter Analysis Project, 48

Obrero Boricua, 121
O'Brien, Frances, 77
Office of the Commonwealth of Puerto Rico, 50, 53, 59, 65, 66, 85, 87, 101, 105–6, 111, 119, 153, 155, 156, 158, 161
Oliver, Fernando, 133
Oliver, Herbert, 74, 78
Operation Friend, 61
Orta, Awilda, 104
Ortíz, Bart, 158
Ortíz, John, 56
Ortíz, María, 88
Owens, Major, 98
Ozone Park, 152

Pacheco, Joseph, 144
Padilla, Elena, 69
Pagán, Antonio, 58
Palmieri, Eddie, 35
Pantoja, Antonia, 20, 23–24, 25–26, 47, 52, 54, 69, 70, 102, 116, 159, 169, 173n31
Parent Advocates for Bilingual Education, 129
Passalacqua, Juan Manuel García, 110
Paxon, William, 145
People's Board of Education, 69
People's Educators, 129
Pepe y Flora, 59
Perales, César, 123
Pérez, Carmen, 106
Pérez, Eddie, 124
Pérez, Madeline, 74
Pérez, Mauricia, 73
Pérez, Miguel, 146
Pérez, Richie, 151, 168
Pietri, Pedro, 35, 130
Podair, Jerald, 74
Pogge, Thomas W., 18
Police Community Relations Board, 63
policy responsiveness, 43
political activities, 43–44
political economy, 36–43, 37
Ponce De León Democratic Club, 51, 57
Poor People's Movement, 80
Por Los Niños [For the Children] slate, 114
Portnoy, Ruth, 73–74
post-modernism, 28
Pounds, William, 110
poverty, 39–40, 42, 160
Powell, James, 62–63
Poynter, Ralph, 164
PRCDP. See Puerto Rican Community Development Project (PRCDP)
PREA. See Puerto Rican Educators Association (PREA)
PRIDE. See Puerto Rican Inter-American Dynamic Educational Foundation, Inc. (PRIDE)
PRISA. See Puerto Rican Students for Action (PRISA)
PRLDEF. See Puerto Rican Legal Defense and

Education Fund (PRLDEF)
Professional Staff Congress, 118
Progress, Inc., 152
Progressive Youth of Puerto Rico, 59
Public Law 94-311, 111
public reason, 160
public philosophy, liberalism as, 22
Puerto Rican Association for Community Action, 122
Puerto Rican Association for Community Affairs, 141, 173, n31
Puerto Rican Bar Association, 81, 87
Puerto Rican Community Council of East Harlem, 87
Puerto Rican Community Development Project (PRCDP), 46, 52–53, 67, 68, 87, 98, 101, 107, 111–13, 119, 154
Puerto Rican community institutions, 24, 25, 33, 47, 119, 156, 159, 166, 169
Puerto Rican Coordinating Committee for the Northeast, 85–87
Puerto Rican Cultural and Social Action, 54
Puerto Rican Education Action Media Council, 92
Puerto Rican Educators Association (PREA), 120, 129, 141, 144
Puerto Rican Family Institute, 46, 68, 98
Puerto Rican Folk Festival, 154
Puerto Rican Forum, 25, 44, 46, 47, 48, 51–52, 68, 75, 97, 110, 153, 155, 160, 173n31
Puerto Rican Inter-American Dynamic Educational Foundation, Inc. (PRIDE), 77
Puerto Rican/Latino Education Roundtable, 141, 145
Puerto Rican Legal Defense and Education Fund (PRLDEF), 103, 104–5, 108, 110, 128, 129, 141, 145, 148, 152
Puerto Rican Legal Institute, 108, 165
Puertoricanness, 28, 30, 35, 47, 64, 66, 71
Puerto Rican Newspaper, Radio, and Television Society, Inc., 107
Puerto Rican Parade, 154, 166
Puerto Rican population growth, in New York City, 35–36;
  political economy, 36–43;
  politics, 31, 43–49
"Puerto Ricans Confront the Problems of Urban Society: A Design for Change," 69–70
Puerto Rican Service Center of New York, 155–56
Puerto Ricans in the United States, An Uncertain Future, 110
Puerto Rican Socialist Party, 35, 86
"Puerto Ricans Re-examining Problems of the Complex Urban Society," 71–72
Puerto Rican Students Association, 118
Puerto Rican Students for Action (PRISA), 78
"Puerto Rican Unity Day," 90
Puertorriqueños Unidos [Puerto Ricans United], 66, 92

Queens House of Detention, riot at, 97
Quero Chiesa, Luis, 75, 92, 101
Quiñones, Nathan, 142, 145, 151
Quintero, Luisa, 51, 68, 72, 75

race, racism, 21, 141, 149–52, 167
race relations, 115, 152
Ramírez, Gilberto, 88
Ramírez, Roberto, 149
Ramos, Eligio, 66
Ramos, Juan, 135
Ramos, Lydia, 124
Ramos, Manuel, 157–58
Rand Institute of New York City, 115
Reagan, Ronald, 148
Realidades (TV program), 92
religion, religious identity, 27, 88–89
relocation, 56
remedial education, 117
Republican Party, 157, 158
Rescher, Nicholas, 17
Rey, Alfredo, 105
Reyes, Luis O., 129, 142, 144
Reyes, Raul, 99
Richardson, Elliot, 91
Ríos, Carlos M., 59, 154–55
riots:
  in 1964, 167;
  in 1967-1968, 80–83;
  El Barrio riot, 80–82;
  prisoner riot, 97;
  at Queens House of Detention, 97
Rivera, Andrés, 89
Rivera, Angel F., 83
Rivera, Dennis, 124, 134
Rivera, Evelyn, 147–48
Rivera, Gladys, 106
Rivera, José, 134, 143, 145, 150
Rivera, Julia, 142
Rivera, Oswaldo, 60
Rivera, Ramón, 149–50
roadmap for politics, 32
Roberts, Sam, 175n12
Robertson, A. Willis, 45
Robinson, Cleveland, 134, 150
Rochester, 123
Rockefeller, Nelson, 99–100, 168
Rodríguez, Ernesto, 58
Rodríguez, Eugene, 51, 159
Rodríguez, Frank, 58, 59
Rodríguez, George, 98
Rodríguez, Helen, 88, 95, 96
Rodríguez, Isidoro, 122
Rodríguez, Joe, 70, 71
Rodríguez, Juan, 148, 149
Rodríguez, Luis, 58
Rodríguez, María V., 85
Rodríguez, Víctor, 58
Rojas, Tony, 107
Román, Anibal Soliván, Jr., 183–84n22
Román, José Lumen, 66
Romero, Rolando, 151
Rosado, Julio, 77
Rosado, Rossana, 152

Rosaldo, Renato, 27
Rosario, Irma, 85
Rose, Lucille, 109
Rossier, Robert E., 129
Rousseau, Jean-Jacques, 65
Ruiz, Félix, 123
Ruiz, Hilton, 130
Ruíz, Israel, Jr., 142, 143
Ruíz, Manuel and Maria, 56
Ruiz, Modesto, 149
Ruiz, Ruperto, 54, 88
Rustin, Bayard, 55
Ryan, William Fitts, 59, 63

Sabater, Julio, 140, 164
Sable, Jack, 100
Saha, Santosh C., 20
Salgado, Luis, 71
Sanabria, Carlos, 173n31
Sánchez, Gil, 51
Sánchez, José, 59
Sánchez, Nick, 119
Sánchez, Yolanda, 54, 106, 112
Santaella, Irma Vidal, 59
Santiago, Flora, 59
Santiago, Juan, 60
Santiago, Wichy, 107
Save Hostos campaign, 116–18
Scelsa, Joseph, 145
Scheinberg, Labe, 95
Schwartz, Harry, 96
Screvane, Paul R., 52, 63, 177n12
Scribner, Harvey, 113
Search for Education, Elevation, and Knowledge (SEEK) program, 78–79
Seda, Dámaso, 124
SEEK program. See Search for Education, Elevation, and Knowledge (SEEK) program
Segarra, Marlín, 146
self-help efforts, 24, 47, 49, 53, 87, 106
self-sufficiency, 25–26, 169;
  vs. identity, 23–24
Seneca Democratic Club, 51
Serrano, José, 88, 112, 142, 143, 145, 146, 147, 149
Seward Park High School, 77
Shanker, Albert, 77, 78, 114
Shapiro, Fred, 63
Shields, Art, 25
Shriver, Sargent, 53
Shulman, Claire, 143
Silva, Antonio, 132, 133
Silverman, Charles, 173, n31
Simpson, Millard, 45
Sklover, Thea, 130
Smith, Joseph, 95
Social Action Committee of Grace Congregational Church, 63
social justice, 19–20, 109, 116, 124, 149
social liberalism, 19, 49

Sociedad Hostos [Hostos Society], 92
Sociedad Maricaeña, 162
socioeconomic status, 38, 42
Soler, José, 124
Solero, Máximo, 58
Solís, Frank, 127
South Bronx Community Corporation, 101
Southern Christian Leadership Conference, 12, 28, 134
Spanish Association of Women Voters, 85
Special Committee on Decolonization, UN, 108
State Association on Bilingual Education, 146
Stein, Andrew, 143
Steingut, Robert, 132
Stewart, Charles E., Jr., 108
"stop and frisk" and "no knock" laws, 59
strategic action, 33, 47
  education, 102-105;
  electoral politics, 50-51, 65-67, 105-106;
  organizational activities, 51-53, 67-72, 84-89, 106-13, 119-28, 137-40
Straus, Nathan, 68
Student Government Organization, 118
Subcomité Neoyorquino Pro Rescate de Culebra [New York Subcommittee to Save Culebra], 89
suicide rate among Puerto Rican convicts, 60, 62
Sullivan, James, 63
Swetnick, George, 51
Synagogue Council of America, 96

Tactical Police Force Units, 83
Tammany Hall, 25
Tanton, John, 146
Teitelbaum, Herbert, 103–4
Terenzio, Joseph V., 92, 93
Think Lincoln, 94
Thomas, Piri, 91, 101
Tirado, Amílcar, 173n31
Torres, Felipe N., 70, 157
Torres, Frank, 140
Torres, George, 150–51, 152
Torres, Héctor, 124
Torres, Lourdes, 109, 120, 134
Torres, Magdalena, 106
Torres, Migdalia de Jesús, 92
Torres, Pablo, 78
Torres, Paul, 70
Torres, Zoilo, 125, 134
Torres v. Sachs, 108
Tower, John, 45
Trifilo Rubero, 58
Trilla, Francisco, 52, 54, 85, 113

UBP. See United Bronx Parents (UBP)
UFT. See United Federation of Teachers (UFT)
unemployment, 38–39, 111
Unidos, Padres, 122
Union of Patriotic Puerto Ricans, 130
Union Settlement, 155
United Bronx Organizations, 54

United Bronx Parents (UBP), 35, 97, 119, 122, 129, 130, 141, 142
United Federation of Teachers (UFT), 55, 74, 114
United Hispanic American Democratic Club, 105
United Parents Against the Wall (UPAW), 150
United Parents Association, 129
United Tremont Trades, 130
University of Puerto Rico (UPR), 122
UPAW. See United Parents Against the Wall (UPAW)
UPR. See University of Puerto Rico (UPR)
Urban League, 120
U.S. Civil Rights Commission, 110

Valentín, Dave, 130
Vanden Heuvel, William, 60
Vargas-Ramos, Carlos, 25
Vázquez, Héctor I., 75, 76, 87, 97
Vega, Angel, 101
Vega, Bernardo, 155
Velázquez, José "Che," 170
Velázquez, Nydia, 53, 141, 145
Velez, Héctor, 59
Vélez, Johnny, 85
Vélez, Ramón, 53, 60, 69, 85–86, 100, 111
Vélez, Ted, 57, 76, 97
Vélez, Vicente, 75
Veray, Amaury, 69
Veteran's Club, 118
Vice, Celia, 157
Vieques, 157, 167
"Vietnam Summer," 72
Villafañe, Hector, 134–35
Votaw, Carmen Delgado, 110
Voters Legion, 101
voting, 48, 66, 155;
    voter registration campaign, 48, 65, 105–6, 117
    See also electoral politics
Voting Rights Act (VRA), 107–8
VRA. See Voting Rights Act (VRA)

wage gap, 39–40
Wagner, Robert F., 35, 37, 60–61, 63, 141, 142, 157
Walker, Thomas J., 130
Walzer, Michael, 160
Ward, Haskell, 112
War on Poverty, 44–46, 53, 71, 102, 167, 169
WBNX, 101
W.E.B. Dubois Club, 73
Wexler, Jaqueline, 92
Williams, Melissa, 18
Wimmer, Andreas, 160
WWRL, 156

Young Lords, 28–29, 35, 93–95, 96, 120

Zapata, César Ruiz, 60
Zarefsky, David, 45
Zayas, Gil, 70
Zuccotti, John, 117

ABOUT THE AUTHOR

José E. Cruz is an Associate Professor of Political Science and Latino Studies at the University at Albany, State University of New York. His areas of interest include Latino and Puerto Rican political participation, immigrant political incorporation, the role of race and ethnicity in the political process, social movements, and radical politics. His first book, *Identity and Power: Puerto Rican Politics and the Challenge of Ethnicity* (Philadelphia: Temple University Press, 1998), explored the causes and consequences of the politicization of ethnicity. In 2000, Cruz co-edited *Adiós Borinquen Querida: The Puerto Rican Diaspora, Its History and Contributions* (Albany, NY: CELAC), with Edna Acosta Belén et al. Professor Cruz is also the editor of *Latino Immigration Policy: Context, Issues, Alternatives* (Albany, NY: NYLARNet, 2008). In the summer of 2015, Professor Cruz began a faculty-led study abroad program in Madrid, Spain, focusing on the comparative study of urban politics and Latin American immigration. He is currently doing research on immigrant political incorporation, celebrations of U.S. citizenship by Puerto Ricans, Puerto Rican radical politics, the mayoralty of Harold Washington, and social movements in Spain. Cruz is also the author of *Puerto Rican Identity, Political Development, and Democracy in New York, 1960-1990* (Lanham, MD: Lexington Books/Rowman & Littlefield, 2017).

Made in the USA
Middletown, DE
23 August 2019